Pictorial Guide
to the Birds
of North America

Pictorial Guide
to the Birds
of North America

Text and Photographs by
Leonard Lee Rue III

Thomas Y. Crowell Company
New York
Established 1834

Drawings by Juan C. Barberis

Maps by Donald Pitcher

Manufactured in the United States of America

L.C. Card 73–109905

1 2 3 4 5 6 7 8 9 10

To my sister
Dorothy Rue Rowe

Contents

Acknowledgments

Knowledge can often be a dangerous thing. When I was ten or eleven years old I could name every bird I saw; or perhaps I should say I thought I could name every bird I saw. It was Amy Luck who first gently corrected my errors of identification. It was only as I grew older and acquired books of identification that I began to realize how often I must have been wrong in my earlier days. It was then I found that there were thirty-nine sparrows and fifty-four warblers and that I would have to check more carefully for the differentiating field marks. I sometimes feel that since my first correction years ago, when I first began to acquire real knowledge, I have been going backward. I do not profess to be an expert at bird identification, but I do believe I get as much enjoyment out of working with birds as the experts do, and perhaps more.

Taking photographs of wildlife started as a hobby and now forms the basis of my livelihood. In the pursuit of wildlife I have crisscrossed this continent many times and have made several trips to distant parts of the world. My life list of birds now exceeds 600 species, although I have seen only slightly more than half of the 645 species found in North America. Of the 75 bird families found on our continent, 41 families are represented in this book, with a total of 82 species being discussed at some length. The birds chosen for representation here are those so common everyone knows something about them, or so rare that most people know nothing about them. They are birds found all over North America, or only in Alaska, or Florida, or some other localized area. They are chosen because they are birds I have spent a great deal of time with, lived with, shared experiences with, and observed extensively; experiences and observations I thought you would enjoy sharing.

I have been gathering the photographs in this book for the past seventeen years; living the experiences all my life. In that span of time I have been helped by so many friends that it is impossible for me to list them all. I am indebted to all who have helped me along the way; not only my personal friends but the authors and artists whose books I have read and studied. Knowledge is the sum of everyone's experience. I can only hope that reading this book will help to enrich someone's life as mine has been enriched by those before me. Perhaps, after all, this is the best way to say thanks to everyone.

I do however want to acknowledge my special thanks to my editor, Mary Irving. Special thanks, too, to my sister Evelyn Rue Guthrie for taking time out of her own very busy life to transcribe the scribbling that I do into a neatly typed manuscript, and to Philip A. DuMont of the Fish and Wildlife Service for his assistance in preparing the appendix.

Leonard Lee Rue, III

Blairstown, New Jersey

Introduction

What are birds? Birds are animals with feathers. One of the five groups
of "higher" animals, birds display singular adaptations to their way of life.
Like the other vertebrates, or animals with backbones, they have a spinal
column made up of small bones known as vertebrae. Birds differ from
fishes, amphibians, reptiles, and mammals in a variety of ways, but their
most distinctive characteristic is that they alone have feathers. Feathers represent a modification of the earlier scales that covered the birds' ancestors,
the reptiles. They insulate the bird's body from heat and cold, give it shape
and balance, and make flying possible.

The forelimbs, or arms, of most birds are modified into wings. Instead of
the five toes originally possessed by most mammals, birds have only three.
The thumb, or alula, is still prominent on the forepart of the wing, but the
third finger is rudimentary and usually covered by the skin of the wing.
The length of forelimbs, fingers, and feathers differ greatly in each order of
birds according to its mode of life and type of flying. With a record wingspan of eleven feet ten inches, the sea-soaring albatross has the longest
wings of any bird. The hovering Helenas hummingbird of Cuba, the world's
smallest bird, has a wingspan of one and one-half inches.

Such flightless birds as the ostrich, the rhea, and the cassowary were
capable of flight at one time, but, through lack of use, their wings and flight
muscles degenerated and atrophied. These birds usually depend for protection upon their speed in running. Most of the flightless birds that could not
run fast enough, such as the dodo and the great auk, have become extinct
or, like the kiwi, rare. The penguins' wings have been modified into efficient
flippers that allow these birds to outswim the fish on which they feed.

The length of the tail seems to have a direct bearing upon a bird's speed.
Some birds with the shortest tails are the speediest fliers. The record is held
by the Indian swift, which was clocked at 219½ miles per hour over a two-
mile course in the Chachar Hills of India in 1934.

As another specialization for flight, the bones of most birds are hollow or are structured with air cells, thus providing reduced weight yet with no loss of strength. Birds also have internal air sacs connected to their lungs, which increase the amount of available oxygen and add extra buoyancy. To the deep, heavily keeled breastbone of flying birds are attached the powerful muscles needed for flight.

Flapping, or power flight, particularly requires a tremendous expenditure of energy. Birds have a high metabolic rate that permits food to be converted into energy in the shortest possible time. Like mammals, birds are homoiothermic, or warm-blooded. To aid the digestion and other bodily processes, however, they have a much higher body temperature than mammals, with the rate ranging from 104 to 110 degrees Fahrenheit according to the species. A large, four-chambered heart and exceptionally large blood vessels circulate the blood at a fantastic rate. In fact, birds have larger hearts in proportion to their body size than do any other vertebrates.

Birds still retain reptilian scales on their legs and feet. Their feet and legs are modified according to the type of life each bird leads. The toes of the swimming birds are either webbed or lobed to provide more purchase against the water. Wading birds have long legs and long toes; the first so they can wade in deep water, the second to prevent their sinking in the soft mud. Perching birds usually have an unusually long claw on the hind toe, the better to grasp the branch while they sleep. The toes of gallinaceous birds are strong so that the feet can be used for scratching in the earth to uncover food. Birds of prey have sharply hooked talons for grasping their prey. The type of feet helps to classify the bird species.

Birds use their beaks or bills to perform such chores as food gathering, grooming, defending themselves, and nest building. Directly related to the type of food eaten and the manner in which it is obtained are the shape and size of the beak, which may be modified to serve as a fish catcher, flesh tearer, nut cracker, nectar sipper, and so on. Lacking teeth, most birds swallow their food whole, storing it in a special throat sac called the crop. The food then passes into the upper stomach and finally into the lower stomach, or gizzard, where it is cracked, ground, and masticated so that it can be utilized by the body. Wastes are excreted through a single opening, the cloaca. Through the female's cloaca, the male's sperm enters the oviduct, or egg-laying tube, to fertilize the egg cells.

Birds are primarily land dwellers. Most birds spend their entire lifetime on land, and even the sea birds must return to land to breed and to nest.

All birds lay eggs that must be hatched by the heat of the parent's body or by artificial heat. After hatching, the young may be either altricial (helpless) or precocial (capable of leaving the nest as soon as hatched), but they must be cared for by the parents until they are able to fend for themselves.

At some time during the early Mesozoic era, about 200,000,000 years ago, the path of mammal and bird ancestors parted. The ancestors of birds were bipedal reptiles that climbed about in the treetops using their forearms as well as their hind legs. Gradually the scales on the forearms split, elongated, and "feathered" out, enabling the first birds to glide from branch to branch or to the ground.

Fossil finds of birds have been extremely rare because of the smallness and fragility of their bones. The earliest fossil definitely identifiable as that of a bird was found in a slate quarry in Bavaria in 1861. Paleontologists have calculated that this reptilelike bird lived during the Upper Jurassic period of 150,000,000 years ago. Called *Archaeopteryx*, this bird had teeth like a reptile, but its body was covered with feathers.

Over succeeding periods of time, various forms of birds developed, gained ascendancy, then disappeared. The ancestors of the majority of our modern birds are believed to have made their appearance during the Oligocene epoch of 40,000,000 years ago. As a group, birds reached their peak during the Pleistocene epoch, about 500,000 years ago, when an estimated 11,500 species were in existence. From *Archaeopteryx* up to the present time, an estimated 2,000,000 species of birds have evolved. Of this total, all but a fraction have passed from the scene.

Considerable disagreement exists among the experts concerning the classification of birds. Some bird groups are so unique in body structure and habits that they are easily identified. Other groups are held together by the dissimilarities between them and the rest of the birds rather than by the similarities within a particular group. The higher the bird is on the scale of evolution, the more difficult classification becomes.

Birds are grouped by order, family, and genera. The black-capped chickadee visiting the feeding station outside my window as I write is classified as *Parus atricapillus atricapillus* according to the Linnean system:

PHYLUM: Chordata, or "having a backbone."

CLASS: Aves, or "having feathers," i.e., a bird.

ORDER: Passeriformes, or "perching birds."

FAMILY: Paridae, referring to the Old English word tit, meaning "small."

GENUS: *Parus,* derived from Paridae.

SPECIES: *Atricapillus,* from the Latin *atratus,* meaning "clothed in black," and *capillus,* meaning "hair of the head," hence "black-capped." The name chickadee comes from the bird's song of *chick-a-dee-dee-dee-dee.*

SUBSPECIES: *Parus atricapillus atricapillus,* given by Linnaeus in 1758 and designating the specific chickadee resident in northern New Jersey.

Most authorities agree that there are twenty-seven orders, 166 families, and approximately 8,600 species of living birds in the world today. In North America, 20 of these orders occur, representing 75 families that include 645 species. Rough estimates place the worldwide bird population at approximately 100,000,000,000, although the actual population may be ten times more or less than that figure, and the breeding population within the forty-eight contiguous states of the United States at about 6,000,000,000.

Birds play a tremendously important part in the lives of most people, even of those who care nothing about them. Their value lies in the fact that they serve one of two basic needs—the utilitarian or the esthetic—or both.

I recall the first time I saw a house sparrow catch and devour a moth; it was years ago, and I was about seven years old. I ran downstairs to prevent the bird from eating the moth but was too late. In my ignorance, I thought the sparrow was "bad" because it ate the moth. On the contrary, we now know that birds are among man's most valuable allies in controlling the hordes of insect pests that would threaten man's very existence were they to remain unchecked.

The most common and most valuable bird in the world is the domestic chicken, developed from the red jungle fowl that still lives wild in considerable numbers in India. In the United States alone, more than 2,000,000,000 chickens are raised for food each year and over 64,000,000,000 eggs are eaten. Added to those figures are the numbers of ducks, turkeys, guineas, and pigeons that also provide man with food and, in their wild form, with sport. Millions of dollars are spent in pursuit of feathered game.

In addition to their ecological, commercial, and economic importance, birds are valuable to mankind in numerous other ways and for a great variety of reasons. To an increasing number of people, birds represent an esthetic rather than a pecuniary interest. From time immemorial, in prehistoric cave paintings through modern works of art and literature, man has recorded his links with birds. More and more people are taking up the study of birds and are making substantial contributions to our knowledge about them. More is known about birds than about any other form of wildlife because they are easier to see and because most are active during the daytime. As with any subject, however, the more we learn about them, the more we realize how much we still have to learn.

The so-called balance of nature, upset since the appearance of the first hominoids, has become increasingly threatened as man has asserted his ascendancy over the lesser creatures. Often man's technological advances outrun his knowledge, and the full extent of the destruction loosed by pesticides and insecticides on the wildlife populations as well as on the human population is not yet known. The mounting evidence of such destruction has aroused a growing human awareness, although it may already be too little and too late.

As our continued human population explosion threatens the existence of all wildlife populations, increased understanding of the interdependent relationship between man and wildlife becomes ever more urgent. Only by fulfilling our obligations as stewards of today's wildlife can we ensure a future for both wildlife and man.

1 Gaviiformes— Loons

Two sounds—the howl of the wolf and the forlorn cry of the loon—uniquely embody all the emptiness and solitude of the northern wilderness. While the wolf has vanished from large areas of North America, the loon, at best, is holding its own.

The long-bodied, ducklike loon has no close relatives among other birds of the world. All four living species of the family Gaviidae are found in North America; only two species, the common loon and the red-throated loon, occur as far south as the United States.

Derived from the old Scandinavian word *loom*, meaning "someone who walks awkwardly," the name loon is appropriately applied to this bird, which is highly specialized for swimming and diving but travels on land with difficulty. The powerful legs with large webbed feet are placed so far to the rear that the loon is unable to stand upright and must toboggan forward on its belly during rare excursions ashore. Because the loon cannot take off from land, it runs across the surface of the water, beating its short, narrow wings rapidly to gain air speed. When airborne, it is a strong, swift flier.

A loon's bones are solid, not filled with air compartments like the bones of other birds. Its body weight roughly equals the amount of water it displaces, and the bird controls its flotation position by controlling the air intake to its body. The loon has a high tolerance to carbon dioxide as well as the ability to store extra oxygen in its blood. These adaptations enable the loon to make deep dives—some birds have been caught in fishermen's nets at depths of 190 feet—and to remain submerged for considerable periods of time.

1

Common Loon
(Gavia immer)

FIELD MARKS:	*Black and white with dark green head in summer. Dark brown and white in winter. Ducklike bird with legs at back of body, short narrow wings, and sharp pointed bill.*
SIZE:	*32 inches long with a wingspan of 58 inches.*
HABITS:	*Only leaves the water to build nest and hatch eggs. Dives to tremendous depths and swims underwater rapidly.*
HABITAT:	*Rivers and lakes.*
NEST:	*Mounds of vegetation piled on sandspit.*
EGGS:	*Dull green, 2 in a clutch. Incubation 29 days.*
FOOD:	*Fish.*
VOICE:	*Forlorn cry.*

The common loon can dive to tremendous depths and swim underwater for long distances. Attached to the rear of its body, the bird has powerful legs, which give extra leverage to its large webbed feet.

The loon swims so swiftly underwater that it can easily outswim fish—even the speedy trout—which constitute the staple item of its diet. For good reason this bird is sometimes called the "great northern diver."

In flight this bird is easily recognized. With head and neck stretched out in front, and big feet sticking straight out behind, the loon resembles a flying cross when viewed from the ground. In profile its drooping head and neck give it a slightly hunchbacked appearance. As the loon flies overhead, it emits its unmistakable, mournful, wild cry.

Male and female are identical in appearance. I can only tell them apart by the fact that the female spends more time brooding on the nest than does the male. The common loon has white underparts; upper parts are glossy black with white spots in summer and grayish brown spots in winter. An adult averages a total length of about thirty-two inches, has a wingspread of approximately fifty-eight inches, and may weigh as many as fifteen pounds. For its body weight the loon has comparatively small wings, yet so rapid is the wingbeat that estimates credit this bird with air speeds of up to sixty miles per hour.

Like other members of this order, the common loon tends to be solitary; I have never seen more than a single family group at one time. It ranges

Loons are always found on water and only come ashore to nest.

from the Atlantic to the Pacific coasts and from the Arctic region south through the United States to Florida and the Gulf Coast.

Venturing ashore only during the breeding and nesting season, the loon constructs its nest of vegetable debris on a sandy spit of land jutting out into the water of lakes, rivers, or coastal areas. The nest constantly increases in size as the brooding loon idly piles additional rotted vegetation onto it. The male is a devoted mate, quick to respond to the female's call for help. On one occasion I photographed a nest while the female brooded and the male fished several hundred yards away. The female became uneasy as I approached, but her mate showed no concern. As I drew nearer, the female emitted a strangled squall. Immediately the male hurtled through the water toward the nest. Sliding out onto the mud, he headed directly for me and struck out with his long, sharp beak. I was amazed that this bird, so awkward and vulnerable on land, would put himself in such jeopardy in defense of the nest, yet he didn't hesitate to do so. In the face of such devotion, I discreetly withdrew.

Two dull green eggs, about three and one-half inches long and a little more than two inches in diameter, are hatched after an incubation period of approximately twenty-nine days. Soon the young chicks are swimming about. I remember finding a two-week-old loon swimming in Chub Lake in the province of Quebec. As my canoe approached, the baby loon attempted to dive beneath the surface, but its efforts were frustrated by the fact that its body was still covered with down instead of with feathers. So much air was trapped underneath the down that the loon was unable to submerge. Its head was underwater and its feet were paddling like mad, but its little rump refused to take the plunge. I was reminded vividly of a can-can dancer.

2 Podicipediformes— Grebes

Grebes belong to an ancient order of birds and still retain many features present in the fossil diving-bird known as *Hesperornis,* which lived 130 million years ago. Of the eighteen living species, six are found in North America, all members of the family Podicipedidae.

The Podicipediformes, "rump-footed ones," have their legs situated far back on their bodies in the classical fashion of diving birds. Grebes are superb divers. Although capable of flying fairly well, they prefer to seek sanctuary in the water, swimming away when danger threatens and submerging quickly when it materializes. Grebes cannot compete with loons as swimmers and divers, but they really don't have to; frequently, when rising to the surface for a breath of air, they hide out among the aquatic weeds.

In place of the skin webbing between the toes found in most water birds, grebes have stiff flaps on each toe. These flaps, known as lobate webbing, provide the foot with an extremely efficient propelling surface. Another conspicuous characteristic is the apparent absence of a tail. The few rudimentary tail feathers serve no functional purpose; whether waterborne or airborne, grebes steer themselves with their feet.

Pied-billed Grebe
(Podilymbus podiceps)

FIELD MARKS: *Fuscous. White beak has black band around the middle in summer. Lobed toes, white underparts, rudimentary tail.*

SIZE: *12 inches long with a wingspan of 23 inches.*

HABITS: *Eats its own feathers. Skillful swimmer and diver. Takes off from the water.*

HABITAT: *Freshwater lakes and rivers.*

NEST: *Decayed vegetation placed on a mat of green vegetation which will float.*

EGGS: *Dull white, 5–7 in a clutch. Incubation 21–24 days.*

FOOD: *Water insects, bettles, larvae, when young; small fish, tadpoles, leeches, snails, crayfish, when mature.*

VOICE: *A series of low, slurred whistles.*

The pied-billed grebe rarely flies and cannot take off from land. It escapes from danger by diving and hiding among aquatic vegetation.

A beak of two colors—white, encircled in summer by a black band—gives the pied-billed grebe its name. This bird is also called dabchick, water-witch, and hell-diver, in tribute to its habit of dabbling around in the water and to its skill in diving and swimming underwater. One naturalist has described the grebe as a fish with feathers.

A full-grown adult measures about twelve inches in length, has a wing-spread of twenty-three inches, a brownish black head and back, a black throat, and whitish underparts. Because its toes are lobed instead of webbed, the grebe cannot swim as fast as a duck, but it has better control of its body in the water.

Like the loon, the grebe can swim at different levels. Although it usually swims high on the surface of the water, by expelling the air from its body it is able to swim partially submerged, with only its head sticking up out of the water like a submarine's periscope. The grebe may submerge by slowly sinking from sight or, as when danger threatens, by diving forward into the water with a slight "plopping" sound. It swims along underwater and surfaces only after reaching the safety of decaying rushes and flags, where its brown coloration blends with the vegetation.

Although this bird is capable of making long-distance flights, I have never seen one fly farther than twenty feet or so before dropping into the water and disappearing. Because it is unable to take off from land, the grebe scoots along the surface of the water to gain the momentum required to become airborne.

The pied-billed grebe is distributed across the continent from Nova Scotia to British Columbia and south to Mexico, wherever open fresh water is

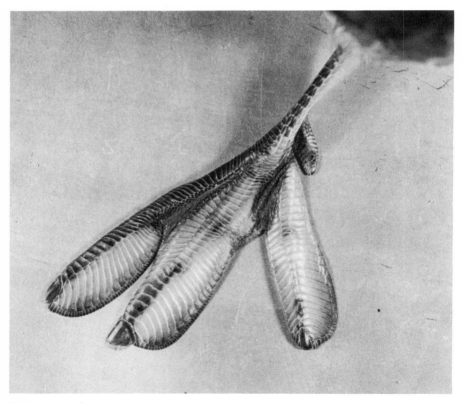

Pied-billed grebes have flat lobes on their toes in place of the skin webbing usually found between the toes of other water birds. The grebes use their feet to steer both in the air and on the water.

found. In winter it ranges only as far south as it must to find the open water it needs for survival. While it has never been numerous in any area, on rare occasions flocks of several hundred individuals have been seen.

As soon as winter's grip has loosened, the grebe returns to the northern lakes and ponds. March and April signal the start of the breeding season and set the stage for an energetic courtship display, in which the bird skitters this way and that over the surface of the water. Sometimes the display is enacted in unison by both male and female.

The grebe constructs its nest of rotting aquatic vegetable matter placed on a floating raft or mat of green vegetation. Bobbing up and down like a cork on the surface of the water, the snug home is safe from the danger of flooding. Most of the time the nest is anchored to reeds and bushes, but occasionally it is allowed to float free.

One brood is raised each year. The five to seven dull white eggs, about one and one-half inches long and one inch in diameter, soon become stained with mud and debris. The cautious grebe usually covers the eggs completely when leaving the nest, thus hiding them from detection by the casual observer. The parents take turns incubating the eggs. Because the incubation period varies from twenty-one to twenty-four days and starts soon after the first eggs have been laid, the young hatch at different times.

The male generally takes charge of the young as they hatch, while his mate completes the incubation. When only a few hours old, or as soon as their down dries, the young chicks are able to dive and to swim underwater. They cannot dive deeply, because the air trapped in the down functions as a life preserver, pushing them back to the surface. Often the little grebes climb onto a parent's back for a ride as the latter swims about.

Young grebes subsist principally upon various types of water insects, beetles, and larvae. Later they develop a taste for small fish, tadpoles, leeches, snails, crayfish, and some vegetable matter. Almost every analysis of grebes' stomach contents reveals that these birds have ingested large quantities of their own feathers. Why they should do so remains a mystery. The feathers may aid the digestion or modify the puncturing action of fish bones in the digestive tract.

Snapping turtles, large fish, eagles, and otters are the chief enemies, and they will take any grebe they can catch. Young birds, not surprisingly, are more easily taken than are adults.

3 Pelecaniformes— Pelicans and Their Allies

These large, fish-eating swimmers differ among each other in habits and appearance yet share certain anatomical similarities. All are short legged and totipalmated, that is, the four toes are webbed; the rear toe is bent forward on the inside instead of projecting to the rear. All have throat pouches and long, strong wings.

All fifty-four species of the six families comprising this ancient order are found in North America. Representatives of three of these family groups are discussed.

The largest members are the pelicans. Of the six species belonging to the family Pelecanidae, only two—the white and the brown pelicans—occur on this continent. In the pelicans the throat pouch reaches its greatest development, functioning as a dip net for scooping up fish and as a serving bowl for feeding the young.

Cormorants, belonging to the family Phalacrocoracidae, are the most numerous representatives of this order, with thirty species, six of which occur on the North American continent. The adult's black plumage led the ancient Romans to call this bird *corvus marinus*, "sea crow," long since corrupted into the English version, cormorant.

The Anhingidae family group is found only in the New World. In the United States it occurs in the southeastern and Gulf Coast regions. Unlike the other families of this order, its members are inhabitants of fresh water. This has led to their sometimes being confused with cormorants, their closest relatives, as both frequent the same areas. The latter are jet black and more compactly built, while the anhingas are light colored in spots. A common characteristic of both birds is that neither has waterproof wing feathers. Following a prolonged spell of underwater swimming, their wings become heavy. Instead of resting on the water, both anhingas and cormorants clamber ashore onto a rock or bush and spread out their wings in the sunshine to dry.

Brown Pelican
(Pelecanus occidentalis)

FIELD MARKS:	*Dark gray and white. 14-inch beak with conspicuous gular pouch. Yellow-white head. Brown stripe down back of neck in summer. Spot bare of feathers beneath eye.*
SIZE:	*4½ feet long with a wingspan of 6–7 feet.*
HABITS:	*Nets fish in its pouch. Catches fish by diving into water. Flies at a speed of 30 miles per hour.*
HABITAT:	*Coastal areas.*
NEST:	*Twigs and other materials piled in a slight depression in the sand.*
EGGS:	*Chalky white, 2–3 in a clutch, Incubation 30 days.*
FOOD:	*Mullet, menhaden, thread herring, minnows.*
VOICE:	*Low, husky chuck sound.*

One of the largest birds found in the United States, the brown pelican is easily recognized by its bulk and by its flight pattern of powerful strokes alternated by short glides.

Most of us would agree with Dixon Lanier Merritt's limerick beginning

A wonderful bird is the pelican,
Its bill will hold more than its belican.

In flight the pelican appears graceful; diving, ungainly; swimming, serene and competent; perched ashore, clumsy and uncertain.

The brown, or common, pelican is one of the largest birds found in the United States, with a total length of up to fifty-four inches and a wingspan of seventy-two to eighty-four inches. From the pelican's great bill, about fourteen inches long, hangs the bird's distinctive throat pouch. When distended, the pouch is six or seven inches deep and may hold several quarts of water.

The adult has a brown body with gray wings and tail. Its head is a bright yellowish white with a stripe of the same color extending down the neck; in winter the entire neck turns white. A spot, bare of feathers and encircling the pelican's eye, gives the bird a quizzical expression as it solemnly watches your every movement. Baby pelicans are white, turning an overall dull gray with maturity.

With its alternately flapping and soaring flight, the pelican frequently skims low over the water at a speed of thirty miles per hour. Small flocks may fly in a V or string formation. This large bird searches for food from a height of about thirty feet, plunging headfirst into the water with a tremendous splash on sighting its finny quarry. As the pelican always seems to spy the fish after passing over it, the backward-angled dive inevitably resembles an afterthought. What amazes me is the way the pelican can get its bulky body into the water before the fish escapes.

Grasping the fish with the bill, or netting it in the pouch, the pelican surfaces, expels water from the pouch, juggles the fish to face headfirst toward its throat, then swallows its meal. Sometimes a laughing gull snatches fish from the pelican's mouth as the bird is in the process of turning its catch in the right direction.

In the past, fishermen slaughtered pelicans by the thousands because of their fish-eating habits. Yet scientific investigation has proved that 98 percent of the fish eaten by these birds—mullet, menhaden, thread herring, and minnows, for example—have no commercial value.

This pelican is a familiar sight from South Carolina southward to Florida and along the Gulf Coast to Texas and California. It is, incidentally, the state bird of Louisiana. A true sea bird, the pelican is not found inland, preferring to nest on offshore islands or as near the coast as it can get.

The dull gray coloring of the immature brown pelican (left) disappears when the bird reaches maturity. The adult bird (right) has a white head and a brown body.

A beach nest is constructed by piling twigs and other material on top of a slight depression in the sand, Such a nest, however, is vulnerable to floods created by storms and hurricanes. More durable is the nest built in mangrove thickets, which offer better protection from natural disasters and thus a better chance of carrying nesting activities through to completion.

The pelican usually lays two or three large, chalky white eggs, approximately three inches long and two inches in diameter. The incubation period is about thirty days. Both parents are active in caring for the young, taking turns feeding them and shading them from the broiling sun. The return of a parent from the feeding grounds—a journey that may necessitate a round trip of one hundred miles or more—creates great excitement in the rookery. Poking their heads into the parent's pouch, the young pelicans with frantic gusto consume the fishy "soup" regurgitated by the weary traveler for their benefit. At eight to ten weeks of age the young pelicans leave the rookery.

The pelican has no natural enemies, but gulls do sometimes destroy the eggs.

Double-crested Cormorant
(Phalacrocorax auritus)

FIELD MARKS:	*Glossy back. Orange face and throat patch. Double crests on top of head. Long hook-tipped beak with serrated edges. Legs placed forward of the tail, webbing between all four toes.*
SIZE:	*30–33 inches long with a wingspan of 50–52 inches.*
HABITS:	*Sits with its body elevated and its neck in an S curve. Uses its tail as a brace while sitting and a rudder while swimming. Male and female share the task of incubation.*
HABITAT:	*Mainly the seacoast.*
NEST:	*Seaweed and kelp with sticks and twigs if available.*
EGGS:	*Bluish white, 2–4 in a clutch. Incubation 28–29 days.*
FOOD:	*Minnows, menhaden, and other trash fish.*
VOICE:	*Usually silent.*

The double-crested cormorant is the most common and farthest ranging cormorant in North America. Often seen on inland lakes and rivers, it is chiefly found along the seacoast from the Aleutians south to Mexico on the Pacific Coast and from Newfoundland south to Mexico on the Atlantic and Gulf coasts.

In spite of the many times I have observed and photographed this bird, I have yet to detect the double crests on top of the head that give this bird its name. This is probably because I have never seen the bird prior to its breeding season, when the two tufts are most prominent. Other names given to this bird are "shag" and "crow duck."

Measuring about thirty to thirty-three inches in length and with a wingspan of between fifty and fifty-two inches, the adult cormorant has glossy black plumage and an orange throat patch bare of feathers. Immature birds have a grayish white neck, breast, and belly.

The cormorant's orange bill is sharply hooked at the tip and has serrated edges. These tiny sawteeth pierce the protective slime encasing the fish and give the bird a better grip on its catch. To prevent fish spines from catching in its throat, a cormorant flips the fish so that it is swallowed headfirst. In flight the cormorant usually holds its beak slightly open, as the external nostrils, which were open at birth, shut when it reaches maturity. This is undoubtedly an adaptation for diving.

This bird characteristically sits with its body upright, its neck in an S curve, and its beak elevated. Like other diving birds, the cormorant's legs are placed well to the rear. The twelve stiff feathers of the short tail frequently function as a brace when the bird sits upright and as a rudder when it swims.

When swimming, the cormorant usually sits low in the water, its tail held on or slightly beneath the surface. The feet provide the main propulsion when the bird swims underwater. For its size the cormorant has a larger webbed foot than any bird I know. The web embraces all four toes, stretching across the three front toes and continuing around the inside to the hind toe. If extra speed is needed, the cormorant flaps its wings as though flying underwater. With such speed, the cormorant can easily outswim most fish.

The cormorant's short, narrow, tapered wings give it a top flying speed of approximately twenty miles per hour. Flocks of these birds maintain a ragged V formation, generally flying much closer to the water than do geese or ducks. To take off from the water, a cormorant spatters across the surface like an overloaded amphibious plane. Even when perched on a tree or a rocky ledge, it habitually drops down to the water, runs along for a few

Like many swimming birds, the double-crested cormorant often perches with its wings half open to dry.

steps, and then becomes airborne. This behavior gives rise to the old wives' tale that a cormorant must wet its tail before it can fly.

During a picture-taking trip to Alaska, I visited Cook's Inlet, which boasts the second highest tide in the world with a difference of twenty-seven to twenty-eight feet between high and low tides. While the tide was out, I walked along the flat to some offshore rocks, where I had noticed cormorants sitting on a number of favorite resting rocks. The birds flew off at my approach, but I was sure they would soon return. Clambering up on a nearby rock, I covered myself and my camera with a camouflaged poncho.

The cormorants flew back, circled around, and did everything but land on the rock under surveillance. Finally, several landed on the far side of the rock. All I could see of them were their heads cautiously poking up for a look, then dropping down out of sight. Eventually a few more birds flew in, lured by their fellows on the rock, and I was lucky enough to take a few photos before being trapped by the rapidly incoming tide.

Easier to work with were the Florida cormorants, which were accustomed to seeing crowds of people. Paddling our canoe out into the warm, blue-green waters of Florida Bay at Flamingo, my son and I discovered every buoy and channel marker occupied by double-crested cormorants. Once over shallow water outside the channel, we tied the canoe to a marker, jammed the tripod legs into the goey marl, and waited. We didn't have long to wait; cormorants were trading back and forth almost continuously. One flew up on our channel marker and began to preen itself, running its long, snaky neck and bill over the oil gland located above the tailbone, and rubbing the oil over its feathers. The oil waterproofed the feathers and added a high gloss to them as well, so the bird's body shone green-black in the sunlight.

Although many double-crested cormorants stay on their breeding grounds all year round, those from the northernmost regions and from the inland areas return there in April. As with most swimming birds, much of the cormorants' courtship takes place on the water. The birds beat the water with their wings, run along the surface, dive beneath it, surface, spin about wildly, and play catch with pieces of seaweed or grass.

These birds build their nests to suit the location. On low-lying offshore islands the nest is built on the ground or on top of the rocks. Where islands or coastline are high and steep sided, a favorite spot is on the ledge of a cliff. The nest is usually made of seaweed and kelp, although sticks and twigs are used if available. In many areas cormorants build their nests in dead trees. If the trees aren't dead when the birds start to nest in them, the excrement soon kills them. If nesting sites are scarce, cormorants may nest within a few feet of each other. I have seen one tree with twenty-seven nests in it.

Visiting a cormorant colony during the breeding season is not for those with weak stomachs. The odor from the excrement of hundreds of birds is overpowering. Young birds that have fallen from the nest and pieces of dropped or regurgitated food rot in the sun, attracting clouds of flies.

The cormorant lays two to four bluish white eggs, two and three-eighths inches long and one and one-half inches in diameter. Both sexes share the task of incubation, which takes twenty-eight to twenty-nine days. The changing of the pair at the nest is accomplished with all the formality of the changing of the guard at Buckingham Palace. The bird reporting for duty bows to the brooding bird, walks around the nest, caresses the other with its beak, and finally tucks its head under the other's body. The brooding bird rises and waddles off as its mate takes over.

Even after the young hatch, they must be carefully brooded. Because they are covered with a jet black down, which attracts and holds the heat, they need shielding from the sun's rays.

At first the young birds are fed a regurgitated "soup," but within a week they are capable of thrusting their heads down the parent's throat to seize larger chunks of fish from its pouch. In a short time small fish are brought in and fed directly to the young.

When they are four or five weeks old, the young leave the nest. They are hesitant to enter the water until they lose their down and feather out. By the time they are two months old, they are capable of flying.

Because the cormorant subsists exclusively on fish, it has gained the undying enmity of many fishermen. Nevertheless, extensive tests have proved that this bird is not detrimental to man's interest, for the bulk of its diet consists of minnows, menhaden, and other trash fish. The cormorant's excrement promotes the growth of plankton, which constitutes the basic food for many fish. In fact, many of the larger fish used by man feed on the small trash fish nourished by plankton.

Although the double-crested cormorant has no real enemies, its eggs are sometimes eaten by gulls and crows.

Anhinga
(Anhinga anhinga)

FIELD MARKS:	*Male: black with white spots on head, neck, back, and wings. Female: buffy brown head, neck and breast; white band on wings and tail; green circles around eyes. Long spearlike orange beak.*
SIZE:	*34 inches long with a wingspan of 47 inches.*
HABITS:	*Spears fish with its beak. Spreads out its wings to dry. Can swim with only its head and neck exposed.*
HABITAT:	*Fresh water and swamplands.*
NEST:	*Heavy twigs lined with leaves and moss.*
EGGS:	*Off-white, 3–5 in a clutch. Incubation 28 days.*
FOOD:	*Fish and occasionally insects.*
VOICE:	*Usually silent.*

The anhinga feeds mainly upon fish, which it spears with its long beak.

The anhinga is called "water turkey" because it resembles a slenderized caricature of our familiar turkey, "snake bird" because of its long, sinuous neck, and "darter" because of the quick, darting motions it makes with its head when fishing.

A full-grown adult has a wingspread of forty-seven inches and measures about thirty-four inches in total length, roughly divided into thirds: one third, beak, head, and neck; one third, body; and one third, tail. Its long legs are placed well to the rear, and the toes of its short feet are fully webbed. The male has glossy black plumage with a greenish tinge; silver spots on head, neck, back, and wings; a white band on wings and tail tip. The female's head, neck, and breast are buffy brown. Around its eyes the anhinga sports a circle of vivid green. Unlike the cormorant's bill, sharply hooked at the tip, the anhinga's bill is long and narrow. Instead of catching fish in its bill, the anhinga impales the fish upon it.

A bird of freshwater waterways and swamplands, the anhinga ranges throughout most of the southern United States where these conditions prevail. It has been found as far north as the Ohio River valley.

During the March breeding season this gregarious bird prefers to nest with others of its own kind or in rookeries with herons and ibises. The nest is well constructed of heavy twigs, to which a quantity of Spanish moss may be added, and is located off the ground in a low bush or in a tall treetop. Just before the eggs are laid, the nest is lined with green leaves. The three to five off-white eggs, overlaid with a chalky encrustation, are two inches long and one and one-quarter inches in diameter. Both parents participate in the incubation process, which takes about twenty-eight days.

Young anhingas feed by sticking their heads down the parent's throat and extracting the regurgitated morsels. As they grow in size, the young birds thrash about in the nearby bushes with beaks and feet, flapping their flightless wings. If they fall into the water, they simply swim back to shore.

Although insects occasionally are taken, fish constitute the mainstay of the anhinga's diet. The anhinga catches fish by direct pursuit, swimming swiftly underwater and chasing the fish in among the weeds and grasses. Using its long, sharp beak as a spear, the bird actually impales the fish instead of grasping it. Then the anhinga surfaces, shakes the fish loose from its beak, and swallows it headfirst. Only rarely does it take a fish valued by man for food or sport.

A peculiarity of the anhinga is the "hairy" lining of its stomach. This may serve to restrain fish bones from being released into the intestines until they have been softened by the digestive processes.

After satisfying its hunger, the anhinga leaves the water and clambers awkwardly into a nearby bush or tree, where it spreads its wings to dry in the manner of fishermen drying their nets. When the feathers are thoroughly dried, the bird busily employs its beak to stroke them with waterproofing oil obtained from a gland above the tail.

Ordinarily the anhinga is extremely wary and quick to make its escape as man approaches. If it can do so unseen, the bird drops into the water like an arrow and disappears beneath the surface to seek refuge among tall weeds or under overhanging brush. Holding its beak and head above water like a periscope, the anhinga escapes detection by remaining motionless. At other times it escapes by taking to the air. This bird is a strong flier and does considerable soaring after gaining sufficient altitude.

The anhinga is a peaceful bird, apparently not sufficiently numerous to bother anyone, yet seen often enough to be interesting. Seldom molested by man or by other creatures, this bird seems to have found the key to peaceful coexistence, although raccoons, gulls, and crows do occasionally take their eggs.

4 Anseriformes— Waterfowl

This order is made up of two family groups. The family Anhimidae has only three members, the screamers, all natives exclusively of South America. The family Anatidae, whose members we shall be discussing, is divided into eight subfamilies—swans, geese, surface-feeding ducks, tree ducks, bay ducks and sea ducks, stifftails, and mergansers—which, in turn, are composed of 145 species.

All members of this family can swim. They have short legs, webbed front toes, and a flattened bill equipped with either strainers or sawteeth. Most have medium long to long necks. Swift, strong-winged fliers, these birds are easily capable of long-distance flight. They keep their feathers heavily oiled and waterproofed. Beneath the feathers, most have a layer of down and a subcutaneous layer of fat for warmth.

These birds are for the most part gregarious and spend much of their time in large flocks, except during the breeding season, when they select individual home territories. In general, where male and female have a similar coloration, the male helps to raise the family. Where the male is the more brightly colored sex, the female usually raises the family alone. One annual brood is the rule.

The members of this order feed chiefly on vegetation in the form of plants, seeds, nuts, grains, and roots. Certain species feed on the surface of the water; others use their long necks to feed underwater. Some tip up and feed with just their tails out of water; others dive completely beneath the surface.

The shallow-water, or "puddle," ducks, which feed by tipping up, can spring into the air and fly away. The deep-water, or diving, ducks must run across the surface of the water to gain speed before they can become airborne. Swans and geese also have to run to acquire lift.

The mergansers are fish eaters, which dive beneath the water and catch their prey by outswimming it. They, too, run across the water before taking off.

Mute Swan
(*Cygnus olor*)

FIELD MARKS:	*Pure white plumage, bright crange-red bill with a large black fleshy knob.*
SIZE:	*40 inches long with a wingspan of 90 inches.*
HABITS:	*Carries its neck in an S curve while swimming. Adults mate for life.*
HABITAT:	*Lakes, ponds, marshes, bays.*
NEST:	*Grass, aquatic vegetation, sticks, twigs.*
EGGS:	*Greenish or dull white, 4–6 in a clutch. Incubation 5–6 weeks.*
FOOD:	*Aquatic insects and plants.*
VOICE:	*Low-pitched grunt.*

The only swans to breed in the eastern United States, mute swans begin nesting in April or May along freshwater inland lakes or ponds.

The name "mute swan" is a misnomer. Although this swan is much less loquacious than either the trumpeter or the whistling swan, it is capable of uttering a low-pitched grunt, a buglelike blare, a snort, and when angry, a hiss.

It is extremely difficult to distinguish between the mute swan and the whistling swan in flight, but the difference is readily apparent when the birds are on the water. The ranges of the mute and trumpeter swans do not overlap, so no confusion exists between their two species. Both trumpeter and whistling swans hold their long necks stiffly erect while swimming, whereas the mute swan carries its neck in the graceful S curve we think of as being typically swanlike. The whistling swan's bill is black, with a bright yellow spot in front of the eye, and is carried pointing straight ahead. The mute swan's bill is bright orange-red, with a large black fleshy knob on top at the forehead, and is usually carried pointed down toward the water. The mute swan also raises its wings up over its back while swimming. This action is used by the male when displaying for the female, as a sign of aggression to rivals, or as a danger signal; it is used by the female when she wishes to brood her young on her back while swimming.

Young mute swans cannot begin to rival the beauty of their parents. This is the essence of Hans Christian Andersen's fairy tale, "The Ugly Duckling." Their down coats are sooty gray, their beaks dull rose, banded with black. Only when they are at least two years old do they attain their full panoply of white plumage. Some mute swans have been reported to live to be one hundred years old.

A full-grown adult measures forty inches in length, has a wingspan of ninety inches, and weighs between twenty and thirty pounds. The swan uses its strong wings as flails when fighting. Although the mute swan has been domesticated for centuries, it is seldom tame, even in captivity. It easily dominates all other waterfowl and is extremely aggressive toward dogs, cats, even man himself.

Since ancient times the mute swan has been held in high regard, as evidenced by Greek mythology. From the union of the supreme god Zeus, disguised as a swan, with Leda, wife of King Tyndareus of Sparta, so legend has it, came Pollux and Helen of Troy.

The mute swan is not native to North America but was introduced during the mid-1800's from Europe, where it had been domesticated prior to the twelfth century. In 1482 England's King Edward IV proclaimed this swan royal game, decreeing: "No person whatever, except the King's son, should have any swan-mark or game of swans of his own . . . except that he hath freehold lands and tenements to the clear yearly value of five marks." To see that his laws were obeyed, the king created the office of swankeeper and appointed deputies to help him enforce the law. Undoubtedly it was this type of protection that prevented the mute swan from being exterminated as the population of Europe continued to increase. To this day all swans on England's Thames River belong to the monarch and to two London companies. Every year the swans are caught and bill marked, and the young are pinioned by having the first joints of one wing tip cut off, which prevents their being able to fly.

By the early 1900's, wild mute swans began to be seen along the New Jersey coast and on the marshes and bays of Long Island. As the wild population continues to grow, these swans have increased their range so that they are now found as far north as the New England states and as far south as Maryland. Mute swans are the only swans to nest in the northeastern United States; whistling swans go north to the Canadian Arctic.

Mute swans do not migrate in the usual sense, that is, they do not travel far when forced to move in the winter. Breeding season finds them on freshwater inland lakes or ponds. When winter's icy grip seals off such areas, the birds move to the brackish coastal areas that remain open, where they can find food and safety.

The wild mute swan population is well established on Swartswood Lake, in Sussex County, New Jersey, only twenty miles from my home. The swans usually return to the lake as soon as the ice breaks up in March; I knew of twenty-eight nesting pairs there during a recent spring.

Adults mate for life, but there is considerable fighting among the young males, or cobs, as they seek to establish a relationship with receptive females, or pens. The young pens form attachments when they are one year old but do not lay eggs until their second year.

The swans begin nest construction in April or May, often on top of an abandoned muskrat house or on a sandspit, or the nest may be built from scratch out in the marsh or swamp. One common factor is that all the nests continue to grow larger the longer they are used. The swan lays four to six greenish or dull white eggs, which are four and one-half inches long, two and three-quarters inches in diameter.

During several days spent photographing mute swans on Swartswood Lake, I watched the female adding new material to the nest—already about five feet in diameter and two feet above water—as she brooded. Part of the time she slept, her long neck curved back so that her head rested on top of one wing and at times was covered by the raised secondary feathers. Awake, she idly reached down and picked up strands of grass, gobs of rotting aquatic vegetation, or bits of sticks and twigs, which she proceeded to pile up around the rim of the nest.

Before the female left the nest to feed and exercise, she stood on the edge, plucking beakfuls of material to carefully cover her eggs as a protection from the hot sun or chill wind, or from crows and other predators. Only when she was satisfied that the eggs would escape detection did she walk stiffly down to the water's edge and swim off to join her mate.

Although the male did not assist his mate in her five to six weeks' incubation vigil, he was always near at hand as a protector. When the young hatched, he proudly convoyed his family through the rushes and reeds, where they fed on aquatic insects and plants.

Trumpeter Swan
(Olor buccinator)

FIELD MARKS:	*Snow white after first year, long neck, black beak.*
SIZE:	*45 inches long with a wingspan of 95 inches; females slightly smaller.*
HABITS:	*The largest bird that flies on the North American continent. Carries neck stiffly upright while swimming.*
HABITAT:	*Lakes.*
NEST:	*Large and bulky, frequently built on top of an old muskrat house.*
EGGS:	*White or pale green, 4–6 in a clutch. Incubation 28–32 days.*
FOOD:	*Aquatic vegetation and insects.*
VOICE:	*Loud, deep call.*

The trumpeter swan, our largest swan, is one of the rarest birds in North America. Once close to extinction, the trumpeter has been reintroduced in many areas and is now increasing in numbers.

Today the trumpeter swan is one of the rarest birds on the North American continent. This was not always so. Early records going back to 1700 show that at one time the trumpeter's loud, deep call, like the notes of a French horn, sounded throughout most of North America. Its breeding range extended south to Missouri; winters found the swan as far south as the Gulf of Mexico and along the Atlantic seacoast. Large flocks of trumpeters mingled with even larger flocks of whistling swans.

As settlers filled the United States, a war of extermination was waged upon the swans. The war was not intentional, rather, inevitable. Young swans made delicious eating, although the older birds, which live to be fifty to sixty years old, were tough and stringy. The quills of the trumpeters, too, were eagerly sought for use as writing pens. Naturalist John James Audubon preferred them for his finest work, saying that they were much stronger and more flexible than any of the steel pens available at the time. Swan feathers and skins were used in the millinery trade. However, it was the trumpeters' conspicuousness and size that really led to their destruction. Then, as now, some people were attracted to a target as large as a swan simply because it existed.

Swan hunting became an organized business. Indian hunters of northern Canada killed the birds during their flightless summer period. In the years between 1853 and 1877 the Hudson's Bay Company bought and sold more than seventeen thousand swan skins.

Under such pressure the swan's range became more restricted. No longer did it range to the Gulf of Mexico, nor was it seen on the Atlantic or the Pacific coasts. In summer it ventured farther north to the Arctic tundra in an effort to escape persecution. By 1933 only sixty-six trumpeter swans were left alive in the United States. Luckily for the swans—and for us—the trumpeters are now protected and are gradually increasing in numbers.

I saw my first trumpeters while on a camping trip into Yellowstone National Park in 1960. A single pair was swimming on the far side of a roadside lake, but I was unable to get close enough to photograph them. Six years later I again located trumpeters on a wilderness lake on Alaska's Kenai Peninsula, but efforts to photograph them were also unsuccessful.

The two adults and four cygnets were as wild as the area. The adults had shed their primary flight feathers and could not fly, while the young were too small to have developed their feathers. Still, the birds had no trouble keeping most of the lake between us. The adults ran along the surface of the lake, flapping their wings, their feet splattering water in all directions, at the same time keeping up a resonant call that made the forest ring. The downy young simply turned tails up and dived beneath the surface to reappear hundreds of feet away.

On a recent camping trip to Yellowstone I finally achieved success. Unlike the others I had tried to photograph, the trumpeters I now had in my lens were intent upon feeding in the shallows of the lake. Although the water was not deep, the mud was so soft and squishy that it prevented me from approaching closer. Despite the fact that I never manage to get as close as I would like, the trumpeter presents a good-sized target.

The trumpeter swan is the largest bird that flies on the North American continent. Large adult males have a total length of forty-five inches, a wingspan of ninety-five inches, and weigh between twenty and thirty pounds; the female is slightly smaller. The trumpeter carries its neck stiffly upright while swimming, unlike the mute swan's graceful S curve, and it is now a western bird, whereas the mute swan is found only in the eastern United States. Slightly smaller than the trumpeter, the whistling swan's range overlaps that of its larger cousin, but the bright yellow spot on its bill serves as an identifying characteristic.

A trumpeter swan's nest is large and bulky, frequently built on top of an abandoned muskrat house. Cradled in the down lining are four to six white or pale green eggs, four and one-quarter inches long and two and five-eighths inches in diameter. Twenty-eight to thirty-two days are required to hatch the eggs, and the cygnets are then carefully shepherded by both parents. The young birds are a sooty gray their first year but the following year acquire the snow white plumage of adulthood.

Aquatic vegetation and insects comprise the trumpeter's principal diet, although it also eats grain. The swan gathers most of its food in the water and often feeds by tipping up in the fashion of dabbling ducks. With its long neck it can easily feed on the bottom, even when the water is three to four feet deep.

By early fall, adult swans have grown their new primary feathers and are again capable of flight, about the same time that the young are learning to fly. Swans cannot leap into the air to fly but must first gain momentum by running along the surface of the water. When airborne, the swan's neck and feet both are extended straight out. With a deep, measured wing stroke, the swan soon reaches a cruising speed of about forty miles per hour. Swans in flight present a beautiful sight. Their glistening white bodies and flashing wings against the blue sky give the impression of a fragment of cloud that has broken loose and drifted earthward.

While these birds are capable of making long flights in a short time, flocks of migrants are no longer seen in the United States. Most trumpeter swans remain on the lakes where they have hatched their young. The Red Rock Lakes Migratory Wildfowl Refuge, in southwestern Montana, is one of the best places to find them the year around. Like some of the lakes utilized by the swans in Yellowstone National Park, the Red Rock Lakes do not freeze in the wintertime, because the water is naturally heated by the hot springs of the region. In this refuge, rangers put out more than one thousand bushels of grain to help the birds during the winter. The Canadian government performs the same task in British Columbia, where the majority of existing trumpeters spend the winter.

Canada Goose
(Branta canadensis)

FIELD MARKS:	*Dark brown on back and tops of wings with lighter underparts; broad white chin strap; black feet, bill, head, and neck.*
SIZE:	*3½ feet long with a wingspan of 5½ feet.*
HABITS:	*Mates for life. Loses all flight feathers for a period during the summer.*
HABITAT:	*Lake shores and coastal marshes.*
NEST:	*Aquatic vegetation lined with down and feathers.*
EGGS:	*Olive green, 5–9 in a clutch. Incubation 28 days.*
FOOD:	*Aquatic vegetation, roots, grasses, grain, insects.*
VOICE:	*Honking.*

32

The Canada goose is easily identified by its black head and neck, its broad white cheek, and its characteristic honking.

The Canada goose is a familiar symbol of approaching spring or autumn. Long, V-shaped bands of geese flying southward are certain signs that cold weather will soon follow, for geese head south when the northern lakes begin to freeze over. In the spring the sound of flocks heading northward heralds advancing warm weather. Long after they have passed by, the honking of these geese as they fly overhead in the night trails down and gladdens the hearts of all who hear it.

One of the largest, most commonly seen, and best-known species of waterfowl in the United States today, the Canada goose formerly bred primarily in the Arctic or near-Arctic regions. It is now found nesting farther south in increasing numbers, owing to the increased protection it is receiving.

This bird is dwarfed only by the larger swans. When fully grown, it weighs up to eighteen pounds, measures forty-two inches in length, and has a wingspread of sixty-six inches. Its upper parts are grayish brown; underparts are lighter. Feet and bill are black. The sexes are look-alikes. Owing to

Canada geese usually mate for life and are very devoted to their young. Families of geese are often seen swimming about with the female in the lead and the male bringing up the rear.

its large size, the Canada goose is deceptive in flight: Each wingbeat appears to be slow and measured, yet this bird can fly at speeds of up to forty-five and fifty miles per hour.

A devoted parent, the Canada goose usually mates for life. It constructs a nest of several bushels of aquatic vegetation it has gathered and piled into a mound. From the brood spot on her breast, the female plucks down and feathers to line the nest. Only one brood of young is raised per year. Both parents take turns incubating the five to nine olive green eggs, each about three inches long and two inches in diameter, for the required twenty-eight days. After the young hatch, they are convoyed by both parents, the female leading the way, with the young swimming behind her and the male bringing up the rear.

For a period during the summer, ducks and geese lose all their flight feathers at once and seek the sanctuary of open water. By September both the adults and the season's young are able to fly; soon afterward they start the trip south. Some geese winter as far south as Mexico, but the majority travel only as far south as they must to escape the freezing of the lakes.

Canada geese feed on all types of aquatic vegetation, roots, grasses, and grain. While they may do some damage by pulling up unharvested or newly sprouted grain, they help to pay for their depredations by eating the destructive insects they find in the grain fields. When feeding, they always post a sentry to watch for danger. Usually the male stands guard for his family and does not hesitate to attack anything or anyone threatening it, striking out with beak and wings. Blows struck with the wings can shatter an enemy's bones. Later, when the geese flock, several of the older males assume this job for the entire flock.

The greatest threat to the Canada goose is the man with a gun. Foxes sometimes prey on the adult, and both raccoons and foxes will try for the goslings.

American Brant
(*Branta bernicla*)

FIELD MARKS:	*Dark brown back and wings, white belly. Black head, neck, and breast. Adult has white semicircle around back of neck.*
SIZE:	*30 inches long with a wingspan of 50–52 inches.*
HABITS:	*Brooding done entirely by the female. Excellent swimmers.*
HABITAT:	*Salt water.*
NEST:	*Down piled in a slight depression among stones on beaches.*
EGGS:	*Grayish white, 3–5 in a clutch. Incubation 4 weeks.*
FOOD:	*Eelgrass, sea lettuce.*
VOICE:	*Guttural honking.*

The American brant breeds along the Arctic coast and winters in coastal bays from Cape Cod south to North Carolina. This sea goose is never found far from salt water.

As the sun's slanting rays turned the wintry sky of New Jersey's Brigantine National Wildlife Refuge to a burnished coppery gold, long, strung-out lines of brant came flying in low. When they came nearer, one could see that their bodies were smaller than those of Canada geese, while their necks were shorter and their wingbeats faster. Scorning the impounded freshwater areas, the brant dropped down outside the dikes into the seawater of the bay. Calling among themselves with a guttural honking, the brant splashed and disported in the water, seemingly aware that here they were safe.

In wintertime this brant can be found from Cape Cod south to North Carolina. New Jersey probably boasts as large a concentration of brant as any single spot, with Brigantine and Barnegat being famous for them.

The brant is a sea goose and never strays far from salt water. Larger than a mallard, it weighs up to four pounds, is about thirty inches long, and has a wingspan of fifty to fifty-two inches. Head, neck, and breast are jet black, in vivid contrast to the characteristic white belly that distinguishes this bird from the black brant of the Pacific Coast. The brant has a white line on either side of its neck, while the black brant has an almost completely white collar.

In early spring, while ice still locks the inland lakes, the brant begins to head north. The southernmost flocks depart first, picking up increasing numbers as they journey on. Some brant follow the coast, others cross Hudson Bay. They breed from Ellesmere Island to Greenland, and as far east as Spitsbergen, nesting along the coastlines among aquatic vegetation. On barren beaches, a slight depression between stones is utilized and filled with down.

Three to five grayish white eggs, two and three-quarters inches long and one and three-quarters inches in diameter, make up the average set, and the brooding is done entirely by the female. About four weeks are required for the eggs to hatch. Although the male does not incubate the eggs, he provides protection for the female while she is setting and helps to care for the young after they hatch.

As soon as their down dries, the baby brant scamper off to the sea and plop in. Right from the start they are excellent swimmers, and their buoyancy permits them to float high in the water like their parents. They feed on insects, some crustaceans, and vegetation. Brant do not dive underwater when feeding, preferring to pluck the vegetation that is exposed at low tide.

The brant now numbers approximately 225,000 birds, but a few years ago it was threatened with extinction. In 1931 eelgrass, which had been the bird's main dietary staple, contributing 90 percent of its food in winter, was almost completely wiped out. With the eelgrass gone, many species of ducks and geese were hard pressed for food, and the brant died by the tens of thousands.

Fortunately, some of the brant began to feed upon a weed called sea lettuce. This weed replaced the eelgrass that had been lost. Little by little the eelgrass recovered, until today it grows almost as abundantly as it did formerly. The brant has gone back to feeding on it but at the same time has retained its liking for sea lettuce. Any species that depends upon one type of food to the exclusion of all others is almost automatically fated for destruction if anything happens to that source. The brant has made the transition to a multiple diet, thus its chances of future survival are better.

The chief predators of the brant are man, raccoons, and foxes; gulls sometimes eat the eggs. Brant are wary birds, make delicious eating, and are attracted easily to properly placed decoys. All things being equal, they should provide shooting sport for many years to come.

Mallard Duck
(Anas platyrhynchos)

FIELD MARKS:	*Male: metallic green head, brownish red breast, white neck band; olive bill. Female: mottled brown with orange bill.*
SIZE:	*24–28 inches long with a wingspan of 40 inches.*
HABITS:	*Male abandons female after breeding season. Change their way of life to conform to hunters.*
HABITAT:	*Ponds and freshwater marshes.*
NEST:	*Down-lined hollow.*
EGGS:	*Greenish buff, about 12. Incubation 28 days.*
FOOD:	*Mainly vegetarians, but also eat insects and small fish.*
VOICE:	*Loud quack by female, whistling sound by males.*

A favorite target of hunters, mallard ducks are extremely abundant and can be found all over the northern parts of the northern hemisphere. The male of this species is recognized by its rusty breast, green head, and white neck band.

To the duck hunter the mallard is king. Sometimes known as the "common wild duck," it is found around the world in the Northern Hemisphere and is the most abundant of all species. With the exception of the Muscovy duck, the majority of our domestic ducks trace their ancestry to the mallard. This duck is also the chief waterfowl of most game preserves.

The mallard is a large duck, weighing up to three and one-half pounds; it has a total length of about twenty-four to twenty-eight inches and a wingspread of up to forty inches. A green head, white neckband, and rusty breast distinguish the drake, or male. The hen is smaller and mottled brown in color. Both sexes have a blue wing patch bordered with two white bars.

Mallards are in the vanguard of advancing migratory flocks. As soon as the ponds are freed from the winter ice, these hardy birds fly in to celebrate the occasion. The breeding season starts almost immediately thereafter, with the ducks quickly pairing off to establish their claims to a particular section of pothole, pond, or slough. Although mallards may be found nesting across the northern tier of states, the bulk of the flocks nest in Canada as far north as the Arctic Circle.

When the breeding season ends, the drake generally abandons the hen and seeks out the company of other males. The hen, meanwhile, has selected a secluded spot among high grass or near water for a nest, which is usually a down-filled hollow or depression. Here she lays an egg a day until her clutch of about a dozen greenish to grayish buff eggs, a little more than two inches long by one and one-half inches in diameter, is completed. The period of incubation is about twenty-eight days.

As soon as the ducklings hatch, the hen shepherds them to the water. The little ones plop right in and commence dabbling and surface-feeding on insects, an excellent source of protein. The young grow rapidly and soon supplement their diet with aquatic plants, wild rice, and other seeds.

It is often a wonder that we have any ducks at all. Crows, raccoons, ground squirrels, foxes, and skunks commonly break up many nests and consume the eggs. The young ducklings themselves are preyed upon by most of the meat-eating birds and animals, in addition to being exposed to the underwater forays of fish and snapping turtles.

Around the first of June the mallards' primary flight feathers fall out all at once, and the ducks can only escape by swimming. Their beautiful breeding plumage is replaced by what is known as "eclipse" plumage. Dressed in this somber garb, it is often difficult to distinguish males from females. The best field identification mark is the female's orange bill compared to the male's olive one.

With the coming of fall, the ducks regain their flying ability, and the males once more color up in their winter plumage. Families come together to make flocks of ever-increasing numbers as the flights wend their way southward. Mallards are capable of flying at speeds of up to sixty miles per hour and could make short work of their long trip if they really exerted themselves. Paradoxically, they meander south, being hurried only by the ice of winter.

Meanwhile the frosty air is sealing up the northern waters and releasing the safeties on the hunters' guns. Mallards change their normal way of life to conform to the activities of the hunters. Under normal conditions, the ducks feed early in the morning and spend the daytime hours in the most isolated and inaccessible spots they can find. They feed again in late afternoon. If the hunting pressure becomes excessive, the ducks may even begin feeding at night under the protective blanket of darkness.

With their mottled brown coloration, female mallard ducks are much less attractive than the males. The female mallards usually lay their clutch of greenish buff eggs in a down-lined hollow in some secluded area.

5 Falconiformes–Vultures, Hawks, and Falcons

Five family groups of day-flying birds of prey make up the order Falconiformes. Four of the families are found in North America.

These large flesh-eaters are characterized by exceptional binocular vision; strong wings for flapping flight or soaring; strong, sharply hooked beaks; and, with the exception of the vultures, strong, sharp, curved talons. Like the eagles and the owls, they have three talons pointed forward and one pointed backward, with the outer talon capable of being turned at will to the front or to the back. The females generally are larger than the males.

To the family Cathartidae belong five vultures of the New World, including the Andean and California condors, the largest flying birds in the world. Both condors have a wingspan of about 120 inches and a much greater wing width than that of any other bird—the turkey vulture has a wing span of 72 inches; the black vulture, 54 inches. The best-known members of this family, which feeds on carrion, are the black and the turkey vultures.

The family Accipitridae is the largest family of this order, boasting 205 species worldwide, 23 of which are represented in North America. This family includes the hawks that we call kites, accipiters, harriers, and buteos; the eagles; and the Old World vultures. Its members come in a great variety of shapes and sizes. Some of the smallest ones feed on insects; many of the medium- to large-size members are fierce predators of small animals, rodents, and birds; the largest members are scavengers.

The osprey is the only member of the family Pandionidae. Truly an international bird, this strong, powerful flier's five subspecies are found near water in North and South America, Europe, Asia, Africa, and Australia.

Most members of this order are becoming increasingly rare, owing to man's unrelenting warfare against them. If the birds are not shot on sight, they are often inadvertently poisoned by eating baits set out for mammals or by widespread agricultural sprayings. Many of these birds are among the wildest of wild creatures and cannot tolerate the encroachments of man and his so-called civilization.

Turkey Vulture
(*Cathartes aura*)

FIELD MARKS:	*Dark brown with naked red head.*
SIZE:	*26–30 inches long with a wingspan of 6 feet.*
HABITS:	*Holds wings in a broad V while flying. Extremely long-lived. Soars for hours without flapping wings.*
HABITAT:	*Fields and roadsides.*
NEST:	*Rudimentary nest of leaves and twigs.*
EGGS:	*White with brown markings, 2–3 in a clutch. Incubation 30 days.*
FOOD:	*Carrion.*
VOICE:	*Hisses.*

Turkey vultures are masters at flying and can soar for hours without flapping their six-foot wings.

The turkey vulture's habit of feeding on carrion makes it repulsive to many, yet the bird is only carrying out the role in life for which it was designed and created. Its feet are too weak to be used for grasping and killing in the manner of many birds of prey. Its flight is too slow and measured to permit it to overtake or plunge down on its prey. This vulture's role of aerial janitor is to feed on dead creatures in order to control disease and tidy up the landscape. So valued is the turkey vulture as a scavenger that it is protected wherever it is found.

The eating of carrion also gives the vulture an effective weapon against some of its enemies, particularly man. If the vulture is attacked, or if man attempts to capture one, the bird regurgitates the putrid carrion it has eaten and sprays it upon its tormentor. Skunks are a favored food, whether through preference or because their scent makes them easy to locate, I do not know. I do know that vultures will feed on a dead skunk in preference to anything else.

Commonly found throughout most of the United States, the turkey vulture winters in its nesting areas except in the northern part of its range. In my area of New Jersey the vulture, not the robin, is the first bird to return in the spring.

The "turkey buzzard," as it is often called, is a large bird, two-toned brownish in color, approximately twenty-six to thirty inches long, and with a wingspread of seventy-two inches. Its distinctive naked red head allows it to feed inside a dead animal's carcass without soiling its feathers. Male and female are look-alikes.

This bird nests on the ground, on high cliffs, in caves, under or inside hollow logs, in cellars of tumbled-down houses, or even in abandoned cabins and houses. Its nest is of the most rudimentary type—perhaps a few leaves or twigs scratched together. Two or three dull brown splotched white eggs, measuring a little more than two and one-half inches long and one and one-half inches in diameter, make up the annual clutch. The female incubates the eggs for about thirty days; not until six or seven weeks after hatching are the young vultures able to join their parents in the effortless flight so characteristic of the species.

In flight, vultures are masters of the art of soaring. Riding high in the sky or sailing low over the fields, they can soar for hours without flapping a wing. Turkey vultures hold their wings on a more marked V angle than do most of the other soaring birds. This is a good identification mark, and one that can be seen at long distance. Seldom do vultures take to the air before eight or nine o'clock in the morning; perched on a fencepost or dead tree, they welcome the rising sun with outstretched wings. As the sun climbs higher in the sky and the earth begins to warm, thermal drafts the birds have been waiting for are created. With a few ungainly flappings of their powerful broad wings, they seek out the thermals and soon are lofted into the sky, where they appear as mere wheeling specks.

Now the search for food begins, each vulture keeping an eye on the others. As soon as one bird locates food and drops out of the sky, its nearest companion notices the action and heads for the feast. The second vulture's departure is noted by the third, and so it goes, until many birds are gathered at one spot.

Many authorities claim that the turkey vulture finds its food by sight alone. While vultures have wonderful eyesight, I have witnessed too many occasions where they found their food or were attracted to it by scent alone to allow that claim to go unchallenged. Once, when conducting a survey on foxes, I hoped to attract my subjects by placing decomposed bait in the middle of a small, raked-over patch of ground. Standing near a high, brushy fence row, I happened to notice several vultures circling the next field. I opened the jar of bait, and as the odor wafted up to the vultures, they came homing in on it like planes on a radio beam. Suddenly spying me as they cleared the fence row, the surprised birds almost bent their pinions double in their haste to regain altitude.

On a large carcass, vultures may become so gorged that they have difficulty flying. When that occurs, they wait on the ground until part of their stomach contents is digested. If molested at this time, they vomit some of

Turkey vultures rarely fly early in the morning, but sit on a fence post or dead tree with wings outstretched, waiting for thermals to develop.

the food to lighten their weight so that they can fly. Many vultures are killed on the highway after gorging themselves on creatures that have fallen victim to the automobile. Too heavy to move quickly, they in turn are often struck by passing vehicles and add their own carcasses to the carnage. I have never seen any animal—not even another vulture—feed on a vulture's carcass. Raccoons, opossums, and skunks will eat the turkey vulture's eggs, and all three of these plus the fox will attack the flightless young vultures.

Despite their unappetizing diet, vultures live many years. Accurate records exist of individuals which have lived more than one hundred years.

Black Vulture
(*Coragyps atratus*)

FIELD MARKS: *Short blackish gray feathers covering back of neck and head; short tail; whitish patch on the undersurface of each wing toward the tip. Naked black face.*

SIZE: *22–25 inches long with a wingspan of 54 inches.*

HABITS: *Courtship displays, flies with several wing flaps and a short sail.*

HABITAT: *Southern part of U.S.*

NEST: *None; lays eggs directly on ground.*

EGGS: *Gray-green, 2 in a clutch. Incubation 28–30 days.*

FOOD: *Carrion, young birds.*

VOICE: *Hisses.*

Black vultures feed mainly on carrion, but they often invade settled areas in search of garbage and small animals.

Like the turkey vulture, the black vulture is common in the southern United States, but its range is more restricted, seldom extending north of Kansas. The two vultures resemble each other from a distance, but closer examination reveals that the black vulture has short black feathers covering the back of its head and neck, while the turkey vulture's red head and neck are naked. The black vulture is slightly smaller—twenty-two to twenty-five inches long—and has a shorter wingspread—fifty-four inches. This disadvantage is immediately apparent when the two birds take to the air. The turkey vulture is much more buoyant and graceful in flight, seldom needing to flap its wings to stay aloft. Unless the thermals are strong, on the other hand, the black vulture must flap almost continuously to remain airborne.

This gregarious bird travels, feeds, nests, and roosts in large colonies of its own kind. Some concentrations number into the thousands. With the arrival of the breeding season, in late February or early March, the black vultures put on quite a courtship display as the males compete for the females. Only the slightly larger size of the males distinguishes them from the females. Circling around the females, bobbing their heads and hissing, the males sometimes display by raising their wings over their backs until the tips meet. When a female singles out one of the males, the couple performs intricate soaring flights, wheeling in tight circles with wings almost touching.

No attempt at nest-building is made. Although the black vulture prefers to nest in large, hollow trees having an entrance hole a few feet above the ground, when such trees are in short supply, the bird lays its eggs directly on the ground, sometimes under dense tangles of thickets and bushes. In many areas the black vulture, like the turkey vulture, lays its eggs in shallow caves or on the rock ledges of steep cliff-sides.

Owing to the long period of care required by their young, black vultures raise only one brood a year. Incubation by both parents begins as soon as the first of a pair of gray-green, smooth-shelled eggs, approximately three inches long and two inches in diameter, is laid. Twenty-eight to thirty days are required for the eggs to hatch, although sometimes incubation may be extended for another ten days until the second egg has hatched.

The young birds are helpless at first and must be carefully guarded against the elements. The parents nourish them with regurgitated food in a liquid state until they are large enough to digest chunks of meat. In about two weeks' time, the youngsters are strong enough to begin wandering about. Better than three months must elapse before they are capable of flying.

In the southern states the black vulture is commonly called "black buzzard" or "carrion crow," because most of its food consists of dead bird and animal carcasses. Yet this vulture also feeds on living creatures and is responsible for a tremendous amount of destruction in the southern heron rookeries, where it feeds on young birds.

At one time many vultures, both black and turkey, were killed because it was thought they spread disease by eating creatures that had died of disease. Today we know that the various diseases that may infect their food cannot survive the vultures' digestive juices and systems. In most areas vultures are now protected by law.

Owls, hawks, eagles, raccoons, foxes, and bobcats are among the predators that will catch and eat young vultures whenever they can. Both young and adult vultures protect themselves by disgorging the contents of their stomachs over anything that scares or molests them. This action constitutes quite an effective weapon. Adults are relatively free from predation, however. As a matter of fact, vultures are among the longest lived of all creatures; several have been recorded that have lived more than seventy-five years in captivity.

Red-tailed Hawk
(Buteo jamaicensis)

FIELD MARKS:	*Mottled dark brown and white back and wings, lighter breast with dark belly band, yellow feet. Upper tail surface is conspicuous brownish red.*
SIZE:	*Male: 20–22 inches long with a wingspan of 50 inches. Female: 22–25 inches with a wingspan of 56 inches.*
HABITS:	*Soars in wide circles, perches on trees and poles. Adults leave young alone in the nest at night after the brooding period is over.*
HABITAT:	*Nests in woodlands, feeds in the open country.*
NEST:	*Platform of sticks. Green twigs of conifer are placed in nest to claim occupancy.*
EGGS:	*Dull white with brown or purple blotches, usually 3 in a clutch. Incubation 28 days.*
FOOD:	*Mainly rats and mice; squirrels, small animals, and insects.*
VOICE:	*Piercing scream.*

49

My first encounter with a red-tailed hawk was back in 1936, the year my parents purchased a hilltop farm in Warren County, in the northwest corner of New Jersey. When I was taken to inspect what was to become our new home, my most vivid recollection was of seeing a large hawk nailed spread-eagle to the side of the barn. The farmer was tremendously proud of his son for having shot the "chicken hawk," as he called it. In later years I recalled the light breast, dark belly band, and brick red tail that identified that hawk as a red-tail.

Even today many rural people lack the most rudimentary knowledge or understanding of the creatures that share their lands. This ignorance persists in spite of the efforts of conservationists, county agents, and agricultural colleges. To many persons any large soaring bird is a "hen hawk" or a "chicken hawk" that should be shot on sight. A few years ago one of my neighbors disgustedly told me how he had just missed shooting down a really big brown hawk. He was fortunate to have missed, because the bird at which he had aimed was an immature bald eagle, the killing of which is subject to a federal fine.

There are no "chicken hawks" as such. Although there are hawks that eat chickens, the red-tail should not be included with these. Most of the damage done to poultry and game birds is perpetrated by the woods hawks, the accipiters, such as the goshawk and Cooper's hawk. These birds are seldom seen, because they customarily perch on a tree, waiting inconspicuously until they spot their prey. Then they swoop with bulletlike swiftness, usually attacking horizontally. If the prey is small enough, the accipiters snatch it from the ground and keep right on going until they reach heavy cover, where they can feed in safety and out of sight.

The buteos, or buzzard hawks, such as the red-tailed, the red-shouldered, and the broad-winged hawks, remain soaring conspicuously in the sky, describing those big, lazy circles made famous in the title song of the musical *Oklahoma!* If a young chicken has just been stolen from the poultry yard and the flock is in an uproar, the vengeful farmer grabs his gun and blasts away at the innocent red-tail. When the bird comes crashing to earth, the farmer neither knows nor cares that he has just shot a valuable ally. The red-tailed hawk was less interested in the chickens than in the rats and mice infesting the poultry yard.

According to United States Department of Agriculture studies made in 1890, 1893, and 1928 of red-tails' stomach contents, we find the following diet: rats and mice, 55 percent; insects, 10.5 percent; rabbits and squirrels, 9.3 percent; poultry, 6.3 percent; frogs and snakes, 6.1 percent; game birds, 2.1 percent; crustaceans, 1.5 percent; and unidentified material or material of minor importance, 9.2 percent. Understandably, the diet of the hawk changes with the availability of food.

Adult red-tailed hawks feed mainly upon rats and mice, although some of the young hawks may attack poultry until they develop the skill to catch wild prey. A young red-tailed hawk, such as the one shown here, may be distinguished from an adult by its finely streaked gray tail.

The poultry that has shown up in the red-tails' diet usually can be attributed to the depredations of immature hawks lacking the skill to catch more wary wild prey. If similar studies were conducted today, the percentage of poultry in the diet would be much less. Poultry farming has become so competitive that most of our poultry is raised in mechanical plants or factories. Many chickens never get outdoors, and those that do are generally so well protected that it would be almost impossible for a hawk to take one, even if it wished to. With the elimination of many of our small marginal farms the dunghill cock and chickens are almost things of the past.

While the numbers of free-running poultry have been reduced, the rodent population has increased. This increase is directly attributable to our soaring human population and to the corresponding accumulation of refuse and edible garbage that we dump. I am convinced that the percentage of mice and rats in the red-tails' diet would be much higher now, because these hawks represent our front-line defense against such rodents. The red-tail actually has no enemies, except man, though it is possible the great horned owl takes young from the nest.

The red-tail is one of our largest hawks, the female measuring twenty-two to twenty-five inches in length and having a wingspread of up to fifty-six inches, and the male measuring twenty to twenty-two inches in length, with a wingspread of up to fifty inches. Male and female have the same coloration. The upper parts are brownish gray; the underparts are white, with a dark band across the lower abdomen. The bright yellow feet have strong, hooked claws. The rusty red tail is not visible when the hawk is soaring directly overhead, but the moment the bird wheels, light strikes the upper portion of the tail and instantly provides positive identification.

The six subspecies of red-tails are found throughout North America, right up to the Arctic Circle. Most common and widespread, and the subspecies with which I am most familiar, is the eastern red-tailed hawk. The western red-tail is much darker. Red-tails migrate from the northern extremes of their range, although they spend the winter over most of the United States. They fly along the ridge directly behind my house on their way to Hawk Mountain Sanctuary, in eastern Pennsylvania, so I get to see them first. We always have resident red-tails, but the migration brings us winter visitors as well.

Although these hawks give definite evidence of remaining paired all year, actual nest activity is noticeable in March. The birds frequently have chosen a nest site and have built their new nest or remodeled an old one long before they lay their eggs. When a nest has been selected, one of the pair places a sprig of greenery—a short bit of twig with pine needles, for example—in the nest. This greenery is replaced as it wilts; when the trees leaf out, deciduous branches are brought in. This action puzzles ornithologists; I believe that is signifies ownership of a nest and is a warning to other hawks not to trespass.

Most red-tails nest in high places. The highest nest I ever photographed set a record: It was located about 120 feet up on top of an electric high-tension tower. This was the first known instance of red-tailed hawks building on a man-made structure.

I first discovered the nest on June 1, 1956. By that time, the brown- or purple-blotched, dull white eggs had already hatched, and the young hawks were well feathered. Red-tails usually lay their three eggs, measuring about two and one-half inches long and one and one-half inches in diameter, in April; a twenty-eight-day incubation period has them hatched in early May. When I first approached the tower, both adults flew off uttering a piercing *kee-er-r*. As I climbed to the top, ever mindful that the three high-voltage lines each carried 225,000 volts of electricity, both hawks ascended higher and higher until they were mere specks in the sky.

While I busied myself photographing the young hawks, they retreated to the far side of the nest, hissing, hunching their wings, and sitting back on their tails, ready to use their talons for defense if need be. Suddenly I heard a whistling sound. One of the adults came plummeting out of the sky headed directly for me, rocketing down at such a speed that its body and pinions whistled. As I looked up, and the bird realized that it was being watched, it "chickened out." Instead of hitting me, it contented itself with zooming to within four feet of my head, then swooped back up. As the hawk hurtled past, it opened its wings, each feather making an audible zzzzzzing. Both birds dove at me repeatedly but never came any closer.

One evening, figuring on getting a photo of the adults on the nest when they came in for the night, I left my camera in position. The adults still hadn't come in by the time darkness threatened, so I set off the camera and flash to photograph the young. The bright flash brought both adults flying up out of the oak forest below. I learned then that adult red-tails do not stay at night with the young when they no longer have to be brooded. The adults much prefer the safety of the thick forest to the exposed nest.

Prior to leaving the nest, the young hawks exercised constantly. They flapped their wings strenuously and finally began to make short, hopping flights around the tower's superstructure. A few days later the nest was empty. Another brood of red-tails had been launched with a flying start.

Red-tailed hawks lay their spotted eggs on a platform of sticks high in the trees. After the young hawks hatch, they exercise their wings constantly and take short hopping flights.

Red-shouldered Hawk
(Buteo lineatus)

FIELD MARKS:	*Mottled light brown and white body, brownish red shoulders, five white tail bars.*
SIZE:	*23 inches long with a wingspan of 44 inches.*
HABITS:	*Frequents the same nesting areas year after year. Deposits a twig in the nest to lay claim to it.*
HABITAT:	*Heavily timbered or wet areas.*
NEST:	*Twigs, sticks, leaves, pieces of bark, moss, and lined with cedar needles and shredded cedar bark.*
EGGS:	*Dull white or pale blue with splotches, 2–3 in a clutch. Incubation 28 days.*
FOOD:	*Mainly small rodents.*
VOICE:	*Piercing whistle.*

Red-shouldered hawks often hunt from a perch for small rodents, snakes, insects, and small birds. Rats and mice are the main elements in the birds' diet.

The red-shouldered hawk is not as large as the red-tailed hawk, nor, because it frequents more heavily timbered wet areas, is it seen as often. Its name derives from the rufous coverlets on the upper portions of the wings. The southern red-shoulder is much paler than its northern relative and sometimes lacks the red coloration altogether. The black-and-white checkering of this hawk's primary wing feathers is particularly noticeable, as are the white bands and tip on the black tail. The red-shoulder is about twenty-three inches long and has a wingspread of approximately forty-four inches.

This hawk ranges across the United States from the Atlantic Ocean to the Rocky Mountains and from southern Canada to northern Mexico. Another relative, the red-bellied hawk, is found along the Pacific Coast.

As winter approaches, most northern red-shoulders migrate southward following the long chain of the Appalachian Mountains. I have often watched large numbers of these hawks heading south over the Kittatinny Mountain ridge behind my home, along the route of one of their main flyways.

By March most red-shouldered hawks have returned to their northern range and have sought out their regular nesting areas. If not unduly molested, these hawks frequent the same areas year after year. Sometimes they use the same nest utilized the previous year, although often they prefer to build an entirely new one. When preparing to use a nest from the previous year, the hawks lay claim to it by depositing a twig or a sprig of greenery within. This serves notice to other birds of the nest-owners' intentions.

When a nest is to be built, the red-shoulder seeks out a good-sized stand of tall timber. It nests in almost any kind of tree but prefers the nest to be high—from twenty to sixty feet above the ground—and snugly settled in a strong fork. About twenty-four inches in diameter, eighteen inches high, and hollowed out to a depth of two to three inches, the nest is well constructed of twigs, sticks, leaves, pieces of bark, and moss and is lined with such softer materials as cedar needles and shredded cedar bark.

These hawks appear to mate for life until or unless something happens to one or the other of the pair, when a new mate is accepted. Both parents share the twenty-eight-day job of incubating the two or three brown-to-purple-splotched, dull white or pale blue eggs, about two inches long and not quite as wide, that comprise the annual clutch. Often, while the female is brooding the eggs, the male can be observed bringing her food and depositing it on the edge of the nest, where she can easily reach it. Sometimes the female feeds while continuing to brood the eggs.

When feeding their young, the parent hawks tear the prey into small pieces to make swallowing easier. The young hawks eat until their stomachs are full, then doze in the warm spring sunshine.

By the time young hawks are two weeks old, they are clambering about in their nest. A month later, almost completely feathered out, they strengthen their wing muscles by moving to the edge of the nest, which they grasp firmly with their talons, and there flap their wings energetically. In another week's time they fly to nearby branches during the daytime, returning to the nest at night. Even after the young leave the nest, the parents continue to care for them until they have learned to provide for themselves.

Instead of being condemned through ignorance as a "hen hawk," the red-shoulder's food habits actually should endear it to mankind. Mice, rats, and other small rodents comprise 65 percent of this hawk's diet. It also takes snakes and sometimes small birds. Poultry or game birds amount to less than 2 percent of its diet by actual stomach analysis. Records exist of the red-shoulder nesting in the vicinity of a poultry yard without ever molesting any of the birds.

The young hawk may be killed and eaten by other predators, among them the great horned owl and the goshawk, but man has always been its greatest enemy. Fortunately, man is finally seeing the error of his ways and, in some states, is giving this hawk the protection it deserves.

Broad-winged Hawk
(Buteo platypterus)

FIELD MARKS:	*Dark brown head, neck, back, and upper parts of wings; white underparts; rusty-red bars on belly; 2–3 alternating black-white bars on tail, broad wing.*
SIZE:	*13–16 inches long with a wingspan of 33–37 inches.*
HABITS:	*Hunts by soaring. Migrates in large flocks.*
HABITAT:	*Unbroken woodlands, swamps, ponds, abandoned fields.*
NEST:	*Like the crow's.*
EGGS:	*Dull white splotched with brown, 2 in a clutch. Incubation 21–24 days.*
FOOD:	*Insects, frogs, toads, snakes, rats, mice.*
VOICE:	*Thin whistle.*

In all my time afield I have found only one nest of a broad-winged hawk. This is not unusual, because the broad-wing is a wilderness hawk, which prefers mature stands of timber for its home. Its nesting range extends from the Atlantic Coast to just west of the Mississippi River and from the Gulf of Mexico to Canada's prairie provinces, north of the Great Lakes and the St. Lawrence River.

As man continues his urban and suburban sprawl, the broad-winged hawk retreats before him. Many areas that once knew the broad-wing have been chopped down, bulldozed under, or paved over. While this hawk is happy in unbroken woodlands, it often frequents swamps and ponds as well as old abandoned fields. Old woods roads are favorite hunting spots, because small mammals must expose themselves when crossing, and the cleared wagon tracks give the food-seeking hawk room to maneuver.

One of the smallest of our buteos, or buzzard hawks, the migratory broad-wing is just slightly larger than a crow. Measuring thirteen to sixteen inches in length, it has a wingspan of thirty-three to thirty-seven inches, but the wing is exceptionally broad. The tail, which this little hawk flares widely when soaring, usually has two to three alternating white and black bands of about equal width. Head, neck, and upper parts are dark brown; underparts are white, the belly being heavily barred with rusty red. Its small size, broad wings, and banded tail make identification of this hawk easy.

There is good reason for more people being aware of this hawk at migration time than at any other time of the year. During late spring and summer, when the birds are on their breeding range, it is unusual to find more than a half-dozen birds. Yet they commonly migrate in large, loose flocks resembling a funnel of leaves blown along by the wind. In mid-September, when the big migrations are underway, as many as three to four thousand broad-winged hawks have been seen in a single day. My neighbor Floyd Wolfarth saw more than ten thousand broad-winged hawks on the Kittatinny Ridge on September 20, 1969.

Leaving the Appalachian ridges, the broad-wings continue into Florida, where a few spend the winter, while the rest fly south to Mexico and Central America. In early April, after spending the winter in a tropical jungle habitat, they reverse their trek and start back north. The flocks are not as concentrated in the spring as they were in the fall migration; the birds seem to straggle north but are usually on their breeding grounds the last of April or the first of May.

This hawk does not nest as high as does the red-tail. The one nest I saw was perhaps thirty feet up in an oak tree, and records show that most

A small, tame buteo, the broad-winged hawk inhabits mixed woodlands and groves, where it preys upon insects, small mammals, and snakes.

broad-wing nests are below forty feet. The nest was not large and could easily have been mistaken for a crow's nest.

Two brown-splotched, dull white eggs, about one and seven-eighths inches long and one and three-eighths inches in diameter, is the usual set for this bird. Incubation takes twenty-one to twenty-four days and is shared by both parents, as is the chore of feeding the young after they have hatched. The young hawks are cared for in the nest for about five or six weeks and for a month or so after leaving it.

The broad-wing has so often been portrayed flying off clutching a wriggling snake in its talons that this has become the stereotyped conception of this hawk. The broad-wing probably catches more snakes than all the other species combined. Many of the snakes taken are water snakes, which feed on fish, mainly trash fish, although it cannot be denied that they also take trout. Less fortunately for man, this hawk also likes garter and ribbon snakes, which feed chiefly on insects.

A United States Department of Agriculture study for 1893 reveals that insects make up 39.7 percent of the broad-winged hawk's diet. Moths and their larvae are most frequently taken, as they are most readily found in a forest. Old fields are prime places for the broad-wing to catch beetles, grasshoppers, and crickets. Frogs, toads, and snakes constitute 30.9 percent of the hawk's diet. Its habit of eating frogs and toads is of negative value, for both these amphibians are mainly insect eaters and extremely beneficial to man. The poisonous secretions of the American toad, its main protection against many predators, has little effect upon this hawk. Rats and mice make up 23 percent of the diet. Most of the mice are white-footed mice of the woodlands and meadow mice of the old fields and swamps. The woodrat is taken in preference to the brown rat, so closely associated with man.

The broad-wing catches some of its food by soaring, but most of the time it sits on a favored perch, spots the movement of its prey, then flies off to catch it. Like that of all hawks, its eyesight is exceptional; tests reveal that a hawk sees with its normal eyesight what man sees only with the aid of 8-power binoculars.

Because this hawk is relatively gentle and unsuspecting, it can usually be approached closer, while perched, than can most other hawks. Its food habits make it a definite asset to mankind. Despite this, the broad-wing has been severely hunted.

Twenty to thirty years ago, during the great mid-September migrations, the broad-wings were forced to run a gauntlet of fire. Every projecting ridge and rocky outcropping on the chain of mountains along which the hawks flew sported a blind from which shooters poured a withering fire. Some wealthy shooters bought or rented such ridges solely for the purpose of shooting migrating hawks. Thousands upon thousands of hawks were killed, with the broad-wings bearing the brunt of the onslaught. Although many hawks still are shot each year, they are getting wider protection.

Osprey
(Pandion haliaetus)

Field marks:	*Sepia above, white below; white head with broad black patch through cheeks.*
Size:	*22–24 inches long with a wingspan of 6 feet.*
Habits:	*Holds wings in an arched position, beats wings to hover over prey and then plunges.*
Habitat:	*Seacoasts, lakes, rivers.*
Nest:	*Reeds, weeds, sticks, driftwood, kelp, cornstalks, innertubes, pieces of plastic, and lined with moss or cedar bark.*
Eggs:	*Pinkish white splotched with reddish brown, 3 in a clutch. Incubation 5 weeks.*
Food:	*Fish.*
Voice:	*Soft* kreeeeeeing.

The osprey should be the most commonly known hawk in North America, because it is the most widely distributed of all the Falconiformes. At least 98 percent of its diet consists of fish taken alive, so it is never found far from waters in which fish may be caught. In many parts of its range the osprey is known simply as a "fish hawk." Most of the fish it catches are carp, suckers, and other trash fish found in shallow waters. This hawk also feeds on bullheads in the South and sometimes takes trout and both shad and salmon, although most of these are eaten after the fish have been weakened by spawning and their life cycle is drawing to a close. The osprey also takes an occasional frog, salamander, or water snake.

This hawk is specialized for its fishing expeditions in several ways. Its feathers, for example, are heavily oiled to make them waterproof. Should the osprey miss its quarry after plunging into the water, it rises into the air and shakes itself vigorously so that water droplets cascade down as though from a lawn sprinkler. Then, lightened and drier, the osprey continues its quest for food. The feet have a spiny inner surface that helps to secure a better grip on such slippery prey as fish, and the talons are exceptionally long and sharply hooked. On a number of occasions an osprey has locked its talons into a fish too large for it to handle. Unable to free themselves, both prey and predator perish and their bodies are washed up on the beach, mute testimony to their battle. The long, strong feathers on the osprey's head are believed to cushion this part of its anatomy when the bird plunges into the water. I'm not sure the head needs such protection, however, because the osprey enters the water feet first, not headfirst, its powerful wings held aloft to obtain the vigorous stroke needed to bring bird and fish to the surface and into the air.

I remember as a youngster watching an osprey circling over the shallow bar that separated the islands in the middle of the Delaware River near Manunkachunk, New Jersey. The bird suddenly swooped to within fifty feet of the water and hovered there, its huge wings beating rapidly to hold it in place. Then, like a stone, it dropped into the water with a small splash and disappeared beneath the surface. With a tremendous splashing, the bird reappeared, vainly trying to lift its catch, only to disappear once more beneath the waters. This time the bird reappeared almost instantly, and the splashing was frenzied, but the osprey could not lift the fish from the water. Now the bird remained on the surface, but its wing strokes lacked their former vigor. At last the osprey was able to free itself from the fish. Aided by the current, and using its huge wings as oars, the bird flapped its way to the island. Struggling onto the rocky shore, the bedraggled osprey collapsed in a heap. Following a ten or fifteen minutes' rest, the bird shook

The osprey feeds primarily upon fish and is our only hawk that dives into the water after its prey.

itself doglike to rid its feathers of excess water, walked along the river's edge, mounted into the air, and disappeared from sight beyond a bend in the river. I did not see the fish that almost caught an osprey but feel sure that it was a carp, for they were plentiful in the area.

The osprey is a large bird, twenty-two to twenty-four inches in length and having a wingspread of up to seventy-two inches. Male and female are look-alikes; unlike most hawks the female is not much larger than her mate. Back and tail are brownish, head and underparts are white. In flight the osprey is often confused with the eagle, despite the latter's dark underparts. Unlike the straight eagle wing, the osprey's wing has a sharp crook at the wrist, and its outer primary wing feathers are widely separated.

Ospreys spend the winter in Florida, the Gulf States, Mexico, and Central America. They begin to work their way northward the latter part of February and are back in New Jersey by the first week or two of March. Apparently mated for life, ospreys appear on the scene in pairs.

Little time is spent in nest hunting, because the osprey returns to the same nest site year after year. Nests in continuous use for 41, 45, and even 125 years are known to exist. Nevertheless the osprey goes through the same formality of adding new material each spring. Large and bulky to begin with, the nests grow to be even larger and bulkier with the passage of time. They are found in all kinds of locations, made of whatever material is available—weeds, reeds, sticks, driftwood, kelp, cornstalks, innertubes, bits of plastic—and are lined with moss or cedar bark. The osprey adds anything it can carry and employs such a random method of construction that the nest resembles a pile of flotsam left stranded by high tide. I have photographed ospreys at Sandy Hook, building nests by momentarily hovering over them, then casually dropping whatever material they happened to be carrying.

While I have never seen an osprey nest built directly on the ground, I have seen nests built on low stumps, atop piles of driftwood and in trees, on telephone pole crossarms and platforms, or on wagon wheels set atop poles by solicitous humans. In some areas power and light companies erect platforms to keep the ospreys from building their nests on the power poles and causing short circuits.

Ospreys usually lay three reddish brown spotted, pinkish white eggs, about two and three-eighths inches long and one and five-eighths inches in diameter. Incubation requires about 5 weeks and is the task of the female alone. When first hatched, the young are fed a regurgitated diet by the

An osprey nest is a large, bulky mass of sticks and twigs located in a dead tree, on a rock pinnacle, or whatever else is available. Ospreys use the same nest every spring.

parents. By the time they graduate to small pieces of fish, they are two weeks old. Although the male helps in catching fish for the young, he generally leaves the actual feeding chore to the female. When the young are a month old, they are strong enough to tear the fish apart for themselves. In another month they are large enough to leave the nest. Daily they have practiced for this event by standing on the edge of the nest, gripping tightly with their talons, and flapping their wings wildly. Even after they have left the nest, young ospreys are fed by the parents for another three to four weeks.

Because of its large size the osprey has only one natural enemy, the eagle. The eagle is not so much interested in attacking the osprey as it is in making the latter drop the fish it has caught. The osprey generally tries to take evasive action, but, being burdened with the fish, it cannot out-maneuver its tormentor. Eventually the osprey drops the fish, which the piratical eagle proceeds to snatch out of the air and carry away to eat. I have seen this happen on two different occasions while photographing osprey nests on the islands in the Connecticut River below Essex. Twenty years ago this area was a main bastion of the East Coast osprey and eagle populations.

Like the eagle, the osprey today is declining over most of its range, despite its apparent increase during migration in recent years. This increase must be the result of a switch in the bird's migratory flight pattern, for on all sides the encroachment of man means the destruction of both the osprey and its habitat.

Belatedly the osprey and most other hawks are receiving well-deserved protection from many of our states. Laws do not prevent people from shooting these birds, however; they merely penalize those who are caught. Along the Jersey coast, many fishermen carry on all-out war against the osprey in the erroneous belief that the bird is harmful to their fishing interests. For years Sandy Hook State Park had a large concentration of osprey nesting out on the spit. In spite of concerted efforts by naturalists and others, the osprey are steadily declining in numbers.

We know that such poisons as DDT build up in the bodies of birds that have eaten fish killed by these poisons. While accumulated poisons do not render the male sterile, new evidence has proven that a buildup of DDT in the female's body prevents proper calcification of the eggshells. As a result the shells of both the osprey and the eagle eggs are so thin that they are broken when the birds attempt to brood them. Evidence exists that the decline in both bird populations coincided with the widespread use of such poisons.

Because the osprey is a migratory bird, it is exposed to additional dangers from irresponsible shooters. The bird is fairly safe on its home grounds, because people who are knowledgeable about it know of its harmless ways and often build special platforms on top of trees and poles to attract the osprey to nest.

Sparrow Hawk
(*Falco sparverius*)

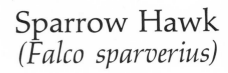

FIELD MARKS:	*Male: Brownish red back and tail (only small hawk with reddish tail), white belly and white breast with buffy brown streaks, blue wings. Female: dull brown back, tail, wings. Long tapering wings and tail.*
SIZE:	*Male: 8–10 inches long with a wingspan of 21 inches. Female: 10–12 inches long.*
HABITS:	*Belligerent in the defense of the nest, hovers on rapidly beating wings.*
HABITAT:	*Open and semi-open country.*
NEST:	*Cavity in a tree.*
EGGS:	*Pinkish white with brown spots, 4–5 in a clutch. Incubation 28 days.*
FOOD:	*Insects, particularly grasshoppers, mice, small birds.*
VOICE:	*Sharp* killy, killy, killy.

Brooding sparrow hawks protect their eggs by rolling over on their backs and striking at intruders with their talons.

In spite of its name this bird is not a hawk but a falcon. It has the long, tapering wings and tail that typify such better-known falcons as the peregrine and the gyrfalcon. This error in terminology can be traced to the early English colonists in the New World, who named the bird after the European sparrow hawk. They should have named it instead after the kestrel, the European counterpart of our sparrow hawk.

As a further complication, insects, not birds, constitute the main food of our sparrow hawk. In fact, insects form the bulk of its diet in the spring, summer, and early fall almost exclusively. A much better name for this little falcon would be "grasshopper hawk." A name I particularly like for it is "windhover." When hunting, the falcon sometimes sits on a fencepost or on a telephone pole or wire carefully watching the grass below for the tell-tale movement of its prey. On sighting a grasshopper, cricket, or beetle, the bird darts down, snatches up its prey, and carries it back to the perch for eating. At other times the bird courses over the field until it spots something edible, then hovers in one spot, wings held high over its back and beating loosely. Hovering effortlessly in this fashion, it suddenly drops down to feed on its catch. This species is the most beneficial to man of all the falcons.

When cold weather puts a stop to insect activity, mice become a staple. Only when snow covers the ground, hiding the mice from sight, does the sparrow hawk live up to its name, feeding on small birds, the one most frequently taken being the one we can most easily spare—the English, or house, sparrow.

Young female sparrow hawks are very belligerent and flare their wings and hiss when approached.

A number of years ago, when I was still in high school, someone brought me a young sparrow hawk that had evidently fallen out of the nest. The bird was fairly well feathered but could not fly. Right from the start the young bird was completely unafraid and would perch wherever I placed it.

My first thoughts were of food for my new charge. The bird was called a sparrow hawk, sparrows it would have. Our barn and wagon house were plagued with house sparrows at the time, so my trusty .22 rifle produced a steady supply of fresh food for the hawk. Pulling the skins from the carcasses, I cut off the meat, which the hawk gobbled as fast as I offered it. I was elated; here was my chance to become a falconer.

I kept the hawk in a large cage in the barn and fed it to repletion every morning and noon and again in the evening. Every time I offered it food, I gave a high-pitched, shrill whistle, trying to imitate the call of the adult sparrow hawks I had heard so many times. Despite my lack of knowledge in hawk training, it was only a matter of days before the young hawk became greatly excited and hopped across its perch to come to me whenever I whistled.

Soon the bird was flying; the transition to becoming airborne seemed almost effortless. Now, when I fed the hawk, I would place it on one of the stalls and move eight to ten feet away, then whistle, holding up my left hand as a perch while offering food with my right. I didn't have to train the hawk; it was anxious to come. In fact, the most difficult part was to get the bird to sit still long enough for me to back away. Many times the bird refused to be perched; it either flew around me or landed on my shoulder, all the while making a soft *kee-kee-kee* sound.

I tried flying the hawk outside the barn, keeping it on a long string. The string proved too much of a drag for the bird's new wing muscles and definitely hampered its activity. Then I flew the hawk up in the hay mow, empty at this time of year. The cavernous barn gave the hawk lots of space to fly, but the bird never failed to come when called.

As the bird grew larger and stronger, so did its appetite. Fearful that perhaps it wasn't getting enough food to tide it over between feedings, I began to leave whole sparrows for the hawk. It plucked the feathers, then ripped off pieces of the meat.

One evening I came into the hay mow and whistled but received no answer. That was odd—the hawk had always responded. Whistling constantly, I checked all through the mow and at last found the hawk's body. Apparently the bird had tried to swallow an entire sparrow leg. The upper leg had gone down, but the lower leg and foot stuck out of the bird's throat. The young hawk had choked to death.

The sparrow hawk is not large. The male is only eight to ten inches in length, with a wingspread of twenty-one inches, while the female is slightly larger. The male is the more brightly colored of the two, having a rusty red back and tail; blue wings; black dots on breast and belly; and single wide black band above the white terminal band on its tail. The female has a dull brown back, tail, and wings; brown-streaked breast and belly; and eight to ten broken black bands on its tail. Both sexes sport rusty caps and a gray fringe, with one dark line running through the eye and another behind the white cheek patch.

The sparrow hawk's three subspecies range over most of North America, stopping just short of the Arctic region and Hudson Bay. Birds in the northern part of the range migrate to the southern United States in winter. In northwestern New Jersey, where I live, the birds may stay all winter, but usually they move to the southern part of the state. In February they are already back in my area, gracing the poles and wires.

Whether the birds mate for life is not known, but they are paired up and breeding in April. Unlike other hawks, which construct a nest or utilize a ledge on the side of a cliff, the sparrow hawk prefers a tree cavity, an abandoned flicker's nesthole, or even a bird box, if the latter is situated in a good spot and has a large enough entrance hole. No material is carried into the nest site; the female lays her eggs in whatever happens to be inside the cavity. Usually the sparrow hawk lays four to five brown-dotted or ringed, pinkish white eggs, slightly less than one and one-half inches long and one inch in diameter. The markings on the eggs suggest that this bird has not always been a cavity-nesting bird, but once needed the protection afforded by such camouflage.

Incubation is largely the chore of the female, requiring twenty-eight days, with the male helping out when and if the mood strikes him. The male usually perches nearby to help protect the nest from attack. Both birds are extremely belligerent in defense of the nest; the female is belligerent most of the time. When I photographed a female hawk and her eggs in a wood duck nest box, I had a feathered fury on my hands. The moment I removed the lid, the female rolled over on her back and was ready to strike at me with her talons, peck at me with her beak, or beat me with her wings. Even the young are belligerent. Although the young males tend to cower in the far recesses of the cavity or box, the females turn aggressively, flare their wings, and hiss. Both the raccoon and the great horned owl eat the eggs and the young of the sparrow hawk.

A friend of mine had a pair of sparrow hawks nesting in an apple tree that stood by his back porch. After the young hatched, the hawks, particularly the female, made life miserable for everyone, including the cat. Anyone or anything that moved out on the back lawn was in for lightning-fast dive-bombing attacks by the birds. Finally my friend began wearing a football helmet in self-defense.

By midsummer the young are fledged and out hunting for food for themselves. In some areas every third or fourth telephone pole is capped with a sparrow hawk, and the soft call of *killy-killy-killy-killy-killy-killy* is heard on all sides.

6 Galliformes— Chickenlike Birds

The birds of this order are what we ordinarily think of as gallinaceous birds, or resembling our domestic fowl. Our common domestic chicken is a member of the pheasant family, an offshoot of the wild jungle fowl of southeastern Asia. Many of our most splendid game birds are members of this order. All told, it includes 240 species, divided into 7 family groups. Only 4 of these families are native to North America.

Despite their strong breast muscles the majority of these birds are not capable of sustained flight. Their broad, cupped wings are not long, compared to body and weight. The pinions are stiff and make a whistling or whirring sound when the birds take off by springing into the air.

The legs of most of these birds are long and strong, so that running is the most effective means of escaping from danger. The most frequently used parts of a bird's body must have a correspondingly larger blood supply to care for the demands made on the muscles, which explains why most birds in this order have "dark meat" on their legs and "white meat" on their breasts.

The family Tetraonidae is comprised of the various grouse and ptarmigan. Most of these birds sport subdued plumage; in some species it is impossible to distinguish the sexes with just a glance.

All the species of this family are subject to cyclic fluctuations in population. A period of peak population is followed by a drastic decline.

The family Phasianidae contains 178 species of quail, partridges, and pheasants. Six species of quail are native to the United States, but there are no native pheasants or partridges. However, some species have been successfully introduced, as in the case of the pheasant.

The family Meleagrididae is represented by the turkey, largest member of the order, which originated in the New World. Although we almost always associate the turkey with Thanksgiving Day, the Pilgrims were familiar with the bird before they saw it in the wild near their Plymouth colony. Centuries before the early Spanish explorers arrived, the Indians of Mexico had domesticated the wild turkey.

Turkey
(*Meleagris gallopavo*)

FIELD MARKS:	*Iridescent brownish olive; similar to domestic turkey except tail feathers are brown and black, not white and black. Males are larger, have a larger tail, and are more colorful than females.*
SIZE:	*48 inches long with a wingspan of 60 inches.*
HABITS:	*Avoids danger by running. Flies as a last resort. Roosts in trees at night.*
HABITAT:	*Open woodlands or forest clearings.*
NEST:	*Hollows scratched in leaves.*
EGGS:	*Brown or buff with fine spots on the large end, 8–14 in a clutch. Incubation 28 days.*
FOOD:	*Insects, wild berries, fruits, acorns, beechnuts, hickory nuts, pecans, hazelnuts, weed seeds, spilled grain.*
VOICE:	*Gobbling, putts and chirps.*

Male turkeys can be distinguished from the females by their larger size, more colorful heads, and the long hairs sprouting from the center of their breasts.

When our new nation was looking for a national emblem, Benjamin Franklin suggested that we use the wild turkey. After all, several European nations were already using the eagle as their device, and the American bald eagle was primarily a scavenger. Franklin felt that the wild turkey possessed the attributes desirable and representative of what we could hope for the country. It was widely distributed, intelligent, fast, and strong when it needed to be, and liberally endowed with native caution.

These virtues were apparently insufficient either to raise the turkey to exalted station or to spare it from slaughter. At the time of the coming of the white man, the turkey was found over most of the United States. It was hunted by the red man, who used the meat for food and the feathers for adornment, but, armed only with bows and arrows, the Indian did the turkey little real harm. In short order the white man and his guns succeeded

Wild turkey hens nest in hollows scratched out in the leaves and lay eight to fourteen eggs in a clutch. The eggs are brown or buff and are finely spotted at the larger end.

in wiping out most of the turkeys over the greater part of their range.

The wild turkey is our largest game bird, measuring forty-eight inches in length and with a wingspread of sixty inches. Some old toms weigh up to twenty or twenty-five pounds. This turkey can be distinguished from the domesticated bird by the color of the tail feathers. The wild bird's tails are black and brown, while the domesticated bird's tail is black and white. The female is about a third smaller than the male, is duller in color and less iridescent. The male has a much larger, longer tail, which he spreads out like a fan at the slightest opportunity; a more colorful head, with a long, fingerlike, pendant caruncle growing from the top; and a long sprout of stiff hairs, called a beard, growing from the center of its breast.

During the breeding season, the tom struts before the hens with widely fanned-out tail raised almost vertically and dragging wings almost touching the ground. He presents a handsome picture as the bronze-tinted plumage and iridescent blue and red head glisten in the sunlight.

Each tom gathers a harem of hens, and bitter, bloody battles between rival males ensue. Death is frequently the fate of the loser. The hen does not stay with the tom during the mating season but sneaks away to lay her egg in a hidden nest, the location of which is known only to her. She joins the tom each day, mates, then retires to the nest.

The turkey nests I've seen have been mere hollows scratched in the leaves. One nest rested against a tree, behind several large rocks. I had walked past the nest without seeing the hen sitting on it and spotted her only on my way back down the hill. She never moved or blinked an eye. After taking several photographs of her, I walked away, leaving her feeling, no doubt, that she had fooled me again.

Eight to fourteen brown or buff eggs, finely spotted at the large end and measuring two and three-eighths inches long and one and three-quarters inches in diameter, are customarily found in a single nest. Two hens may use the same nest on occasion and may even take turns incubating the eggs for the twenty-eight days required to hatch them. The tom has been known to smash the eggs deliberately to prolong his sexual activities with the hen.

Although the wild turkey is a bird of the forests, it needs grassy fields in order to raise its young. There are always more grasshoppers and crickets in the fields than in the woodlands, and these insects provide the protein needed by the young turkeys for growth. In a huge grass-covered field belonging to the state and located near my home in New Jersey, turkey family groups could be seen a few years ago at almost any time of the day, busily feeding on insects. Then the state opened up this field to the general public for use as a picnic ground. That put an end to the turkey visitation and effectively sealed the birds' doom. To see a turkey in that area now is most unusual.

In addition to feeding on all types of insects, turkeys eat wild berries and fruit in season. They subsist principally on mast crops—various types of acorns, beechnuts, hickory nuts, pecans, hazelnuts, seeds of diverse weeds, and spilled grain. These birds come readily to feeders baited with whole corn. During the winter of 1968–1969 a hen turkey came to my feeder daily. On one occasion (December 2, 1968) she ate 589 dried kernels of whole corn.

To avoid such predators as foxes, raccoons, bobcats, hawks, and owls, the turkey in southern swamps roosts over water whenever possible. Adverse weather also takes a tremendous toll, especially of the young poults, which are difficult to rear. Man, of course, has always been this bird's greatest enemy. Today, through wise conservation management and practices, the wild turkey has been brought back to many of its former haunts.

Wild turkeys use their strong, powerful feet to turn over the forest floor in search for food.

Spruce Grouse
(Canachites canadensis)

FIELD MARKS: *Male: Mottled dark gray and white or dark brown and white back; black throat, breast, and tail; orange-red skin patch above eye. Female: buffy brown and white, with light brown terminal band on black tail. Feathers down to tips of toes.*

SIZE: *17 inches long with a wingspan of 22 inches.*

HABITS: *Has no fear of man. Drums in the breeding season.*

HABITAT: *Coniferous forests.*

NEST: *Slight depression in the earth lined with grasses or moss.*

EGGS: *Buffy brown with spots, 8–12 in a clutch. Incubation 17–18 days.*

FOOD: *Insects and berries in the spring, needles, buds, and tips of the spruce, fir, and tamarack trees in the cold weather.*

VOICE: *Clucks and putts.*

This female spruce grouse is walking out on a limb to take a look at the author.

Called "fool hen" by those who know it well, the spruce grouse really lives up to its name. A denizen of the northern coniferous forests, where it comes into little contact with man, this grouse doesn't consider him an enemy. Man, sorry to say, takes advantage of this lack of fear, and where he establishes himself, the spruce grouse stock is depleted. This bird allows man to approach so closely that it can easily be killed with a club or snatched off a branch with a snare.

I well remember the time, up in the bush country of Quebec, I actually caught a spruce grouse alive. The bird displayed great curiosity and showed no alarm at my stealthy movements. When I was close enough, I simply reached up and grabbed the grouse with my hand. After taking a few photos, I released it. But I had been convinced that this bird was indeed anybody's fool—a sort of living dodo.

Measuring about seventeen inches in length and with a wingspread of about twenty-two inches, the spruce grouse is smaller than the ruffed grouse. Like the ptarmigan, this bird has legs feathered down to the tips of its toes. Its back may be a dark brown or gray; its tail is black, as is the throat and breast, giving the grouse the appearance of wearing a bib. The skin patch above the eye is a bright orange-red. The hen is smaller and lighter colored than the male.

The spruce grouse's "drumming" during the breeding season is not nearly as accomplished as is that of the ruffed grouse. It is better described as a fluttering flight. To put on his show, the male flies to the top of a spruce or tamarack tree, then flies to the ground with a tremendous beating of his wings. Apparently the performance is satisfactory to the female, because she soon mates with him.

The nest is a slight depression in the earth lined with grasses or moss, usually situated at the foot of a tree or stump. Eight to twelve buffy brown, spotted eggs, about one and three-quarters inches long and one and one-quarter inches in diameter, comprise the annual brood. For seventeen to eighteen days the hen incubates the eggs and, like the ruffed grouse, raises her chicks by herself. The young develop quickly and fly within two weeks.

The mother spruce grouse does not attempt to lure anyone away from her young when danger threatens. One hen that I surprised out on the Alaska Peninsula gave a warning cluck to her chicks; they scattered to hide, while she flew into a nearby evergreen tree. There she clucked and putted, fluffed out her feathers, and walked around the tree, stepping from branch to branch. When I stood still, she walked out along the branch as if to get a better look at me. When I approached the tree, she retreated back up the branch and walked around the limbs to the opposite side of the tree. She evidently wanted a better look, but she wanted to be the one to do the looking.

In the summertime insects and berries form a large part of this grouse's diet. During cold weather the grouse falls back on its main staples, such as the needles, buds, and tips of the spruce, fir, and tamarack trees. When the birds are on this winter diet, their flesh actually tastes like turpentine, making it disagreeable to most human palates. At other times the spruce grouse is an important food source for wilderness people.

Foxes, lynx, wolves, wolverines, woods hawks, falcons, and owls all take a heavy toll of the grouse. Still, the bird can cope with this natural predation. Man, the despoiler, who kills the bird wantonly and destroys its habitat, is the greatest enemy.

Ruffed Grouse
(Bonasa umbellus)

FIELD MARKS:	*Mottled tawny and white or dark gray and white. Male has an outer ring of unbroken black feathers on the tail; female has two brown feathers in the center of the tail.*
SIZE:	*19 inches long with a wingspan of 25 inches.*
HABITS:	*Male flails wings to create drumming sound while courting. Subject to wild flights.*
HABITAT:	*Woodlands and brush-covered upland fields.*
NEST:	*Rounded depression in the leaves against a tree.*
EGGS:	*Tan or buff, 8–12 in a clutch. Incubation 21–24 days.*
FOOD:	*Leaves, twigs, buds, insects.*
VOICE:	*Putts.*

In the early fall, ruffed grouse develop scales along the sides of their toes. These scales form effective snowshoes enabling the grouse to walk across the top of the snow.

In my opinion the ruffed grouse has really earned the title "king of game birds." It is a bird that can hold its own against predation and hunting pressure, providing its habitat is not destroyed. It is a wily bird, where hunted; its thundering flight is usually in the opposite direction from that being watched by the hunter. Thanks to its beautiful mottled brown plumage, the ruffed grouse blends in with the fallen leaves on the forest floor and thus is rendered practically invisible. (In my home area of New Jersey, some of the grouse are gray instead of brown.) Its crowning achievement is that it makes such tasty eating.

Although both sexes are marked alike, the cock is quite a bit larger, has a longer tail, a longer crest on its head, and a larger neck ruff than the hen, and usually has, as well, an unbroken wide black stripe on the tail. The length of the tail is the most accurate method of sexing the grouse without internal inspection. The female's tail is about five and one-quarter inches long or less, while a tail length of five and one-half to eight and one-half inches proclaims its owner to be a male. The longest tail feathers in my collection measure eight and one-half inches long, the former property of a really handsome bird. A full-grown adult weighs up to one and three-quarter pounds, measures nineteen inches overall, and has a wingspread of about twenty-five inches. As an aid to living in snowy regions, scales grow along the sides of the grouse's toes in the early fall, forming snowshoes that effectively double the foot size and allow the grouse to walk on top of the snow instead of sinking into it. By spring, the scales have worn off.

The ruffed grouse ranges from the Atlantic to the Pacific coasts and from Georgia and Arkansas north to the tree line in Canada and Alaska. Strictly a bird of the woods and brushland, it is not found in the prairie and high plains states.

In the early springtime the sonorous roll of the male's courtship "drumming" may be heard. Perched on a large, fallen, usually moss-covered log, he beats the air rapidly with his wings. The female is attracted to the sound and breeds with the male following his performance. A male mates with as many females as he can entice into his area.

In April or June the female makes her nest—generally a rounded depression in leaves at the base of a tree trunk or stump or under brush—and starts to lay her eggs. Eight to twelve slightly spotted, tan or buff eggs, about one and one-half inches long and one inch in diameter, comprise the average clutch of the one annual brood. The hen incubates the eggs alone, for twenty-one to twenty-four days, sitting so tightly on the nest that it is

The female ruffed grouse lays her eggs in a slight depression in the forest floor. The eight to twelve eggs are buff or tan colored and take twenty-one to twenty-three days to hatch.

exceedingly difficult to locate. When leaving the nest, she usually covers the eggs lightly with an effective camouflage of leaves.

The chicks are about the size of golf balls when they are first hatched. Their primary feathers grow rapidly, allowing them to fly short distances in little more than a week. The female guards the chicks well; at the first sign of danger she gives off an alarm note that sends them scurrying into hiding. I have often surprised such family groups, and, although the mother tried to decoy me away by pretending to be injured, I stayed to look for the chicks. Like magicians performing sleight of hand tricks, the chicks' escape movements were almost too swift to observe. It was only by careful searching that a chick could be discovered tucked under a fallen leaf or a clump of grass. To allay the frantic mother's fears, I retreated from the area and allowed her to regroup her family. By fall little grouse are almost fully grown, and the family group begins to disperse.

Ants, moths, spiders, grasshoppers, crickets, and other insects—all high in protein—are the main food of the young. I have seen the little ones jump

When first hatched baby ruffed grouse are about the size of golf balls.

The wing primaries on a ruffed grouse develop very quickly and the baby birds are able to fly short distances a little more than a week after they emerge from their shells.

six to eight inches off the ground to snatch an insect from a tree trunk or a high blade of grass. In the fall, berries play an important role in the grouse's diet. In winter and early spring the ruffed grouse, like the deer, is a browser and feeds mainly on buds, twigs, and leaves of such trees as the maple, birch, willow, apple, and poplar. Starvation is extremely rare among grouse, because they can eat almost any type of vegetation found in their region. Yet much of their food has such low nutritional value that the birds must eat large amounts merely to sustain life. I have counted as many as seventy-six droppings from a single grouse in one night. That required a tremendous amount of food passing through its body for the small value received. To gather this much food, grouse often feed long after dark, especially on moonlit nights. This exposes them to great danger from their chief enemy, the great horned owl.

In fact, the ruffed grouse's life is fraught with danger. Snakes, skunks, coons, opossums, foxes, and bobcats seek the eggs and the young, while hawks and owls take old and young alike. Because its population is cyclic, this grouse is abundant in some years and scarce in others.

Grouse are subject to wild flights that send them crashing through windows, killing themselves. I know of dozens of such cases and recently have had to replace one of the storm sashes on my own house. We still are not sure what causes the birds to act in this manner.

Willow Ptarmigan
(Lagopus lagopus)

FIELD MARKS: *Both sexes white in winter, with black eyes, beak, and tail. In summer, male is brownish red with white wings and underparts; female is mottled buffy brown and white.*

SIZE: *17 inches long with a wingspan of 22 inches.*

HABITS: *Males help care for the young. Shed their toenails each summer.*

HABITAT: *Tundra or deep thickets.*

NEST: *Hollowed-out spot in moss or grass.*

EGGS: *Red to purple, 8–10 in a clutch. Incubation 24–25 days.*

FOOD: *Insects, berries in summer; twigs, tips of the willow and dwarf bushes at all times.*

VOICE: *Deep raucous call, almost like bullfrog.*

The male willow ptarmigan is white with a black tail in the winter, but becomes a reddish brown during the summer months. The ptarmigan pictured above is in the process of changing its colors.

I first encountered the willow ptarmigan in June 1965, on the brush-covered flats east of Lake Iliamna, Alaska. The birds had already changed from their winter coats of white to summer brown. What amazed me was that the males were still with the females and chicks. Only then did I learn that the males help to raise the young—a rare occurrence among game birds, the males usually maintaining no family ties after mating with the female.

Ptarmigans are the grouse of the circumpolar regions. Largest of the three species is the willow ptarmigan. Measuring up to seventeen inches long, including a five-and-one-half-inch tail, it has the short, cupped wings of the grouse family and a wingspread of about twenty-two inches. The winter garb of both sexes is white, except for the black eyes, beak, and tail. In summer plumage the male is a dark reddish brown; the female is buffy brown. Both are heavily barred with darker colors. Characteristic of the ptarmigan is the shedding of their toenails in late spring. The long outer covering comes off, and the new sets start to grow immediately. The claws are used in winter to scratch through snow and ice in search of food and, like the "snowshoes" of the snowshoe rabbit, to serve as ice creepers when the winter world is frozen over. The *lagopus* in the ptarmigan's Latin name means "rabbit-footed."

You can often hear ptarmigan even when you can't see them in the dense willow tangles, for they are exceedingly noisy birds. During the mating

Willow ptarmigans breed in May and hollow out a spot in the grass for a nest. Eight to ten reddish purple eggs are laid and incubation takes twenty-four to twenty-five days.

season, the cock's hoarse hooting and calling reverberates on all sides, and his enlarged reddish orange comb is often prominently displayed. Breeding takes place in May. The nest is usually a hollowed-out spot in the moss or grass of the tundra. Eight to ten rich reddish to purple eggs, about one and five-eighths inches long and one and one-quarter inches in diameter, are common, and incubation takes approximately twenty-four to twenty-five days.

The chicks leave the nest as soon as their down is dry. Their flight feathers develop so rapidly that they are able to make short flights in about ten days. Shepherded along by both parents, the young are well guarded. At the first sign of danger the parents give an alarm call, and the chicks scatter like windblown leaves. The male becomes aggressive in defending the family and may even try to drive off the enemy. Once danger is past, the parents will call the chicks together, so that the family can proceed on its way. As they travel about, the birds keep up an almost continuous stream of calls and clucks that help to maintain the entire group intact and, very possibly, may aid to alert many of the ptarmigans' enemies.

Wolverines, foxes, wolves, and lynx are among the four-footed predators that prey upon ptarmigan eggs and chicks. Gulls and jaegers also attack both eggs and young, while hawks, owls, and eagles feed on chicks and adult birds. In spite of this heavy predation, the ptarmigan population is so large, and its reproductive capacity is so great, it is able to maintain its numbers.

Such insects as flies and mosquitoes are important items of diet in early summer. As soon as they ripen, berries probably take over first place. At all times, but particularly in winter, willow and dwarf birch buds and twig tips are avidly eaten. Plant seeds of all types are also utilized.

In early fall, ptarmigan families begin to concentrate and may form flocks numbering into the hundreds; at times, ptarmigan seem to be everywhere. To the Eskimo and Indians living in the regions where these birds are found, they represent an important food source.

Rock Ptarmigan
(*Lagopus mutus*)

FIELD MARKS: *Both sexes white in winter, with black tail; male also has black line through eye. In summer, male is sepia with white wing tips and orange-red patch above eye; female is buffy brown and white.*

SIZE: *15–17 inches with a wingspan of 20 inches.*

HABITS: *Feather pads on feet serve as snowshoes in winter. Male stretches head and tail horizontally when sounding call.*

HABITAT: *High, rocky outcroppings of subarctic regions.*

NEST: *Bowl-shaped depression in grass.*

EGGS: *Variously colored from buff to brown to almost black; 8–12 in clutch. Incubation 21–22 days.*

FOOD: *Leaves, twigs, buds, seeds, berries. Insects in summer.*

VOICE: *Guttural, coughing call.*

In winter the male rock ptarmigan is white with a black line through the eye and a few black tail feathers.

In Latin the rock ptarmigan's name is *lagopus*, or "rabbit-footed." Like the snowshoe rabbit (or varying hare) this bird grows "snowshoes" each fall to help it walk over the soft snow. Whereas the rabbit grows long hair on its toes, the ptarmigan grows degenerate feathers. These feathers remain on the feet all year, but are usually badly worn by the time summer rolls around.

The "rock" in the name is also descriptive, for these birds inhabit the highest rocky outcroppings of the Alaskan range. Although smaller than the willow ptarmigan, the rock ptarmigan is more readily seen because of the lack of cover in the areas it frequents. This ptarmigan measures fifteen to seventeen inches in length and has a wingspread of twenty inches.

From a distance the black line through the eye of the male helps to distinguish it from the willow ptarmigan. Except for this black line, black beak and tail feathers, the rock ptarmigan turns almost completely white in winter, starting in September. Late in June the males change to their brown summer plumage, the females having made the change much earlier. Both sexes retain their white wing tips. These tips show up conspicuously when the bird takes to the air but are hidden when it is at rest.

The rock ptarmigan and its subspecies are found in circumpolar regions wherever mountains or rocky outcroppings occur. At different times of the year, this ptarmigan descends from the peaks and may mingle with the willow ptarmigan on the grassy slopes.

Late May through June is the breeding season. On June 14, 1966, Mike Smith and I had a chance to witness a courtship performance of the rock ptarmigan at Highway Pass, Alaska. We were taking photos of a male on a snowfield, when he became alarmed and flew off. A few minutes later Mike discovered a female sitting beneath a clump of grass, probably, we assumed, on her nest. She never moved as we took her picture. I walked around her in a circle, trying to get her to raise her head so it would show up better in the photograph, while Mike clicked both of the cameras we had set up on tripods. All of a sudden we noticed a ptarmigan soaring about 500 feet overhead. It wheeled and glided to a landing a foot or so away from the female, then circled her several times, stopping on a little hummock every so often to call in a deep, guttural voice, which sounded almost precisely like a bullfrog's. When this coughing call is uttered, the male stretches out his neck

Male rock ptarmigans change to their brown summer plumage in late June. The females of the species change color much sooner.

until head, neck, body, and tail are lowered horizontally to the ground. After a while the female rose, circled the male, and the two flew off together. There were no eggs in the nest, which was simply a bowl-shaped depression in the grass.

Eight to twelve variously spotted, buff to dark brown eggs, one and five-eighths inches long and one and one-quarter inches in diameter, comprise a clutch. Incubation, which lasts twenty-one to twenty-two days, and care of the chicks are shared by both parents.

In summer a great many insects are eaten. In other seasons vegetation is the mainstay of the ptarmigan's diet. Leaves, twigs, buds, and seeds of birches, willows, and various berry bushes are favored foods. With its strong claws, the ptarmigan can scratch down through the snow to reach vegetation covered by drifts.

After the snow melts off the ground, rock ptarmigans do not turn brown immediately. During this period they stand out like white beacons. Only their large populations allow them to withstand the tremendous predation upon them at this time. Foxes, wolves, bears, and lynx feed on the young, while jaegers, hawks, owls, and eagles are able to catch the adults. I could always tell when an aerial predator was near, because the ptarmigans would sink to the ground, turning one eye skyward. I have also seen them flush for the cover of a willow thicket at the sight of a golden eagle in flight.

Bobwhite
(Colinus virginianus)

FIELD MARKS:	*Light brown and white. Male is only quail with white throat. Female has buffy throat.*
SIZE:	*11 inches long with a wingspan of 12–14 inches.*
HABITS:	*Runs rapidly with their bodies held erect. Draws into a tight circle with their heads pointed out at night.*
HABITAT:	*Brush, abandoned fields, pinelands.*
NEST:	*Simple nest roofed over with grass.*
EGGS:	*Off-white, 14–16 in a clutch. Incubation 23–24 days.*
FOOD:	*Weed seeds in the fall, winter, and spring; insects and wild berries in the summer.*
VOICE:	*A whistled* bobwhite, bobwhite, bobwhite.

Bobwhites are usually found in coveys of up to twelve birds, and all burst into flight immediately when disturbed. The birds then emit a gathering call and the flock is regrouped in a short time.

Some of my pleasantest memories of years ago are of bobwhite quail. I remember walking along the back lanes of our farm after having driven the cows to pasture, hearing the male birds perched on a stump or post in the brushy fence rows cheerily calling again and again *bobwhite, bobwhite, bobwhite*. By whistling back to them, I could often approach within ten or fifteen feet before they broke for cover.

The bobwhite were plentiful in my area of northern New Jersey during the 1930's, but they began to decline during the next decade. Now they are very scarce. I always attributed their decline in part to the shift in farming practices, from raising multiple small grain crops to concentrating on a few such standards as corn, wheat, and hay. Farmers no longer raise rye, oats, buckwheat, or other grains that the bobwhite used to glean when they were spilled on the ground by reaper or combine.

Familiar to New England and Deep South sportsman alike, the bobwhite is found throughout most of the eastern United States from Massachusetts to Florida westward almost to the Rocky Mountains and northward to the Dakotas. It is the sportsman who shows the deepest concern for the bobwhite, one of the most popular and most heavily hunted game birds in the United States. This quail is a strong flier, exploding out of cover as if launched from a rocket, though it holds well for a dog. Throughout most of its range the bobwhite can easily be found near the haunts of man. It would much rather nest in the proximity of man's own rural areas than frequent mountains, prairies, or forests. And to top it off, the bobwhite provides scrumptious eating for the successful nimrod.

Most of the year bobwhites stay in coveys of a dozen or more, but as the returning warmth of spring stirs new life, the winter coveys split up, and the birds begin to pair. At no other time of the year do the males' calls ring out so clearly and so continuously. Bloody battles are often fought over the females.

Within a two-week period after pairing up, male and female construct a simple nest on the ground, hidden in a dense tangle of undergrowth. So well are these nests hidden that I have never been successful in finding one. The nests are usually roofed over with leaves, grass, or similar local vegetation.

Fourteen to sixteen off-white eggs, one and one-quarter inches long and one inch in diameter, comprise a clutch. While larger numbers of eggs have been found in one nest, this generally occurs because more than one female is utilizing the same nest. Two broods a year are common in the south and many occur in the north, although one brood is standard in the latter region.

Incubation occupies twenty-three to twenty-four days and is shared by both male and female. The chicks leave the nest as soon as they hatch. Their growth is so rapid that in a matter of days they are capable of short flights. Males can be distinguished from females at an early age because the former have richer, darker brown plumage and a pure white throat, while the females' throat is tawny yellow. Adults of both sexes weigh between six to eight ounces, have a wingspan of about twelve to fourteen inches and a total length of eleven inches.

All of the bobwhites' feeding habits are beneficial to man. The bulk of their diet consists of weed seeds in the fall, winter, and spring months. In summer insects rank first; vast quantities of grasshoppers, chinch bugs, cutworms, weevils, beetles, flies, and mosquitoes are consumed. One quail has been recorded as eating 1,000 grasshoppers and 532 other insects in the course of a single day. Wild berries also are eaten in quantity.

When a covey is disturbed, the quail scatter in all directions. They fly at speeds of up to thirty miles per hour, but only for short distances. Quail can run very rapidly. I always enjoy watching them dart across a road, their tiny legs and feet mere blurs beneath their erect, chunky bodies, looking almost like mechanical toys. At night a bobwhite covey draws into a tight circle, tails pointing in, heads pointing out. In this position the quail can watch for danger from all sides.

Snakes, skunks, opossums, raccoons, cats, foxes, bobcats, hawks, and owls prey on quail. Nevertheless, in spite of predation and hunting pressure, the bobwhite is capable of holding his own, so long as its food and cover requirements can be met.

Ring-necked Pheasant
(*Phasianus colchicus*)

FIELD MARKS:	*Male: bloodred cheek patches and wattles, iridescent back and head, 22-inch tail, white neck ring. Female: mottled brown.*
SIZE:	*34–36 inches long with a wingspan of 32 inches.*
HABITS:	*Male has a harem of 3 or 4 hens. Roosts in trees.*
HABITAT:	*Open woods, on farmland in brush, hedgerows, cornfields.*
NEST:	*A few blades of grass and weeds in a slight depression.*
EGGS:	*Olive buff, 12 in a clutch. Incubation 23 days.*
FOOD:	*Grain and weed seeds.*
VOICE:	*Loud two-syllable calls,* k-kuk, k-kuk.

Male ring-necked pheasants maintain harems of three to four hens, which they must defend from rival cocks. Fights between the cocks are frequent and bloody.

The United States has no native pheasants. Of the various species that have been introduced, none is as well known as the ring-neck. A native of China, Mongolia, and Korea, this bird was reared for years in countries bordering the Mediterranean Sea and in Europe. Its Latin name, *colchicus*, derives from the ancient country of Colchis on the Black Sea.

The ring-neck was first introduced into the New World in 1760 by Benjamin Franklin's son-in-law, Richard Bache. Mr. Bache had a large plantation south of Camden, New Jersey. In spite of the efforts expended to provide sufficient shelter and food, the experiment failed.

The first successful importation occurred in 1881, when Judge Denny, the American consul general at Shanghai, China, sent thirty birds home to Oregon. Twenty-six of the birds survived and were released in the Willamette Valley. From the beginning the birds prospered. Two years later the judge sent over another shipment, and these, too, were released in the valley.

In the eastern United States the first effective stocking was accomplished in 1888, a year after Rutherford Stuyvesant had brought over from Scotland a game breeder named Dunn. Mr. Dunn, his family, and his birds were ensconced on the Stuyvesant estate in Allamuchy, New Jersey, which is located just a few miles from my home. Dunn's efforts were successful, and soon large numbers of the birds were being released for hunting. Those that escaped into the surrounding area began to propagate naturally on their own. When the state of New Jersey finally decided to raise pheasants for its hunters, Mr. Dunn was hired to head the project. His descendants have been in charge of New Jersey's pheasant program ever since.

Other states joined in the ring-neck experiment, which was crowned with success in the Dakotas and Nebraska. It has been found that the birds do well in states roughly north of the Mason-Dixon line. Below that line success has been limited. The pheasant, therefore, has not been a threat to the bobwhite, neither does it compete with the ruffed grouse in the northeast. In the midwestern states, on the other hand, it may drive out both quail and prairie chicken.

Even in those states where the ring-neck does well, it has undergone population reversals. I recall how plentiful pheasants were on my family's farm outside Belvidere, New Jersey, during the mid-1930's. The decline in numbers became noticeable in this region during the 1940's. By the end of the forties the pheasant was rare under natural conditions, and only continual releases of birds from the state hatchery kept them in evidence. Similar declines have occurred at various times throughout the pheasant's range. These have been attributed to a variety of factors, but in my area one of the most important was the transition of the farms from multiple small-grain crops to hay and corn. Clean farming practices destroyed much of the brushy fence rows where the birds formerly nested. Fortunately the trend has reversed itself in New Jersey. The pheasant is probably more populous today than ever before in most parts of its range.

Each spring, from April to June, the cock collects a harem of as many hens as he can defend from rival males with roving eyes. Fights are frequent and bloody. Arrayed in their finest plumage, the males are veritable fashion plates with their bloodred cheek patches and wattles, iridescent backs and heads, and long tails trailing behind them. Their tails make up about 50 percent of their total length of approximately thirty-four to thirty-six inches; cocks also have a wingspread of thirty-two inches and weigh almost three pounds. Hens are smaller and have a more subdued coloration.

Like gladiators of old, the cocks eye each other warily before doing battle. Then they attack. Beating their wings, they jump into the air to strike at each other with their needle-sharp foot spurs. The beaks are also used for pecking and grabbing the adversary. The battle continues until one cock is defeated and leaves the area. Meanwhile the objects of all this commotion continue about their business with an "I-couldn't-care-less" attitude. Three or four hens comprise the average harem.

While the breeding season is in progress, the hen has been selecting a nest site, which may be in a hay field, a fence row, or a brush-filled gully. Each hen retires daily to her nest, made of a few blades of grass and weeds set in a slight hollow, to lay another olive buff egg, about one and one-half inches long and one and one-quarter inches in diameter, until her clutch of about one dozen eggs is complete. She incubates the eggs alone, her brown body blending in with her surroundings so well that she is practically

In the face of danger ring-necked pheasants depend upon their legs to escape. However, they can fly for short distances at speeds of up to 40 miles per hour.

invisible. After twenty-three days the little chicks emerge. The precocial chicks are able to leave the nest as soon as their down dries and follow after the hen in search of food. While the adults feed primarily on grain and weed seeds, owing to their need for protein, the chicks' diet consists mainly of insects. The hen continues to brood her flock each night to protect them from the cold, and she broods them as well on rainy days. Not until the fall molt can the young males be readily identified.

The ring-neck is prey for foxes, goshawks, and great horned owls. The eggs are eaten by snakes, skunks, raccoons, opossums, and crows.

Civilization has been kind to the ring-neck; it fills the void left by game birds forced to retreat before its onslaught. That so gaudy a bird can hide so completely is nothing short of a miracle. It almost seems to dissolve right before your eyes. Rather than take to the air, the pheasant runs to safety whenever the opportunity presents itself, usually circling around so as to come behind the hunter. Many a good bird dog has been ruined by the ring-neck's refusal to stand his ground. When flight becomes imperative, the ring-neck springs from the earth like a mallard from a pothole. With a great beating of stubby wings not built for sustained flight and a loud *k-kuk, k-kuk, k-kuk, k-kuk*, he soon reaches speeds of up to forty miles per hour, which quickly take him out of shotgun range as the hunter watches with mouth agape.

7 Ciconiiformes—
Herons and Their Allies

The 7 family groups that make up this order include 114 species. Of the 4 families and 19 species found in North America, we discuss 2 families and 10 species. All these long-legged, long-necked, long-billed birds are waders. With the exception of the flamingo, which has webbed feet, all have long, widely separated toes.

The family Ardeidae—herons, egrets, and bitterns—have straight bills. In flight they carry their long necks drawn back on their shoulders in an S curve and trail their long legs and feet behind to help steer. Their flight is strong but slow and appears labored.

Bitterns have only two patches of powder-down compared to the herons' four. They also depend primarily on their coloration for concealment and protection, while herons depend on flight.

Handsomest members of this group are the egrets. Most are pure white. All have the beautiful breeding plumes, known as aigrettes, which were sought by plume hunters, and for which these birds were slaughtered by the tens of thousands almost to the point of extinction.

Unlike herons, egrets, and bitterns, the family Ciconiidae, storks, lack powder-down patches and serrated toes. Not only are their toes shorter, but the hind toe is elevated above the other three and so does not give the walking support it provides in the herons. The long, heavy bill is either decurved or upturned. Storks fly with necks and legs fully extended.

The only American representative of this family is the wood ibis, or wood stork. It is a distant relative of the European stork, long considered a symbol of good luck and famed for nesting on house chimneys. The long-legged bird's nesting habits gave rise to the myth that it delivered human babies by dropping them down the chimney—certainly a rough way for a youngster to get a start in life.

Great White Heron
(*Ardea occidentalis*)

FIELD MARKS:	*Pure white plumage, bright yellow bill, light greenish yellow legs.*
SIZE:	*54 inches long with a wingspan of 70 inches. Largest North American Heron.*
HABITS:	*Does not flock. Has a long nesting season. Remains in one spot for hours on end.*
HABITAT:	*Off the southern tip of the Florida mainland and in the Florida Keys.*
NEST:	*Small twigs and mangrove leaves.*
EGGS:	*Pale blue-green, 3–4 in a clutch. Incubation 28 days.*
FOOD:	*Fish.*
VOICE:	*Hoarse croak.*

The largest American heron, the great white heron, inhabits an extremely restricted range off the Florida mainland and in the Florida keys.

The great white heron, with its pure white plumage, bright yellow bill, and light greenish yellow legs, is the largest member of the heron family. It often reaches a total length of fifty-four inches and has a wingspread of seventy inches. Male and female are look-alikes. This species has the most restricted range of any of our herons, occurring chiefly off the southern tip of the Florida mainland and in the Florida Keys, which represents the northern extremity of its range.

My first sight of this heron was on a birding trip out into Florida Bay from Tavernier in the Florida Keys. Most of the bay is so shallow that the mucky white bottom mud clutches and clings to anyone foolish enough to try walking on it. The multicolored waters of the bay have a fantastic array of tones and shadings. Its beauty is breathtaking. The darker color marks the deep channels created by currents of the various streams that pour into the bay. Here and there, in the shallowest water, red mangroves drift aground, sprout, take root, and commence to grow. Soon a mangrove key is formed.

The mud flats and warm, shallow water teeming with fish furnish the great white heron with ideal fishing spots. When seeking food, the heron wades out to an advantageous spot and stands absolutely motionless until the first fish ventures within range. Then the bird quickly spears its catch and slides it down its long gullet. The heron remains in one spot for hours on end; only when the incoming tide has the bird afloat does it cease activity. With measured strides it wades up to a shallower spot, or, if its appetite is appeased, wings its way to a mangrove clump to settle down for a snooze. This bird seldom frequents areas where other food is available and thus feeds almost exclusively on fish.

Living in a continuously warm climate, this heron has an exceptionally long nesting season, and eggs have been found in nests built in the tops of mangrove thickets at almost any time of year. The nests are lined with small twigs and dry mangrove leaves and measure about thirty-five inches in diameter. The three or four pale bluish green eggs, two and three-eighths inches long and one and five-eighths inches in diameter, are almost indistinguishable from those of the great blue heron. The young can easily be told apart, however; great white heron chicks are pure white, while great blue heron chicks are gray. The parents share the job of incubation, which lasts about twenty-eight days.

The gluttonous young eagerly swallow the food brought to them by the parents. They grow rapidly, and by the time they are five weeks old they are clambering about in the thickets.

This gregarious species shares nesting sites with the great blue heron. When these two herons mate, as they occasionally do, the resultant hybrid is known as Würdemann's heron. It has the general slate blue body color of the great blue but the white head and neck of the great white.

Although great white herons are numerous in Cuba, Yucatán, and Jamaica, seldom are more than one thousand individuals found in the United States. Great white heron flocks were reduced to a mere handful during the Depression years because many of the poorer Floridians hunted them for food. Timely intervention by the National Audubon Society guarded and preserved the few that remained, allowing the species to restore its populations. While these birds do not possess the beautiful aigrettes that brought about the destruction of the egrets at the hands of plume hunters, tropical storms often take their toll by destroying heron nests and have been largely responsible for keeping heron populations in check. The heron young are in danger from black vultures and gulls, the eggs are sought by gulls and crows, and raccoons eat both the young and the eggs.

American Egret
(*Casmerodius albus*)

FIELD MARKS:	*Pure white with long plumes, yellow bill, black feet and legs.*
SIZE:	*38–42 inches long with a wingspan of 55 inches.*
HABITS:	*Feeds only in the daytime. Elaborate courtship ritual.*
	Builds a poor nest.
HABITAT:	*Streams, ponds, marshes, mudflats.*
NEST:	*Poorly made; lined with mangrove leaves, Spanish moss.*
EGGS:	*Pale blue-green, 3–4 in a clutch. Incubation 28 days.*
FOOD:	*Small fish and young snakes.*
VOICE:	*Hoarse croak.*

102

During the breeding season, the American egret uses its long white plumes to attract a mate. The male egret erects his plumes and struts before the female for hours, making gurgling noises in his throat.

At the turn of this century egrets by the hundreds of thousands were slaughtered in the name of fashion to decorate milady's hats. The common, or American, egret and the snowy egret were the staples of the plume business, both species being hunted so relentlessly for their breeding plumes, or aigrettes, they were pushed to the brink of extinction.

Known to plume hunters as the "long white," this tall graceful bird has pure white, delicate plumes, which grow from the middle of its back and extend well below its tail feathers. Measuring between thirty-eight and forty-two inches in length, it has a wingspread of fifty-five inches, a long, yellow bill, yellow legs, and black feet. The sexes look alike.

This egret nests from South and Central America as far north as New Jersey and Oregon. After nesting duties have been completed and the annual brood is ready to fly, the common egret starts its late-summer trek northward. In its summer travels it strays northward into Canada, but winter finds the bird restricted to the southern limits of the United States.

The egrets' plumes play an important role during the breeding season in early spring. Arriving in small flocks of eight or ten individuals, the birds gather on a sand bar or other cleared area. When a goodly number have assembled, the males strut back and forth before the females, displaying their plumes and uttering deep-throated noises. The show goes on for hours, enlivened occasionally by temperamental fireworks when rival males try to settle their differences by fighting. At the end of a week's time, mate selection is completed, antagonisms are forgotten, and nest construction has begun in the rookeries.

Large numbers of common egrets nest in favored areas alongside other species of egrets, herons, and cormorants. In a family of notoriously poor nest builders, this egret wins the prize. The nest is usually situated in a tree twenty to forty feet from the ground. Only rarely, when the the tree is sufficiently low—a mangrove bush, for example—will the nest be sited at the very top. About twenty-four inches in diameter or even smaller, the nest is often lined with mangrove leaves and the Spanish moss that grows so profusely in most of the birds' nesting areas.

Male and female take turns incubating the three to four pale bluish green eggs, two and one-quarter inches long and one and five-eighths inches in diameter. Both the common egret and the snowy egret are affectionate and demonstrative, and both perform most activities with some kind of little ceremony. An example is the "changing of the guard" ceremony performed by the incubating adults. When one parent returns from feeding to relieve its mate, it flies over the nest and lands on an elevated branch or perch. Both birds utter harsh croaks and display their plumes. Then, wings widespread, the returning bird hops down from its elevated position to the nest's edge. Here the two birds caress each other by rubbing their bills together and sliding them over one another's body. They exchange positions, and the relieved mate is free to fly off to forage for food.

Unlike the great blue heron, which often feeds at night, the common egret feeds only in the daytime, taking suckers, carp, sunfish, dace, and other small fish. Frogs, lizards, mice, crabs, snails, crayfish, and grasshoppers are included in its diet as well. This egret also takes a heavy toll of young cottonmouth moccasins. By helping to control the population of this deadly reptile, the egret performs a great service to man.

When the young hatch, after a twenty-eight-day incubation, the parents feed them a predigested meal of souplike fish directly into their beaks. Later the parents deposit larger chunks of food for them on the edge of the nest; as time passes, entire small fish are brought in as food.

A bird rookery is no place for anyone suffering from a weak stomach. A general odor of rotting fish and excrement pervades the area, and often young birds fall from the nest to their deaths. It seems incredible that the beautiful and graceful egret can be the product of such an environment.

Now that man has taken protective measures to save the egret, its chief enemies are crows and vultures. Crows are perhaps the most destructive because they quickly puncture the eggs in any nest left unguarded for as long as a minute. Both crows and black vultures kill and feed on the young birds that have just hatched.

Snowy Egret
(Leucophoyx thula)

FIELD MARKS: *Pure white feathers and plumes, jet black bill and legs, bright yellow feet.*

SIZE: *24–28 inches long with a wingspan of 38 inches.*

HABITS: *Prenuptial molt, devotion to young, gregarious nature.*

HABITAT: *Marshes.*

NEST: *Loosely assembled sticks and twigs.*

EGGS: *Pale blue, 4–5 in a clutch. Incubation 18 days.*

FOOD: *Small fish, grasshoppers, cutworms, small snakes, lizards, frogs, crayfish, and shrimp.*

VOICE: *Squawk.*

The most beautiful and most graceful member of the attractive heron family is the snowy egret. The dazzling brightness of its pure white plumage accentuates its jet black bill and legs, while its yellow feet make clear the origin of its nickname, "golden slippers." Second largest of the white herons, after the great white, this egret measures about twenty-four to twenty-eight inches in length, has a wingspread of thirty-eight inches and a bill between three and three and one-half inches long. Male and female are identical and cannot be told apart at a distance.

It was the beauty of the snowy egret's breeding plumes, or aigrettes, that came close to being the bird's undoing. Starting in January or February, the plumes commence to grow from a small, elongated patch on the bird's neck and extend down its back. The delicate, filigree-textured aigrettes vary in length from ten to fourteen inches and in number between thirty and fifty. At the height of the plume trade, between 1902 and 1903, these aigrettes brought about $32 per ounce. An ounce required the plumes of four birds. The aigrettes could only be obtained by killing the bird, then pulling out the feathers or "scalping" the small flap of skin with the aigrettes attached. Because the snowy egret was more common and less shy than its cousin the common egret, it bore the brunt of the slaughter.

Compounding the problem was the fact that the egrets only had their dorsal plumes during the breeding and nesting season. Because the birds abandoned an area if they were molested when starting to nest, the hunters did not shoot them at that time but waited for the young to hatch. It was then a simple matter for the hunters to wipe out an entire colony, killing the parent birds as they tried to return to the nests to feed the hungry young. The hunters showed no concern for the young thus fated to die a slow death from starvation. More fortunate were those that fell out of the nest and drowned. Many eyewitness reports describe areas littered with the bodies of slaughtered adult egrets, some floating in the water, others strewn upon the land. The air was filled with the protesting squawks of the starving young and the putrid odor of death.

Such shocking accounts, recorded by expert observers, were given wide publicity. The National Audubon Society was in the forefront of the battle to prevent the sale of plumes and to protect the birds. In 1905 the society hired Guy Bradley, a young Floridian, to patrol the region of Cuthbert Rookery to protect the few surviving egrets. Bradley was murdered by a neighbor whom he had tried to restrain from shooting the birds. The storm of protest arising over Bradley's death gave the final impetus to legislation prohibiting the killing of wild birds for their plumage and the use of such plumage on articles of clothing.

Snowy egrets nest as far north as New Jersey, westward to Nebraska and

The snowy egret, the most beautiful of our egrets, has been nicknamed "Golden Slippers" because of its bright yellow feet. This egret was almost exterminated by the plume hunters.

Utah, southward to South America. In winter they seldom range farther north than South Carolina. After the nesting season, most of the birds migrate northward, many into southern Canada. With the approach of cold weather, they retreat southward to their winter range.

These gregarious egrets like company; their rookeries are frequently shared with the little blue and the Louisiana herons. Their nests are crude affairs composed of loosely assembled twigs and sticks, ten to fifteen inches in diameter, and usually built in a tree or bush five to fifteen feet off the ground. Instances have also been recorded of nests on the ground constructed of the surrounding reeds and rushes.

Incubation starts as soon as the first of the four to five pale blue eggs, one and three-quarters inches long and one and one-quarter inches in diameter, is laid, usually at two-day intervals. If not instantly protected, the exposed first-laid eggs could easily be ruined by the broiling sun or stolen by thieving crows. Both parents participate in the eighteen-day incubation period. They are devoted to their young; from the time the first egg is laid until the young are ready to leave the nest, one or the other parent is always in attendance. The adults spend hours each day hovering over the babies, with their wings extended to serve the purpose of sunshield or beach umbrella. The young are fed regurgitated fish by the parents, and they grow rapidly. By the time they are three weeks old, they begin to clamber about the nest and flop around in the adjoining branches.

The snowy egret feeds on small fish of all types as well as on shrimp, grasshoppers, cutworms, lizards, frogs, crayfish, and small snakes. While feeding, it dances around in the shallow water, darting this way and that, wings raised over its back, spearing the elusive prey with its sharp bill. When disturbed, its strong wings easily and lightly carry it to a more secluded spot. Raccoons will eat both the eggs and the young snowy egret.

Cattle Egret
(*Bubulcus ibis*)

FIELD MARKS:	*White. Light brown patches on head, chest, and shoulders. Yellow beak and legs.*
SIZE:	*17 inches long with a wingspan of 37 inches.*
HABITS:	*Close association with cattle. Feeds in short grass.*
HABITAT:	*On land, but nests in swampy thickets.*
NEST:	*Loosely assembled collection of twigs with no liner.*
EGGS:	*Pale blue-green, 3–4 in a clutch. Incubation 18 days.*
FOOD:	*Grasshoppers, flies, crickets, and other insects.*
VOICE:	*Croaks.*

The spread of the Old World cattle egret into North America has generated a vast amount of interest among those who study birds as well as among other outdoor enthusiasts. While we now have a number of bird species from other lands, most of these were imported by man. The cattle egret made its own way over here. It is thought that the trade winds or even a hurricane blew the birds from their native haunts in Europe and Africa to South America, where they first became established in the late 1800's in British Guiana. While this bird is steadily expanding its range in the Americas, it is spreading out considerably over the Old World as well.

The first cattle egrets to reach the United States touched down in Florida in 1942. Ten years later they had been seen in Massachusetts and New Jersey. By 1960 they had spread westward as far as Wisconsin; the following year they were on the Canadian prairies. The bird is now fairly common all along the Atlantic Coast, and the only bird watchers who haven't seen it are those who haven't bothered to look.

A great help to man, the cattle egret is a most welcome immigrant. It feeds mainly on grasshoppers, crickets, flies, and other insects, which it gleans from pastures, meadows, and grasslands. Its name is derived from its preferred close association with cattle. The egret feeds right in among its bovine hosts. In moving about, the grazing cattle stir up insects that are hidden in the grass. As the insects scatter before the movement of the cattle, the egret is right there to gobble them up.

In feeding like this, the cattle egrets are duplicating the role that used to be enacted by the cowbirds with the bison herds. When the egrets become established in the regions of our western cattle ranches, they should skyrocket in numbers, for any wildlife species can greatly increase in population when it has an unlimited food supply.

While most other herons and egrets include insects in their diet, they spend the greater part of their time in or near the water. The cattle egret, by contrast, has made the successful transition from fishing bird to insect eater on land. Still, this species prefers to nest in the company of other members of its family. Its nest is usually in a swampy thicket, on top of a bush ten or twelve feet above the ground. The nest is a loosely thrown together collection of twigs, with no apparent attempt made to provide a liner. Male and female evidently take turns incubating the three to four pale blue-green eggs, one and seven-eighths inches long and one and three-eighths inches in diameter, and caring for the young. Incubation takes eighteen days.

Slightly smaller than the snowy egret, with which it is most commonly confused, the cattle egret is distinguishable by the slight brownish coloring

Cattle egrets may be found in flocks in pastures where they feed on insects stirred up by the movement of cattle.

around its neck and shoulders. Its bill and legs are yellow, while those of the snowy egret are black. This egret measures seventeen inches in length and has a wingspread of thirty-seven inches.

This bird does not allow man to approach too closely, yet it is not shy and retiring, merely cautious. On the lawns of homes in Homestead, Florida, I have seen flocks of thirty to forty of these cattle egrets feeding. An inquisitive dog might send them flapping to the tops of a nearby tree, but as soon as the dog has disappeared, the birds fly down to resume their search for food. The mowed roadside edges and highway center strips in the same area are other good places to see this species. This egret prefers to feed over short grass, because high weeds and grasses hamper both its movements and its ability to see approaching danger. Crows, gulls, and raccoons eat the egret eggs, and raccoons also attack the young.

Great Blue Heron
(*Ardea herodias*)

FIELD MARKS:	*Dark gray. Bluish tinge on top of back, darker underparts, white head. 6½-inch bill. Largest dark heron.*
SIZE:	*50–52 inches long with a wingspan of 80 inches.*
HABITS:	*Courtship dance. Draws back its head while flying. Always wary and alert to danger.*
HABITAT:	*Lakes, ponds, marshes, seacoast.*
NEST:	*Sticks and twigs, lined with fine twigs and rootlets.*
EGGS:	*Pale green, 4–5 in a clutch. Incubation 28 days.*
FOOD:	*Mainly fish; also frogs, tadpoles, eels, salamanders, snakes, insects, young birds, mice, and small rats.*
VOICE:	*Loud croak.*

The great blue heron stands about four feet tall and is the largest of the dark herons.

I am a long-time admirer of the majestic great blue heron, largest of our wading birds. Wary and always on the alert, it is difficult to approach.

One spring I was photographing a group of wild mallard, wood, black, and pin-tail ducks on a hidden pothole located on Poxono Island in the middle of the Delaware River. From a concealed bird blind right at the water's edge, I snapped away as the ducks swam about, rested, and fed. Suddenly, a great blue heron flew in and landed on the other side of the pothole, about one hundred feet away. Spotting my blind instantly, it peered intently at me. Although all but the very tip of my camera lens was hidden, and I moved the lens very cautiously, I was mistaken in thinking I could get a picture of the heron. At the first slight movement of the lens, the heron uttered a loud squawk and took off. Yet the ducks remained undisturbed. The southern member of the family, Ward's great blue heron, is less suspicious of man.

This heron is found along waterways throughout most of Canada and the United States. While it stays as far north as possible, cold weather forces the heron south to open water, where it can feed. You may encounter it on Canadian wilderness lakes or along the edge of a pond in the center of town. Not too long ago I found several great blues down in the New Jersey Pine Barrens. They seemed so out of place on the snow-covered ground with most of the water turned to ice that I remember thinking how foolish these birds were to put up with the cold when a day's flight would have taken them to warmer climes. Evidently the herons were finding enough fish to eat, or they would have moved.

This large, long-legged bird stands about fifty to fifty-two inches tall and has a wingspread of eighty inches. Head and neck are mostly white, upper parts are slate gray, and underparts are dark. The sharp bill, six and one-half inches long, is a lethal weapon with which the heron spears its prey or fights its rivals. Male and female are identical in size and coloration. In flight the great blue strokes the air with strong, measured wingbeats. Its

The great blue heron often hunts by remaining immobile until an edible fish or insect comes within its range. The heron then spears its prey with its bill.

head is hunched down on the shoulders, while the long legs trail behind to act as a rudder.

With the approach of the breeding season in early April, the great blue herons become more sociable and begin to gather in flocks. Assembling on a flat mud bank or sandbar, they circle about in performance of their court-ship ritual or dance. While the "dancing" is in progress, the birds extend and flap their wings. Males challenge and attack each other, bills flashing like swords. Only the dexterous parrying and counterthrusting of the bills prevents the rivals from being bloodied. Females participate in the dancing, but not in the fighting, though their loud croakings cheer on the combatants to greater fury. Eventually the birds pair off and retire from the area. After mating, the herons become less pugnacious and ultimately nest as a colony.

Isolation is the prime requisite of a heron's nesting site. Although some nests have been found on the ground or in low bushes, most are built in the topmost branches of the tallest trees. Often located over one hundred feet above the ground, the nests are large—perhaps forty inches in diameter—bulky, crudely built affairs of sticks and twigs. The center, slightly hollowed, is frequently lined with slender twigs and rootlets. Because the nests are used from year to year, they grow larger with age as new layers are added each season.

The four to five pale green eggs, about two and one-half inches long and one and one-quarter inches in diameter, are incubated by both parents over a period of twenty-eight days. At first the ugly, helpless little herons are fed soft, regurgitated foods. As they mature, they are fed whole fish by their parents.

Fish is the staple food of the great blue heron, which eats any kind it can catch. Few trout are taken, chiefly because the bird does not frequent the cold, fast-moving streams that trout inhabit. Instead, this heron prefers the warmer, sluggish bodies of water favored by trash fish. Frogs, tadpoles, eels, salamanders, snakes, young birds, mice, and small rats also are taken. Crickets, grasshoppers, and other insects fall victims to the heron as it searches through pastures and woodlands.

The great blue employs two hunting methods. Sometimes it stands im-mobile in one spot for hours on end, waiting for an edible prey to stray within range. At other times it stalks its prey slowly and sedately through the shallows, its long neck hunched on its shoulders, until a movement is detected, then suddenly the bill flashes out to seize or impale its prey. Small fish are quickly flipped about and swallowed headfirst, but the heron must often subdue larger prey before it can be eaten, striking at it repeatedly with its bill or seizing it with the bill and smashing it to the ground.

Because of its food preferences this heron comes into little conflict with man and has been afforded protection by law in most of the states where it is found. But crows, gulls, and raccoons eat great blue heron eggs, and raccoons and great horned owls prey on the young.

Louisiana Heron
(Hydranassa tricolor)

FIELD MARKS:	*Slate blue head, wings, and tail; white body and underside of wings; reddish tan long feathers on back of neck and throat.*
SIZE:	*26–28 inches long with a wingspan of 36 inches.*
HABITS:	*Takes an active part in hunting for food. Entwine necks during the courtship ritual.*
HABITAT:	*Wherever water is in range.*
NEST:	*Sticks and twigs.*
EGGS:	*Light blue-green, 4–5 in a clutch. Incubation 21 days.*
FOOD:	*Fish, particularly killifish, grasshoppers, cutworms, lizards, beetles, small frogs, crayfish.*
VOICE:	*Loud cry.*

The Louisiana heron, the most abundant heron in North America, breeds near the coast from Texas to North Carolina. The birds perform an elaborate courtship ritual and nest-building ceremony.

The Louisiana has the distinction of being the most abundant heron in North America. Even the most casual observer to our southeastern states cannot help but notice it wherever there is water—in roadside ditches, swamps, marshes, coastal areas, ponds, rivers, or streamsides.

The *tricolor* in this heron's Latin name derives from the bird's three basic colors. Head, wings, and tail are bluish gray; underparts are white; and neck and throat feathers are reddish tan. Measuring about twenty-six to twenty-eight inches in length, this heron has a wingspread of about thirty-six inches and a bill more than four inches long. Male and female are look-alikes.

The Louisiana heron does not have the long, graceful dorsal plumes displayed by the showier egrets and herons. The extra-long feathers on the back of its head have never possessed any commercial value to the millinery industry. While countless thousands of snowy and common egrets were being slaughtered by plume hunters in the late 1800's, the Louisiana escaped unscathed.

Despite its name this bird is no more plentiful in Louisiana than elsewhere. It breeds from North Carolina southward to and around the Gulf coastal area. This heron follows the example of many other herons by wandering north after the breeding season, but it seldom travels farther north than New Jersey or farther west than Indiana.

These herons breed in April and May, building their nests in heavy brush or in low trees, usually about five to fifteen feet above the ground. Along the Louisiana coast they have been known to build their nests directly on the low sand islands. The birds perform a courtship ritual in which they entwine their long, graceful necks. Even nest building is a ceremony, involving the finding and presentation of a stick or twig by one bird to its mate, accompanied by loud cries and bowing. Although the ceremony delays nest construction, the birds start early enough so that the nest is usually completed before it must be put to use.

Where thousands of Louisiana herons nest in a limited area, a shortage of nest-building material frequently occurs. When this happens, the birds are not above helping themselves to a neighbor's nest. Caution must accompany such outright theft, because one of each pair of birds is generally in close proximity to its own nest. When a bird is caught stealing a twig, the nest owner sets up a clamor and attacks the intruder. Eventually, one bird succeeds in getting possession of the stick and carries it to its nest.

Although this heron often nests in rookeries occupied by other species, it has been known to deliberately destroy the eggs of some of the other birds. This habit is not widespread and, rather than condemn all Louisianas, we should take the realistic view that it is probably the individual trait of a single offender.

Both parents take turns incubating the four to five light bluish green eggs, one and three-quarters inches long and one and three-eighths inches in diameter, which hatch in approximately twenty-one days. The young are fed regurgitated food, and they grow rapidly. Soon they are strong enough to clamber about on the nest and eventually over the nearby bushes, employing their beaks as well as their feet, flapping their flightless wings wildly. If a young bird falls into the water, it may swim back to safety, yet it still may starve to death, because the parents may be unable to locate or to recognize it in an unfamiliar location. When they feather out, the young have bright brown throats. This bright color tones down with their prenuptial molt, and by the postnuptial molt the youngsters are carbon copies of their parents.

Fish make up the bulk of this bird's diet, yet it seldom eats any fish desired by man. This is fortunate, for its sheer numbers could offer a real threat to the fish population. Little killifish are the favored food, although minnows of all types are taken. Unlike some herons that prefer to let their prey come to them, the Louisiana heron actively hunts down its food. Striding purposefully along the streamside, it herds small schools of fish into shallower water, where it frenziedly stabs at its wriggling catch with its long, sharp beak.

The Louisiana also feeds on lizards, small frogs, cutworms, grasshoppers, beetles, and crayfish. Few people realize the tremendous numbers of grasshoppers that are eaten by most members of the heron family.

Because this heron has never been persecuted, it is one of the friendliest of all the herons. Many of the other birds fly away at the approach of man, but the Louisiana usually continues with its fishing. The Louisiana heron has the same predators to fear as have the other herons—crows, gulls, raccoons, which feed on the eggs, and the great horned owl, which feeds on the young.

Little Blue Heron
(*Florida caerulea*)

FIELD MARKS:	*Adult: dark slate blue with chestnut head and neck. Immature: white.*
SIZE:	*20–25 inches tall with a wingspread of 36–42 inches.*
HABITS:	*Breeds in its immature plumage. Stalks prey with the neck pulled back into the shoulders.*
HABITAT:	*Freshwater lakes and ponds.*
NEST:	*Sticks and twigs loosely assembled.*
EGGS:	*Pale blue-green, 4–5 in a clutch. Incubation 24–28 days.*
FOOD:	*Minnows, frogs, lizards, crayfish, cutworms, grasshoppers.*
VOICE:	*Croaking sound.*

Contrary to its name, the little blue heron is medium sized and has a wingspan of thirty-six to forty-two inches. The adult heron is primarily blue with a purplish maroon head.

The little blue heron's title is something of a misnomer, for neither is this bird particularly small nor is it blue until maturity. It measures twenty to twenty-five inches in length, has a wingspread of thirty-six to forty-two inches, and a bluish, black-tipped bill, three to three and one-half inches long. The adult plumage is slate blue; head and neck are a purplish maroon. Male and female are identical in size and coloration. In the immature stage, however, this heron is almost pure white and is often mistaken for an egret. My first sighting of this bird sent me back to my Peterson's field guide. The identifying marks in the immature stage are the dark wing tips and greenish yellow legs and feet.

The white plumage is worn until the bird is two years old. In fact, this heron is one of the few birds that breeds while in its immature plumage. In its first breeding season, the heron usually has a mottled appearance, primarily white with big patches of blue. At this stage it is often called the "calico heron."

The little blue's breeding range has shrunk over the past forty or fifty years. Formerly, it extended as far north as New Jersey to Illinois; now the heron seldom nests north of North Carolina and Missouri. After the breeding season, many birds venture northward to Canada before turning south for the winter season. This bird prefers freshwater lakes and ponds to saltwater regions.

The gregarious little blue usually nests in good-sized rookeries with others of its species and with other herons. Some rookeries have contained as many as fifteen hundred nests. Mid-March signals the start of the nesting season, with the construction of a typical heron nest—not overly large, composed of sticks and twigs loosely jumbled together, and located four to eight feet off the ground in a willow tree or bush. The four or five pale blue-green eggs, a little over one and one-half inches long and one and one-quarter inches in diameter, are incubated for twenty-four to twenty-eight days.

Agile, quick and light of movement, the little blue heron feeds on all types of minnows, frogs, lizards, crayfish, cutworms, and grasshoppers. It stalks its prey carefully, neck folded down into the shoulders. When close enough for the kill, the bill strikes out with a rapierlike thrust. So swift and accurate is the heron's aim that it seldom misses its target.

I spent an enjoyable day photographing the little blue in Corkscrew Swamp Wildlife Sanctuary, in western Florida, where it was the most common species seen. Walking over the water lettuce that almost blankets the swamp, the bird carefully chose and spaced each measured step as it scanned the area ahead. On spying an edible tidbit, the body moved forward, while head and neck coiled back. Then, like a snake striking at its prey, the bill darted out. When a crayfish, the main item of diet that day, was captured, the bird flailed it around, pecked at it, moved it back in its beak, and chomped down on it in an effort to crack the shell. Success achieved, the heron gulped down the sizable morsel, whose passage along the bird's throat could be clearly noted.

This heron is particularly popular in the rice-growing areas of Louisiana and Texas, where it is called the "levee walker," after its habit of walking up and down the dikes surrounding the rice fields in search of crayfish. Because crayfish burrow into the dikes and weaken them, the farmers welcome the help of the little blue heron.

Little blues remain susceptible to predation by natural enemies, more so while nesting than at any other time. Crows and sometimes grackles regard any unguarded nest as an open invitation and are quick to eat whatever eggs they can find. Raccoons and opossums often feed on both eggs and young. Frequently chicks fall out of the nest and are unable to return or catch their necks in the crotch of a tree in falling and suffer death by strangulation. During the early years of this century many young herons were eaten by people living in the areas frequented by these birds. Now such practices are outlawed.

The immature little blue heron has a pure white plumage, which is very similar to that of the snowy egret. When changing to adulthood, the white birds become boldly patched with blue.

Yellow-crowned Night Heron
(Nyctanassa violacea)

FIELD MARKS: *Blue-gray body. Yellow crown during the breeding seasons, white crown at other times; black head with broad white streak beneath and beyond the eye; bright orange-red eyes; yellow feet and legs.*

SIZE: *28 inches long with a wingspan of 44 inches.*

HABITS: *Feeds during the dawn and twilight.*
Nests in bushes and shrubs.

HABITAT: *Freshwater ponds, sloughs, and lagoons.*

NEST: *Mainly sticks and twigs.*

EGGS: *Dull blue, 3–4 in a clutch. Incubation 26–28 days.*

FOOD: *Small crabs and crayfish, snails, small snakes, lizards, leeches, mice.*

VOICE: *A single* kwawk.

Although it sometimes hunts at night, the yellow-crowned night heron prefers to feed at dawn or in the evening. Small crabs and crayfish comprise the bulk of the bird's diet.

In spite of its name, the yellow-crowned night heron feeds only occasionally at night, doing most of its feeding during daylight, with a preference for the dawn and the twilight hours. In addition it has a white crown throughout most of the year. Only during the breeding season does this heron display a bright yellow swath down the center of its head, from which two or more long feathers, or plumes, extend backward.

This heron measures up to twenty-eight inches in length and has a wingspread of up to forty-four inches. Its bill is about two and one-half to three inches in length, shorter than that of its cousin, the black-crowned night heron. Beneath the crown, the head and throat are black, with a broad white streak running laterally from the bright orange-red eyes. Body and neck are blue-gray, wings have dark brown markings, and legs and feet are yellow. Both adult male and female have the same coloration. The immature bird has an overall dark brown body coloration resembling that of the American bittern.

A bird of freshwater ponds, sloughs, and lagoons, the yellow-crowned night heron breeds as far north as New Jersey, westward to Illinois, then southward to Texas. After the breeding season, the young are capable of flight, and the birds migrate northward as far as Novia Scotia, Maine, and Ontario. Winter finds most of them in Cuba and Mexico, a few remaining in southern Texas and the tip of Florida.

This heron is less common than its relatives, prefers to keep to itself, and is usually solitary in feeding. If several pairs nest in the same area, they do not join forces with the other herons and egrets. The nests are seldom high off the ground, preferably being located in lower bushes and shrubs. Approximately eighteen to twenty inches in diameter, they are composed of sticks, twigs, and sometimes a few rootlets and leaves. On occasion this heron has been known to nest on low, rocky islands where no bushes were available and nests were built on clumps of prickly pear. Some birds have been reported considerably more than two hundred miles inland from the coast. In New Jersey some favor Lake Tranquility as a nesting spot, and others nest around the Cape May rookeries.

From March to April three to four dull blue eggs, two inches long and one and one-half inches in diameter, are commonly laid. One brood a year is usual, and incubation takes about twenty-six to twenty-eight days.

Unlike most heron, which feed on fish, the yellow-crowned night heron prefers small crabs and crayfish. It also takes snails, small snakes, lizards, leeches, and an occasional mouse. To split apart the shell of large black crabs and expose the interior meat, the heron hacks away at the shell with its beak. Because of its food preferences, this heron is neither an asset nor a liability to man. Crows, gulls, and raccoons hunt for the yellow-crowned night heron's eggs, and its young are food for the raccoon and the great horned owl.

With the exercise of a little caution, this bird can be approached quite closely by water. I use a canoe in photographing it, and as long as every movement is slow and deliberate, the heron remains perched on a dead stick or mangrove branch and dozes peacefully in the sunshine, opening its eyes from time to time to check on possible danger, then grabbing a few more catnaps. It is difficult to approach the bird by land, because the slightest rustling of the bushes puts it to instant flight.

American Bittern
(Botaurus lentiginosus)

FIELD MARKS:	*Light brown with white lines and spots under throat and on breast, yellow eyes.*
SIZE:	*26–28 inches long with a wingspan of 36–48 inches.*
HABITS:	*Expert at camouflage. Makes noise by gulping down air and ejecting it.*
HABITAT:	*Swamps.*
NEST:	*Flattened platform of dead flags and rushes.*
EGGS:	*Olive brown, 3–5 in a clutch. Incubation 28 days.*
FOOD:	*Fish, lizards, salamanders, small snakes, eels, crayfish, frogs, grasshoppers, crickets, meadow mice.*
VOICE:	*Loud guttural call.*

Since its buffy brown plumage blends in with the tall vegetation of its habitat, the American bittern can easily disguise itself by freezing into position with its head held upward.

The bittern spends most of its life sneaking and skulking around in the reeds and flags of its swampy habitat. Its slow, deliberate movements allow it to go undetected while sneaking up on its prey. This bird is also a past master at the art of using camouflage. The buffy brown body blends amazingly well with its habitat, while the throat and breast are marked with white lines and spots that resemble light reflecting on the vegetation. To heighten the illusion, the bittern stands with its beak raised skyward, presenting a long, slim silhouette. The yellow eyes stare at one intently. If the reeds are still, the bittern is still. If the reeds sway in the wind, the bittern sways. It is little wonder that so few people actually see a bittern.

Sometimes called "stake-driver" and "thunder-pumper," the American bittern utters distinctive loud guttural calls, which sometimes sound as though a large hardwood stake were being pounded into soft ground and at other times resembles the noise made by old hand pumps after priming. It is difficult to localize the point of origin of the call—produced when the bittern gulps down and then forcibly ejects vast amounts of air—and thus to determine whether the bird is near or far away.

The bittern measures about twenty-six to twenty-eight inches in length, of which about three and one-half inches is its long, strong bill. It has a wingspread of from thirty-six to forty-eight inches, depending on the age of the bird. Male and female are identical in appearance. In flight this bird resembles the other herons, with neck drawn back into its shoulders, long legs extended backward. Its wingbeats are slow but strong and steady.

In the summer this bittern's breeding range extends just below the Arctic Circle from the Atlantic to the Pacific, southward to New Jersey and westward to California. It winters from California to South Carolina and southward into Central America.

The breeding season takes place in late April, and the nest is constructed by the first of May. Usually a flattened platform of dead flags and rushes, the nest is about a foot in diameter, raised three or four inches above the water to prevent its being flooded. So well hidden is it in a clump of dead cattails or flag that it is difficult to locate.

One clutch of three to five olive brown eggs, about two inches long and one and one-quarter inches in diameter, is laid per year. Both parents participate in the incubation period, which lasts approximately twenty-eight days. Where the ground around the nest is dry, the bittern usually tramps out two pathways. One path is used when the bird comes into the nest, the other when it leaves, the reason being that the bird prefers to land and take off some distance from the nest, then sneak over to it. The young are fed a variety of food by the parents and grow rapidly. They are ready to leave the nest about sixteen to eighteen days after hatching, fairly well feathered out but still unable to fly. Now they begin to supplement the parental feeding by catching some of their own food, already having acquired the parents' habit of "freezing" when disturbed. The young bitterns are capable of flying when they are four to five weeks old.

At no time and in no place is this bird so plentiful as to constitute a problem to man, even though it feeds on fish. It spears the fish or seizes it with its beak, then swallows it whole. Lizards, salamanders, small snakes, eels, and crayfish are taken, and frogs also are important food. Often the bittern forsakes the swampland and feeds in hay fields or grain fields, where it gulps down grasshoppers, crickets, and even meadow mice. By this service alone the bittern more than earns its way.

Although the bittern has no need to fear man as an enemy, it has good reason to be wary and watchful of natural predators. On the ground it is stalked by mink, muskrats, and water snakes, while from the air it is hunted by eagles, hawks, and owls.

Wood Ibis
(*Mycteria americana*)

FIELD MARKS:	*White with black flight feathers; unfeathered blackish gray head and neck, long thick bill.*
SIZE:	*48 inches long with a wingspan of 66 inches.*
HABITS:	*Walks with measured steps, nests in colonies.*
HABITAT:	*Fresh and salt water ponds, marshes, and sloughs.*
NEST:	*Green twigs lined with Spanish moss.*
EGGS:	*White, 3–4 in a clutch. Incubation 21–24 days.*
FOOD:	*Small trash fish and insects.*
VOICE:	*Humming notes.*

The only American stork, the wood ibis inhabits southern ponds, swamps, and marshes. It prefers fresh water, but sometimes may be found in saltwater ponds.

My first good look at a wood ibis occurred in 1954, in the famed Cuthbert Rookery, on the Southern tip of Florida. I was a member of a group touring bird locations under the direction of the National Audubon Society. As our small launch cruised into the lake, the ibises, which had been perched in the mangrove tops, took to the air, soaring on the hot thermals. The day was crystal clear, the sky cobalt blue, providing a perfect backdrop for the sight and sound of these large, snow white birds with black flight feathers and tail, wafted aloft.

The strikingly beautiful picture presented by the wood ibis in flight is not duplicated on the ground. Measuring about forty-eight inches overall, with a bill nine and one-half inches long and a wingspread of sixty-six inches, this ibis strides along with deliberate steps. When standing still, as it often is for several hours at a time, the ibis rests its heavy beak against its chest as though both the beak and the cares of the world were more than it could carry. When perched or standing, the bird's naked head and upper neck are instantly noticeable, presenting a grotesque appearance that has given the wood ibis such local names as "flinthead" and "ironhead." Male and female are identical in plumage, but the male is larger, weighing up to eleven and three-quarters pounds, while the female weighs about nine and one-quarter pounds.

The wood ibis has a limited nesting range in the United States, being confined to the southern portions of Texas, Louisiana, Mississippi, Alabama, and Florida. When the young are large enough to leave the nest, the ibis occasionally wanders as far north as southern Canada.

The breeding season begins in January and February, although nesting activity has been recorded as early as December. The favored nesting spot is in the uppermost branches of the tallest cypress trees. Thousands of birds may nest in a given area; as many as thirty-two nests have been counted in a single tree, and often a single tree limb harbors three or four nests. Unlike most birds, which pick up dead twigs and branches from the ground, this ibis often snaps off small live twigs, particularly from the willow, with which to build its large, bulky nest. Spanish moss is used to provide a soft liner for the nest.

Three to four chalky white eggs, two and one-half inches long and one and five-eighths inches in diameter, are laid, and the parents apparently take turns incubating them. Soon after hatching, the young are covered with a dense, woollike down of a white to dusky gray color. Their heads and necks are feathered, although in lessening amounts each year; when they become adults, at three years of age, these parts will be bare.

The ibis feeds in both freshwater and saltwater ponds, marshes, and sloughs, but apparently prefers the freshwater locations. A favored spot is a pothole of water in the process of drying up, where fish are therefore concentrated. Stalking into the water, the ibis stirs the mud around with its feet. This has the double effect of forcing the fish to the surface to gasp for oxygen, which has become depleted in the muddy water, and of hiding the bird from the fish. As the fish come to the surface of the water, the ibis strikes out wildly with its thick, decurved beak, and soon the water is filled with floating dead minnows. Gorging on this bounty, the bird then retreats to shore to rest and to digest the catch. Small trash fish make up the bulk of the ibis' diet. Insects are also eaten. I have watched ibises gathering grasshoppers, for example, out in the dry grasslands. Occasionally, too, a little vegetable matter, such as the seeds of certain water plants, is consumed.

Man has no conflict with the wood ibis over its food preferences, neither has he coveted this bird for its feathers or for its flesh. While other species were being eradicated, the wood ibis was left relatively unmolested. Seldom does this wary bird allow man to approach. When feeding or nesting, several alert individuals always act as sentries and give the alarm as soon as danger threatens. Still, fish crows, the chief predators, manage to steal a goodly number of eggs during the nesting period.

8 Gruiformes—
Cranes and Their Allies

The order Gruiformes has three representative families living in North America: the Gruidae, cranes; the Armidae, limpkins; and the Pallidae, rails, coots, and gallinules. Most of these birds are aquatic marsh-dwellers, although some have adapted to life on the dry prairies. Several members of this order have long legs and are capable of strong flight, while others are better swimmers than fliers.

The most aquatic member of its family—and the only member of this order to be discussed—is the coot. This bird is notable for the lobed webs or flaps on either side of its toes that help the bird in swimming. An expert diver as well, the coot spends much of its time underwater gathering the vegetation on which it feeds. To take off from water, the coot runs along the surface, its broad toes splattering water at every step. Whenever possible it prefers to escape by diving and swimming underwater rather than by flying. A number of birds of this order have become flightless, possibly owing to similar preferences. Coots usually breed on freshwater ponds, lakes, and marshes, although they often winter along the coast.

American Coot
(*Fulica americana*)

FIELD MARKS:	*Blackish gray, white beak and marking beneath tail, red eyes.*
SIZE:	*14–16 inches long, wingspan 24–28 inches.*
HABITS:	*Spatters along surface of water before taking flight. Dives beneath surface when threatened.*
HABITAT:	*Marsh grasses by lake or pond.*
NEST:	*Platform of swamp tules and reeds.*
EGGS:	*Dull pinkish buff, peppered with blackish spots; 5–12 in a clutch. Incubation takes 21–27 days.*
FOOD:	*Variety of vegetation and animal matter, especially favors wild celery and foxtail grass.*
VOICE:	*Clucking, grunting, or squawking sounds.*

The American coot is the only slate-colored bird with a whitish bill. The coot's other distinguishing features are its lobed toes and bright red eyes.

The bright white beak and red eyes of the coot show up in striking fashion against its slate blue plumage and black head, making it one of the easiest birds to identify. Male and female are look-alikes. The coot is the only bird I know of that has a white beak. The ivory-billed woodpecker was a rival for this distinction, but it has been years since anyone has seen an ivory-bill, and the species is thought to be extinct.

A member of the rail family, the coot is fourteen to sixteen inches in length and has a wingspread of twenty-four to twenty-eight inches—about the size of a small duck. Its habits, too, are more like those of a duck than of a land bird. It is a fine swimmer and spends most of its time in the water. Because of this the coot is sometimes called "mud hen" or "water hen."

The coot propels itself through the water by means of lobed, fleshy pads on its toes, which serve the same function as the skin webs between the toes of ducks. When the coot is in an exceptional hurry, it beats the air wildly with its wings, thus gaining enough momentum to "run" or "spatter" across the surface of the water. The "spattering" may also serve as a takeoff for flight. The coot, however, is a versatile bird and may adopt another strategy when it is disturbed. Frequently, instead of swimming or spattering away over the surface, it merely "plops" underwater and swims off beneath the surface.

The coot is the embodiment of perpetual motion, seldom sitting still for more than a moment or two. When it clambers out on land or rests on floating vegetation, it immediately starts preening and grooming its feathers. An exceptionally noisy bird as well, it is forever clucking, grunting, and squawking.

American coots are commonly found from British Columbia all across Canada to New Brunswick and south to Central America, as breeding or wintering birds or both. The northern limits of their winter range are ruled only by the freezing of the freshwater lakes and ponds.

As soon as the ice goes out of the northern lakes, the birds return for the breeding season. Upon their arrival at the breeding grounds, each male selects a section of reed- or tule-bordered pond or lake, which it claims for its home territory. Frequently the males engage in bloody and vicious battles, striking at each other with their sharp beaks and kicking each other with their powerful legs and long claws. With no holds barred, these battles often degenerate into real donnybrooks involving three or four males and sometimes even a couple of females. Everything quiets down after mates have been selected.

The female constructs the nest out of various swamp tules and reeds bent over to form a platform. More vegetation is added until the nest is deeply hollowed. Five to twelve black-speckled, dull pinkish buff eggs, one and one-half inches long and a little over an inch in diameter, comprise a clutch. Only the female incubates the eggs, which takes twenty-one to twenty-seven days, commencing as soon as the first egg is laid. The male guards the nest during this period and attempts to drive off any intruder that approaches. As the first chicks hatch, the male cares for them while the female continues the incubation. After a week or two the entire clutch is hatched, and the little family is reunited. The young are adept at taking care of themselves at an early age. If danger threatens, they seek safety by diving underwater, often grasping hold of pieces of underwater vegetation to help anchor themselves and surfacing only when they need another breath of air.

Not a fussy eater, the coot has a healthy appetite all the same. It eats almost any type of vegetation that a duck eats, favoring especially wild celery and foxtail grass. From inland fields it sometimes pulls up newly sprouted grain. It also feeds on such animal matter as small fish, snails, water bugs, tadpoles, and worms.

Coots are taken for food by snapping turtles, alligators, otters, and sometimes by fish, but the bald eagle is their chief enemy. An eagle will fly over a flock of coots, forcing it to scatter. When a lone bird splits off from the flock, the eagle instantly singles it out. If the coot tries to fly, the eagle snatches it out of the air. More frequently the coot tries to escape by diving. Undaunted, the eagle follows its underwater passage until the coot is forced to come up for air. When it does so, the eagle drives it under again. At last the exhausted coot surfaces and is easily picked up by the eagle. (I have often watched eagles use these same tactics to catch bufflehead ducks.)

As the cold weather increases in the fall, the icing over of their aquatic habitats forces large flocks of coots to head south to open water. In some areas coots by the thousands form huge rafts where their numbers appear to be beyond counting. Although they are considered legal game, most duck hunters don't bother to hunt for coots. They are clean birds, and their flesh is considered palatable by some, an opinion that seems to depend upon each individual's personal taste. I know some hunters who swear by coots as food, while others simply swear at them.

In winter the coots often gather in large flocks where they can find enough vegetation for food and where the ice can be kept open.

9 Charadriiformes—
Shore Birds, Gulls,
and Alcids

The large, complex, and diverse order of Charadriiformes consists of 16 family groups and 301 species. Of the families 10 are represented in North America, and of these we discuss 6. Although most are considered to be sea or shore birds, they are found throughout the world in many different types of habitat.

The principal food of these birds is of an animal nature—insects, marine life, or the eggs and young of one another.

The family Charadriidae embraces the sixty-three species of plovers and lapwings, ten of which are found in North America. The name plover comes from the Latin *pluvius*, meaning "rain," although no one has satisfactorily explained any basis for associating that word with these birds.

Thirty-three species of sandpipers belonging to the family Scolopacidae inhabit North America. Most of them have long legs, and bills that are not only longer than their heads but in several instances several times longer.

The gull-like birds of the family Stercorariidae are long-winged swimmers and hawklike in manner. Their large size and aggressiveness combine to make them extremely efficient hunters.

The eighty-two species of gulls, twenty of which are found in North America, belong to the family Laridae.

Gulls are primarily scavengers, although they do considerable fishing on their own and feed on numerous insects as well. They can swallow larger pieces of food for their size than any other bird I know.

The terns belong to a subfamily of Laridae. One member, the Arctic tern, is discussed. These birds are best described as smaller, more graceful counterparts of the gulls.

Most pelagic of this order is the family Alcidae. Of the twenty-three species, nineteen are inhabitants of North America, and of these we discuss two, the common murre and the tufted puffin. Alcids spend most of their time at sea, coming ashore only to lay their eggs in splits and crevices in the rocks, to hatch them, and to raise the young.

American Golden Plover
(*Pluvialis dominica*)

FIELD MARKS:	*Mottled gold and brown back, black belly, white stripe over eye and down side of neck.*
SIZE:	*11 inches long with a wingspan of 23 inches.*
HABITS:	*Migrates long distances. Male helps female incubate the eggs.*
HABITAT:	*Open tundra, pampas, pasture lands.*
NEST:	*Pebbles and moss laid in a hollow depression in the ground.*
EGGS:	*Cinnamon or light buff heavily spotted with dark brown and black, 4 in a clutch. Incubation 28 days.*
FOOD:	*Insects, berries, seeds.*
VOICE:	*Short, clear whistle.*

Although it is a comparatively small bird, the American golden plover is capable of making a round-trip migration flight of 25,000 to 28,000 miles annually.

Golden plovers are truly international birds, their migration record being eclipsed only by that of the Arctic tern. By late July or early August the adults forsake their northern tundra nesting grounds and fly eastward toward the Atlantic Ocean, where they funnel down to Nova Scotia. Unless bad weather blows them off course and over the mainland of the United States, the plovers fly over the open ocean from Nova Scotia south to British Guiana. They can land and feed on the open ocean if they become too tired or hungry to continue flying. After coming ashore at the northern tip of South America, the birds cross the eastern Amazon Basin and continue down to the pampas of Argentina, where they spend the winter.

Immature birds stay on the northern nesting grounds for almost a month after their parents have departed.

The plovers follow spring back to the Northern Hemisphere. On their northward flight the birds fly up the La Plata Valley, cross the western Amazon Basin, and fly up over Central America. Then they cross the Gulf of Mexico and fly up the Mississippi Valley flyway, across the Prairie Provinces of Canada, thence north or northwest to their breeding grounds.

A golden plover weighs about nine ounces, is eleven inches long, and has a wingspan of about twenty-three inches. That this bird is capable of making a round-trip migration flight of 25,000 to 28,000 miles annually seems almost unbelievable.

Primarily a bird of the open tundra, pampas, or pasture lands, the golden plover feeds mainly on insects. Grasshoppers, caterpillars, beetles, crickets, wireworms, grubs, and flies are all standard items of diet. When feeding along the water's edge, the plover consumes many aquatic insects. Some berries and seeds also are eaten.

On a rare bright day in Alaska's Mount McKinley National Park, three of us—Mike Smith, my son Lenny, and I—set out to photograph a plover's nest we had previously spotted. No living plant grew taller than three or four inches on the high, dry tundra we traversed, which extended, like mountain-to-mountain carpeting, as far as the eye could see. Approaching the area where we thought the nest was located, we were startled by a plover suddenly bursting up from the tundra and flying off to join its mate. We were in luck: The bird arising from the same spot proved that a nest was in the area. A few minutes' careful searching located the nest, which we probably would never have found had we not flushed the bird.

The four eggs, about one and nine-tenths inches long and one and three-tenths inches in diameter, were sharply pointed so they could not roll out of the nest. Cleverly camouflaged by their cinnamon or light buff coloration, heavily spotted with dark browns and black, the eggs closely resembled the few surrounding pebbles and moss that comprised the nest.

We hurriedly photographed the eggs, then retreated for a short distance to await the female's return. Within minutes she was back. Alighting about fifty feet from the nest, she advanced in the general direction of, but not directly to, the nest, running forward for ten feet or so, stopping, bobbing her head up and down, peering around, then advancing again. She made no attempt to hide, which was just as well, for there was nothing behind which to hide.

The plover did not stop at the nest but continued past it. This is a typical action that fools many people if they haven't already located the nest. Although we were aware of the exact location of the nest, still we were ready to admit that this deception was most effective. As we remained motionless, the plover was soon reassured and went back to her nest. The male continued to run about on the tundra some distance away. Carefully straddling the eggs, the female fluffed out her feathers and backed down onto her treasure. The backward thrust bent her feathers in the opposite direction, allowing closer bodily contact with the eggs.

Squatting on her eggs, the plover's bright, golden yellow spring breeding plumage closely matched the golden bits of plant material in the surrounding tundra. The only conspicuous marking on the bird was the white line starting across the crown, running down both sides of the neck, and separating the yellow back markings from the black belly. When the female settled on her nest, she tucked her head down, thus minimizing the white and rendering her practically invisible.

As we inched forward, the entire performance was repeated several times, until at last we were within range for the photographs we wanted. Finally realizing we meant no harm, the plover settled herself on the eggs and submitted to being photographed.

Both the male and the female incubate the eggs, a process requiring approximately twenty-eight days. We could not tell the sexes apart but assumed the female to be the one to return to the nest almost immediately, while the other bird stayed farther away. This is the usual reaction of most birds and has been proved when the sexes are of different colors or markings; the female is the bolder of the two. The young are precocial, capable of scrambling about shortly after hatching.

The golden plover is in danger from the hawks and falcons which will eat the adult, and the jaeger, which will eat both the eggs and the young birds.

Once considered a table delicacy, the golden plover was slaughtered by the tens of thousands during both spring and fall migrations. The population was reduced to a point where it was thought this plover might become extinct. International laws now protect the bird, and its population has made a tremendous comeback.

Whimbrel
(*Numenius phaeopus*)

FIELD MARKS:	*Mottled light brown and white, head stripings, pale underparts, long curved beak.*
SIZE:	*14–18 inches long with a wingspan of 30 inches.*
HABITS:	*Fly low over the water in long strings when migrating.*
HABITAT:	*Coastal or tundra areas.*
NEST:	*A hollow depression.*
EGGS:	*Brown spotted and streaked, 3–4 in a clutch. Incubation one month.*
FOOD:	*Insects and shore life.*
VOICE:	*High-pitched tweetling call.*

At one time the whimbrel was almost wiped out by market hunters, but that situation has changed. Today this large shore bird, measuring about fourteen to eighteen inches in length and having a wingspread of thirty inches is on the increase and is found on both the Atlantic and the Pacific coasts.

In June 1966 Mike Smith, my son Lenny, and I were riding in my camper on the main road of Alaska's Mount McKinley National Park. Just before reaching the Sanctuary River Campground, we noticed a roadside sign stating that this was the area to watch for a Hudsonian curlew. None of us had ever seen this bird, and we were anxious to add it to our life lists. After about forty-five minutes of searching, we neared the nest area. Both parent birds soon appeared, giving their high-pitched tweetling call and flying around and at us. When they finally landed, I got a good look at them. I was certain I had seen birds like that before. Of course, I had—the Hudsonian curlew and the whimbrel are one and the same bird.

Its long, slender beak is yellowish and decurved and immediately classifies the whimbrel as a member of the curlew family. This American counterpart of the European whimbrel shares its coloration of blackish brown upper parts, streaked and spotted with white, ochre, or pale brown; pale brownish white underparts; and grayish blue feet.

Whimbrels spend the winter on the Pacific coast of South America and start north in early spring. The Atlantic flock reaches Florida by the middle of March and Massachusetts by the middle of May. While some birds stay along the coast, many more go inland and nest on the western shore of Hudson Bay. The Pacific whimbrels reach lower California about the middle of March and are on Alaska's Arctic coast by the end of May. The birds I saw in interior Alaska were nesting by the eighth of June. In migration the birds fly low over the water in long strings. The flocks are never very large, and apparently males and females migrate together.

Like most shore birds, the whimbrel does not make a nest but utilizes any hollow depression located in a convenient spot. The nests in Mount McKinley National Park were right out in the wet tundra, where the terrain was boggy with pockets and pools of water on all sides.

Three to four eggs, two and one-quarter inches long and one and five-eighths inches in diameter, make up the usual clutch. Their brown-spotted and streaked coloration is such artful camouflage that they are rendered almost invisible. Both parents incubate the eggs over a period of about one month. One annual brood is customary, for there simply is not sufficient time to raise two broods during the short Arctic summer. By late August the ice that is beginning to form starts the birds on their southward trek.

Whimbrels are large brown shore birds with decurved beaks and a distinct strip-
ing on the crown. They are found in marshes, mud flats, shores, and prairies on
both the Atlantic and Pacific coasts.

The whimbrel feeds on all manner of insects and shore life. Along the
coast, fiddler crabs, sand fleas, worms, and all kinds of small mollusks and
crustaceans are eaten. During the summer, when the bird ranges inland, the
bulk of its diet is made up of insects, including moths, butterflies, grasshoppers, crickets, spiders, and all types of beetles.

Both the adult whimbrel and its young are preyed upon by hawks and
falcons, and jaegers and gulls will eat the young and the eggs.

If shot at, the wary whimbrel soon becomes as hard to approach as a
crow. It is this wariness, as well as the inaccessibility of most of its nesting
sites, that has allowed the whimbrel to make a comeback from the brink of
extinction, to which it was all too close.

Greater Yellowlegs
(*Totanus melanoleucus*)

FIELD MARKS:	*Mottled light brown and white, whitish rump and tail, long bright yellow legs.*
SIZE:	*11 inches long with a wingspan of 26 inches.*
HABITS:	*Act as sentries warning other birds of danger. Fly with their long legs trailed out behind them.*
HABITAT:	*Seacoast and marshlands.*
NEST:	*Slight hollow scratched out by the female.*
EGGS:	*Buff streaked and spotted with dark brown, 4 in a clutch.*
FOOD:	*Fish, tadpoles, water insects, worms, snails, fruits, berries.*
VOICE:	*High-pitched tweetling.*

A large, slim sandpiper, the greater yellowlegs acts as a sentry for other birds and sets up a clamor when it senses potential danger.

"Tell-tale," "tattler," and "yelper" are a few of the greater yellowleg's descriptive nicknames. Most birds protest whenever they are disturbed at the nest. Many may protest when the nesting area is invaded, and a few display themselves conspicuously. While common among a number of the shore birds, these traits are concentrated in the actions of the greater yellowlegs. Another appropriate nickname would be "sentry," after the self-appointed role assumed by this bird.

While bird-watching one winter along Lake Mattamuskeet in North Carolina, I observed many water and shore birds. Invariably, it was the yellowlegs that spotted me first and set up a clamor, alerting all the other birds to what it considered a potential danger.

This bird ranges throughout the Western Hemisphere. The northern limits of its breeding grounds stretch from Alaska eastward to the Atlantic Coast. In winter it is found along the southern tier of states down through South America. In April the yellowlegs is commonly found along the seacoast and marshlands of New Jersey. I have seen this bird come in to the small freshwater pond in front of my home. It never stays more than a few hours, but feeds, rests, and then is lured northward by the siren song of migration.

The greater yellowlegs is a strong flier, traveling a distance of twelve to sixteen thousand miles or more during its round-trip migratory flights. It flies with its long legs trailing out behind. With its powerful wings, this bird can fly at speeds of up to fifty miles per hour, although it appears to be going much faster when it zooms down at you on set wings like a strafing fighter plane. The length of yellowlegs is about eleven inches and it has a wingspan of twenty-six inches.

The arrival of yellowlegs in the north usually coincides with the breaking up of the ice. Most of the birds nest within ten days of their arrival. No one has had much luck locating yellowlegs' nests, so the information we have on their activities is scant. One thing we know is that the greater yellowlegs' nest is never far from water. Nesting in the tundra in the early spring precludes this possibility, for most of that area is a giant sponge. The nest, situated on a tussock or hummock, is usually a slight hollow that has been scratched out by the female.

Four dark brown spotted buff eggs, a little more than one inch long and not quite as large in diameter, comprise the usual clutch. The eggs have the tapered points that one expects of the sandpipers. No one knows whether the male assists in the brooding, but he is in close attendance to the nest and assists the female in feeding the young.

When feeding, this bird makes good use of its long yellow legs and long black, slightly upturned bill. Often it wades out into the water until its white belly touches the surface. Even when it gets into water too deep for walking, this is no problem for a bird that is an excellent swimmer. The yellowlegs dashes and gyrates about wildly when chasing minnows. Several birds occasionally team up to drive a school of minnows into shallow water, where they become stranded and are quickly gobbled up. In addition to fish, tadpoles, water insects, worms, and snails, some fruits and berries are eaten.

In 1965 I was able to observe the greater yellowlegs in its far northern nesting grounds during an expedition to ninety-five-mile-long Lake Iliamna with Stan Lee, of Kodiak, Alaska. Our camp on one of the wilderness lake's large eastern islands was pitched in a little gully as a measure of protection from the ever-present wind, which, coupled with the deep winter cold, had impeded tree and plant growth. Most of the island was carpeted with the mosses, lichens, and dwarf vegetation only three or four inches high that are characteristic of the Arctic tundra. Here and there a few straggly trees protruded.

Every moment I could spare after finishing camp chores was spent taking photographs. Although I often went on these treks by myself, I was never alone. As soon as I ventured out on the tundra, a pair of greater yellowlegs flew up to greet me. They were obviously nesting somewhere on the island, but I never found their nest. I never even knew where to start looking, because the birds followed me for miles and showed no indication of favoring any particular spot. Always they kept up their high-pitched tweetling, wheedling, needling, calling. I would have loved to have had the chance to sneak up on the red-throated loons on one of the little ponds. But that was

The lesser yellowlegs is similar to the greater yellowlegs but is considerably smaller and has a slimmer beak.

out of the question—the calling of the yellowlegs had alarmed everything within hearing distance long before I put in an appearance.

Principal enemies of the yellowlegs are jaegers and gulls, which take their eggs and their young, and hawks and falcons, which prey on the young and even on the full-grown birds.

Widely hunted in former years, the gray and white greater yellowlegs was a favorite of old-time gunners. The bird is sociable, although not overly gregarious, and decoys well. Many hunters imitated the whistling call of the bird and lured the yellowlegs in from considerable distances. Today the bird has been given the complete protection it deserves, thus assuring us of being able to see the yellowlegs flocks as they pass through our area on their long migratory flights.

American Woodcock
(Philohela minor)

FIELD MARKS:	*Cinnamon belly and sides, light brown and black mottling on back. Long bill, short rounded wings, short legs, eyes far back in head.*
SIZE:	*8¼ inches long with a wingspan of 20 inches.*
HABITS:	*Performs most activities at night. Permits close approach. Courtship displays.*
HABITAT:	*Bogs and swamps.*
NEST:	*Recessed spot in the leaves.*
EGGS:	*Buffy brown with dark blotches on the large end, 4 in a clutch. Incubation 21 days.*
FOOD:	*Earthworms, slugs, grubs, grasshoppers.*
VOICE:	*Raspy, buzzing call and a peenting sound.*

The American woodcock's eyes are placed far back in its head, enabling it to watch for danger when probing with its beak beneath the soil. The birds feed mainly on earthworms.

With its short, pipestem legs, very long beak, and big eyes located far back on its head, the plump little woodcock is one of the oddest looking birds I have ever seen. There is no discernible difference between the sexes; both are about eight and one-quarter inches long and have a wingspread of twenty inches.

The woodcock's beak measures between two and one-half to three inches in length and has a flexible tip as well as an upper mandible whose forward half can be bent upward. The bird uses the tip like a pair of fingers and can dexterously pull out of the ground the earthworms that form the mainstay of its diet. You can always detect the presence of woodcock in the vicinity by the bore marks of its bill and the large, whitewash splashing of its droppings.

The female American woodcock's blotched brown and tan coloration forms a dead leaf pattern, thus providing excellent camouflage for the bird. This disguise is so effective that the woodcock often nests in open areas.

Because the woodcock does not need to see what it is doing, since all the action takes place beneath the soil, its eyes have been placed toward the rear of its head. As the bird probes in the earth for worms, its eyes can watch all around for danger coming from any direction.

Sometimes called "bogsucker" or "wood hen," the woodcock frequents boggy, swampy places. Streamsides covered with alders and birch are favored spots. It has to feed where the earth is moist and soft enough for easy drilling. In the north the bird can stay in the area where it was hatched until frost begins to harden the ground. Drought, too, forces the woodcock to seek other areas.

Woodcock are found as far north as New Brunswick and Nova Scotia to Manitoba in Canada, westward as far as Colorado, south to Texas, Louisiana, and Florida. Probably the majority of the birds are reared in Canada, because so much of their habitat in the United States has been destroyed through development.

By April the birds are on the nesting grounds and have paired up. Every night just about late dusk the male goes to a cleared area in its home range and puts on a courtship display. Uttering his raspy, buzzing call to attract the female, he proceeds to fly high into the air or in a large circle, then falls back to earth with a fluttering flight and twittering whistle, landing approximately at his original takeoff point. After witnessing a number of these flights, the female sneaks out to join the male in the cleared area, where they mate. The entire performance takes about half an hour and is repeated nightly for about three to four weeks.

The woodcock's nest is merely a recessed spot in the leaves; practically no attempt is made at nest construction. A clutch consists of four buffy brown eggs, blotched on the large end and measuring one and one-half inches long and one inch in diameter. The female depends upon her beautiful blotched brown and tan pattern to conceal her from enemies while she is brooding. So successful is this camouflage that the nest is seldom found, even though it may be in a fairly open area. The female sits tightly on her nest and generally refuses to flush unless you practically step on her.

When photographing a pair of woodcock nesting in my area, I could actually reach out and touch the female's beak before she hopped off the nest. Then she walked or flew away, returning in a short time to resume her duties.

Incubation takes about twenty-one days. Although I saw only the female on the eggs, both parents are said to incubate them. Both take care of the young, as I discovered, for I usually flushed out two birds whenever I saw the young.

Little woodcock are precocial and leave the nest a short time after hatching. These tiny bits of fluff lie immobile if discovered. Though you know exactly where they are, they are almost impossible to see; even when you touch them, they won't move. The parents may carry the young away between their feet if molested.

In addition to man the woodcock is preyed upon by raccoons, skunks, foxes, bobcats, hawks, and owls. For that reason this bird carries on most of its activities under the protective mantle of darkness. It supplements its earthworm diet with slugs, grubs, and such insects as grasshoppers.

The sporty woodcock is avidly hunted. Owing to this bird's migratory nature, the hunting season for "big eyes," as it is sometimes called, is usually the first one allowed by law each fall. In my part of New Jersey the main flights take place in October.

Long-tailed Jaeger
(*Stercorarius longicaudus*)

FIELD MARKS: *Medium gray. White underparts, dark crown and upper wings; two central tail feathers stick out about 8 inches behind others.*

SIZE: *18 inches long with a wingspan of 34 inches.*

HABITS: *Uses tail feathers as a rudder.*
Robs other seabirds of fish.

HABITAT: *High windy steppes and arctic coasts.*

NEST: *Slight hollow.*

EGGS: *Deep green with brown spots, 2 in a clutch.*
Incubation 23–24 days.

FOOD: *Mice, voles, lemmings, birds' eggs, small birds, small fish, crustaceans, insects, and occasionally berries.*

VOICE: *Generally silent.*

154

When searching for food, long-tailed jaegers hang motionless in the air and scan the ground below for a possible meal.

The long-tailed jaeger is a gull-type bird with predatory habits. Most gulls hunt for and actively kill mice, nesting birds, and insects, but they are primarily scavengers. The jaeger, on the other hand, hunts almost constantly.

Adults measure twenty-three inches in length and have a wingspread of thirty-four inches. They have beautiful pure white underparts, and dark, purplish slate heads and upper wings. Two central tail feathers develop and protrude about eight inches beyond the other tail feathers. These two feathers serve as a rudder for steering and give this bird its descriptive name. Its Latin name, *longicaudus,* means "long-tailed," and *jaeger* is the German word for "hunter."

A bird of the high, windy steppes and Arctic coasts, the jaeger has a worldwide distribution below the polar regions. Winter forces it as far

Long-tailed jaegers begin nesting in June and lay two brown-spotted deep green eggs in a clutch. Both parents participate in the incubation process, which takes 23–24 days.

south as Florida, the Mediterranean region, and the Kurile Islands.

The jaeger nests in June. Two brown-spotted, deep green eggs, about two and one-eighth inches long and one and one-half inches in diameter, comprise the clutch. No attempt is made to use dry material in constructing the nest, which is merely a slight hollow made by the bird's body. The eggs blend in with the tiny tundra plant life so well that they are exceedingly difficult to locate. The parents take turns incubating the eggs, a process requiring twenty-three to twenty-four days.

Like the gulls, young jaegers scramble out of the nest soon after hatching. They grow rapidly on the varied fare fed them by their parents. During the first year the youngsters are brown in color. In the second year they acquire their adult plumage.

Mice, voles, lemmings, and similar small mammals provide a large part of the jaegers' diet. They also take birds' eggs, young birds, and even small adult birds when possible. When around water, jaegers take small fish and crustaceans. In summer insects are added to their menu, and occasionally berries are eaten. In winter jaegers often consort with gulls and terns, making piratical attacks on these smaller birds to rob them of whatever food they have found or captured.

Although the jaeger is a threat to so many other creatures and birds, it has little to fear from any save the fox, which occasionally takes its eggs and young.

I first encountered the jaeger on the dry, open tundra at Highway Pass, in Alaska's Mount McKinley National Park, and I remember thinking that, of the many birds adept at soaring, here was the master. With wings outstretched, it commanded the air currents to do its bidding, hanging motionless in the sky, then, with just a slight shift of its wings, peeling off and gliding on a new angle, like a fighter plane going in for an attack. Just as abruptly the bird checked its flight and again hung motionless, its eyes intently scanning the terrain below for a sign of food.

As we searched for jaeger eggs, the parents floated in the air above us. They uttered piercing cries and dived down at our heads, assuring us that we were getting close to the nest. The birds came down to within two or three feet of our heads and hung there in the air. It would have been an easy matter to reach up and catch them by hand. Because we did not attempt to duck or wave our arms, the jaegers became bolder. Eventually they dropped down and hit me on the head with their feet. I wasn't hurt, because their gull-like feet are webbed and do not have talons, but the birds succeeded in knocking off my beret and carrying it for several feet before dropping it.

Upon discovering the nest, we sat down a short distance away. In a few minutes the jaegers calmed down, and the female returned to her brooding. She continued to be on the alert and flew off several times when we moved. Her mate apparently felt that he had done his part and unconcernedly went back to his hunting. After getting our photos, we left the female to her maternal chores.

Glaucous-winged Gull
(*Larus glaucescens*)

FIELD MARKS:	*Mainly white with pearl gray wings, pinkish feet and legs, yellow bill with a red spot on the tip of the lower mandible.*
SIZE:	*24–27 inches long with a wingspan of 50–54 inches.*
HABITS:	*Primarily scavengers. Strong powers of flight.*
HABITAT:	*Seacoast.*
NEST:	*Hollowed out spot in tall grasses.*
EGGS:	*Olive green with black splotchings, 2–3 in a clutch. Incubation 26–28 days.*
FOOD:	*Garbage and refuse, fish scraps.*
VOICE:	*Raucous squawking.*

Glaucous-winged gulls derive their name from the bluish color of their wings.

The glaucous-winged gull is the most common and most frequently seen gull of the Pacific Northwest. It can be found from the Bering Sea to southern California.

Like the rest of their family these gulls are for the most part scavengers, searching the shoreline and following after ships looking for garbage and refuse. I have seen them gather by the countless thousands around the salmon canneries when the packing was in progress. All fish scraps from the canneries were promptly cleared away by the hungry throngs.

One July I had the opportunity of watching glaucous-winged gulls on the McNeil River in Alaska. The gulls from Augustine Island, situated out in Cook's Inlet, used to fly to the falls on the river to share in the salmon caught by the big Alaska brown bears. The McNeil River is famous both for its salmon runs and the brown bears.

Daily, thousands upon thousands of dog, silver, and jack salmon pounded themselves against the falls trying to ascend to their spawning grounds. The bears took a daily toll of hundreds of fish. As soon as a bear seized a fish, it retired up on a bank to eat it. Often a female salmon's eggs were forced from her body by the pressure of the bear's jaws. Immediately the gulls trailed after the bear and consumed the eggs as soon as they hit the ground. You could always follow the bear's progress through the high grass and thickets by watching the gulls flying over its head. The gulls soon cleaned up any scraps left by the bears. When the bears became glutted, they continued to catch salmon, but only to rip out and eat the eggs, leaving the entire carcass to the gulls. The area also abounds in ravens. Although a smaller bird, a single raven doesn't hesitate to walk into a flock of gulls, chase them away from a fish, and eat its fill.

Glaucous-winged gulls are among the largest of all the gulls, having an overall length of about twenty-four to twenty-seven inches and a wing-spread of fifty to fifty-four inches. Their wings are pearl gray. Head and underparts are white. Feet and legs are pinkish, and the yellow bill has a red spot on the tip of the lower mandible. Male and female are alike in size and coloration.

Their nests are crude, hollowed-out depressions in the high grasses of the offshore islands or coastal headlands. Bits of seaweed and other vegetation are used in the construction. The gulls are always careful to build their nests with enough space between them so that the adults can't pick at each other while brooding. The two to three large, black-splotched, olive green eggs require an incubation period of twenty-six to twenty-eight days, in which both parents participate.

The chicks are precocial and run about as soon as they hatch. This is a period of great danger for the chicks, because they may be killed by other parent glaucous-winged gulls whose territory they invade. An adult gull would not hesitate to kill and even to eat a strange young gull that had wandered from its nest. Foxes, too, sometimes raid the gull nest for eggs and young.

Immature glaucous-winged gulls are pale buffy or cream colored and their prima-ries are a shade lighter than the rest of the wing.

Ring-billed Gull
(*Larus delawarensis*)

FIELD MARKS: *Mainly white, dark gray wings with black tips, yellow bill with band encircling lower and upper mandibles, greenish yellow legs.*

SIZE: *16 inches long with a wingspan of 49 inches.*

HABITS: *Usually found in large numbers. Breeds in the wild.*

HABITAT: *Coasts, bays, estuaries, lakes, rivers, fields.*

NEST: *Water weeds, feathers, grasses.*

EGGS: *Brown with dark splotches, 2–3 in a clutch. Incubation 3 weeks.*

FOOD: *Small fish, garbage, small rodents, insects.*

VOICE: *Squealing cry.*

The ring-billed gull's best identifying characteristics are a conspicuous black ring on the bill and greenish yellow legs.

At one time the ring-billed gull was thought to be the most widely distributed and commonly seen of all the gulls. This is not the case today. Its numbers have been reduced drastically, although it is still found in many of its old haunts from Labrador to British Columbia south to Florida and Mexico.

This gregarious gull is usually found in large groups, preferring the company of its own kind, yet frequently associating with other gulls as well. In the West the ring-billed gull is often confused with the larger California gull. On the East Coast it resembles the much larger herring gull. The black band that circles the yellow upper and lower mandibles almost at the tip of the beak gives this bird its name and is one of the best identifying characteristics. An adult measures approximately sixteen inches long and has a wingspread of forty-nine inches, gray upper parts with black wing tips, white head and underparts, and yellowish green legs.

In the wintertime this gull frequents the haunts of man in the southern portion of its range, whereas in the summer it prefers to breed in the wild. As man has moved farther into the wilderness areas, the gull has forsaken many of its original nesting sites with a resultant drop in its numbers.

I first encountered the ring-bill on Lac Camachigama, in the Quebec wilderness. The lake is about ten miles long and five miles wide, and the

Soaring low over fields, ring-billed gulls zero in on grasshoppers, which they consume in large quantities. The gulls snatch them out of the air as the insects leap.

wind blows almost constantly across it. I have never been on the lake when the water has not piled up into at least four- or five-foot waves. As waves this size make canoeing difficult, few people venture out across the lake, most of them skirting the shores instead. The few rocky islands out in the middle of the lake were thus relatively unmolested by man, and it was on these islands that the ring-bill chose to nest.

On my first visit to the rookery the gulls rose from the island in a screaming, protesting mass. Gulls are so accustomed to protesting any kind of disturbance that it has become a habit with them. Against the blue sky the ring-bills' white underparts flashed like rapidly moving clouds. Although it was late in the season, I hoped that perhaps a few late-hatched birds would still be grounded, but I failed to locate any.

The ring-billed gull has usually chosen a mate by the time it arrives on the breeding grounds, which generally coincides with the spring ice breakup. In Quebec this occurs in late May. The gull prefers to nest on the higher part of the small islands, utilizing water weeds, feathers, and grasses in the construction of the nest. Two to three brownish, dark-splotched eggs, measuring two and three-quarters inches long and one and three-quarters inches in diameter, represent the annual brood. Incubation takes about three weeks and is shared by both parents. The young stay in the nest for only a short period after hatching, then scramble out among the grasses and shrubbery, where their mottled down gives them excellent camouflage protection. If threatened by danger, the young do not hesitate to plop into the water, where they swim buoyantly and well.

As with so many birds, the ring-bill's worst enemy is man, who keeps pushing farther and farther into the wilderness area that the gulls need for their nesting activities.

Small live fish, dead fish, garbage, small rodents, and insects are consumed by the ring-bill, which feeds on whatever food is available. In the prairie states and provinces, this gull eats a tremendous number of insects, particularly grasshoppers, which represent an excellent source of protein. Soaring low over the fields, the bird snatches the grasshoppers out of the air as they leap.

Mew Gull
(Larus canus)

FIELD MARKS:	*Mainly white, dark gray wings with black tips. Very similar to ring-billed gull but smaller and lacks ring on bill.*
SIZE:	*14 inches long with a wingspan of 42 inches.*
HABITS:	*Scavenging. Male aids female in incubating the young.*
HABITAT:	*Coastal areas in winter, inland in summer.*
NEST:	*Twigs and grasses.*
EGGS:	*Olive brown, splotched with black or dark brown, 3 in a clutch. Incubation 3 weeks.*
FOOD:	*Insects, small fishes, seafood.*
VOICE:	*Mewing.*

Named for its mewing call, the mew gull inhabits coastal waters, estuaries, and beaches all along our western coast from California to Alaska.

Probably the most common gull of Europe and northern Asia, the mew gull is found on the North American continent along the West Coast from Alaska south to California. About fourteen inches long and possessing a wingspan of forty-two inches, this gull is not as large as the ring-bill and its bill resembles the plover's. It has greenish legs and a grayish mantle over its wings. The underparts are white. This gull nests in colonies and may be found in large flocks.

Gulls are commonly associated with oceans, but in Alaska's Mount McKinley National Park, hundreds of miles from the ocean, I saw gulls by the dozens perched on top of evergreen trees. This I had to photograph. The gulls were skittish and took to the air as soon as I had approached within a certain distance. As I walked closer, the gulls dived at my head, looking for all the world like miniature kamikazes. Although appearing committed to a collision course, they veered aside at the last moment. The mew gull is not as large as the herring gull, but it looks plenty big enough when it zooms down to within two or three feet of your face. I'll admit I ducked.

The air was filled with gulls flashing by and with the sound of their screaming voices. Alarm caused their screams to be higher pitched than the more common mewing call that gives these gulls their name. As I approached the bank of the Sanctuary River, they redoubled their efforts to drive me away. It soon became apparent that the mew gulls were using the small island in the middle of the river for a nesting ground. Sitting down among the bushes, I gave the gulls time to calm down and in a little while a few of the gulls dropped down to their nests and began to incubate the eggs.

In a well-constructed nest of twigs and grasses, the mew gull usually lays three olive brown eggs, heavily splotched with black or dark brown and measuring two and one-quarter inches long and one and five-eighths inches in diameter. Incubation is shared by both parents and takes about three weeks. Both the adults and the young are relatively free from predation.

Mew gulls feed heavily on insects, searching the tundra carefully for their prey. In settled areas they often follow the plow, as crows do, snatching up the earthworms and insects exposed in the new earth. They also consume small fishes that they catch as well as all edible types of seafood. Scavenging also plays an important role in their diet. Like gulls the world over, mew gulls gladly accept handouts. In Mount McKinley Park, a complement of these gulls usually gathers at each of the campgrounds and parking areas. Table scraps and bread are eagerly sought and eaten. The Eielson Visitor Center is a considerable distance from water, yet the gulls sit around on the ground waiting for a dole from the visitors, and generally they are rewarded.

Mew gulls construct a nest of twigs and grasses where they lay three eggs, spotted with dark brown or black, in a clutch. These gulls usually nest in colonies.

Laughing Gull
(*Larus atricilla*)

FIELD MARKS:	*Mainly white, dark gray wings with black tips; black head in breeding season.*
SIZE:	*13 inches long with a wingspan of 41 inches.*
HABITS:	*Scavenging. Takes fish from the mouths of pelicans. The young leave the nest almost immediately.*
HABITAT:	*Seacoast.*
NEST:	*Grasses, seaweeds, and similar vegetation.*
EGGS:	*Olive green splotched with brown, 3–4 in a clutch. Incubation 20–21 days.*
FOOD:	*Garbage and refuse, eggs of smaller sea birds, small fish.*
VOICE:	*Raucous, hoarse laugh.*

Laughing gulls lose the black feathers from their heads in the winter and grow white feathers with markings. They have a dark gray mantle and white underparts.

At one time the laughing gull was common along the eastern and northeastern coastlines of North America, but it has become relatively scarce nowadays north of Virginia. I first encountered this gull along the Jersey coast at Brigantine National Wildlife Refuge in late spring when it was resplendent in its breeding plumage, its head a jet black. Measuring thirteen inches long with a wingspan of forty-one inches, the laughing gull has dark gray wings, dark wing tips, and pure white underparts. Its raucous, hoarse laughter explains the origin of its name.

These gulls arrive on their northern breeding grounds around the middle of April. Courtship and pairing takes place almost immediately. Offshore islands and sandspits are favored nesting spots wherever such isolation can be found. Otherwise the birds utilize the dunes of the coastal regions.

The nests are well constructed of grasses, seaweed, and similar vegetation. Three to four olive green, brown-splotched eggs, two inches long and one and one-quarter inches in diameter, are laid by the first week in May. Incubation takes twenty to twenty-one days, with both parents in attendance.

Like the young of all gulls, the little laughing gulls remain in the nest for only a couple of days. Afterward they crawl about in the surrounding vegetation. This abandonment of the nest is an important survival protection. Many kinds of aerial and terrestrial predators frequent every rookery, among them hawks, owls, foxes, and raccoons. The young gulls' chances of survival are therefore much greater if they are hidden rather than sitting in an exposed nest. By the latter part of July the young are able to fly. Their immature brown plumage gradually turns gray and white with the succeeding seasons, but they do not acquire the black breeding hood of the adults until they approach the age of two. In the winter these breeding feathers are replaced by mottled ones.

The laughing gull frequents the fishing docks where fish scraps are fought over and quickly eaten. Often the gull tries to share in the fish caught by pelicans; it has even been seen putting its head inside the pelican's mouth and removing small fish from the throat pouch. If necessary, the gull can catch small fish on its own. It also occasionally robs the nest and eats the eggs of such smaller seabirds as the terns and noddies. The gull is, of course, a first-rate scavenger, feeding on any garbage or refuse that is palatable.

Early one morning in Flamingo, at the southern tip of mainland Florida, I had stepped from my camper to check the sky for weather conditions. A huge flock of laughing gulls soared and flapped about over the campground. All of us promptly tore slices of bread into small pieces and threw them into the air. The gulls usually managed to snatch the bread out of the air, performing marvelous aerial acrobatics in the process. We enjoyed watching them so much that as soon as anyone ran out of bread, he would dash for more. I'm willing to bet that the bulk of the bread purchased in Flamingo does not get into human stomachs.

Arctic Tern
(*Sterna paradisaea*)

FIELD MARKS: *White throat, breast, and belly; wings are light gray above and white beneath, with black tips; black cap on adult; bright red beak and webbed feet; long, deeply forked tail.*

SIZE: *15–16 inches long with a wingspan of 31–33 inches.*

HABITS: *Extremely long migratory flights.*
Strong defenders of eggs and young.

HABITAT: *Beaches.*

NEST: *Lays eggs directly on the beach and in the open.*

EGGS: *Range from pale greenish buff to dark olive brown and have irregular spots, 2–3 in a clutch.*
Incubation 21 days.

FOOD: *Fish and small crustaceans.*

VOICE: *High pitched scream.*

The arctic tern sports a jet black cap, which contrasts with its bright red beak. Entirely white underneath, the bird has gray upper wings with dark tips.

To watch an Arctic tern in flight is to watch a butterfly in bird form. Its mastery of the art of flying has earned it such nicknames as "sea swallow" and "paradise tern."

A strikingly handsome bird fifteen to sixteen inches in length with a wingspan of thirty-one to thirty-three inches, the Arctic tern has a long, deeply forked, swallowlike tail. Its throat, breast, belly, and the undersides of its wings and tail are a dazzling white, while its upper wings are gray with dark tips. Both the beak and the webbed feet of this tern are bright red, and it sports a black cap that extends below the eyes.

Many birds travel long distances in migration, but the Arctic tern holds the record. These birds nest along the northern coasts of North America from the Atlantic to the Pacific. During migration, about the end of August, some of these birds fly south along the west coast of the Americas. The others fly east, across the Atlantic Ocean, south along the west coasts of Europe and Africa, and thence to Antarctica, arriving in November. At the end of February the terns have started north again and arrive on their breeding grounds in May or June. Depending on which route the terns take, the round-trip migration may be between 22,000 and 28,000 miles. If the miles these birds fly searching for food and carrying on their daily lives are added, the figures are almost incredible.

While the Arctic tern sometimes mingles with other terns and even nests along with the others' colonies, it is found for the most part exclusively with its own kind. In fact, this tern more frequently nests by itself in an isolated spot than do other terns. Generally speaking, the Arctic tern makes little attempt to construct a nest. Its two to three pale greenish buff to dark olive brown, darkly splotched and spotted eggs, about one and three-quarters inches long and one and one-eighth inches in diameter, are commonly laid on a gravelly or sandy beach. A few pebbles may be placed around the circumference of the area and bits of dried grass or seaweed may serve as a lining. The eggs are well tapered, which prevents them from rolling out of the nest.

Birds that build their nests on the ground are most susceptible to predation, because even such nonclimbing mammals as the fox can raid them. Such birds as the Arctic tern, which build their nests on the beach out in the open, are even more vulnerable. The coloration of the eggs and the parents' ability to find safe islands on which to nest are main factors in the success of the species—that, plus the courage of the parents.

These terns are noted for their valor in defense of their eggs and their young. Skuas, jaegers, and gulls, as well as foxes and members of the weasel family, eat the eggs, the young, or both. Although the terns can seldom prevent their nests from being destroyed, they at least make the effort. They are equally fearless of man at such times. Many reports tell of these birds diving upon and actually hitting people who had ventured near their nests.

I came in for a personal strafing attack on Alaska's Kenai Peninsula when I inadvertently disturbed a family of terns. In trying for photographs of trumpeter swans, I waded across the shallow end of a lake to a small island. One tern was in flight, another was perched on a dead snag. As I neared the island, both birds began diving at me. The air was filled with their high-pitched, screaming *keek, keek, keek*. As I walked across the island, three downy little blobs ran to the far side, plopped into the water, and swam off. Now all fury broke loose, as the parent birds dived low, actually hitting my hat. When the young terns were about two-hundred feet from the island, the parents called off the attack and flew over to them, shepherding the youngsters to a long spit of land, where they scrambled to safety and concealment in the long grasses.

Both parents protect the nest and the young and also participate in incubation, which takes about twenty-one days. At first the young are fed regurgitated fish but soon are brought small whole fish. In addition to fish, terns also feed on small crustaceans and insects.

I recall watching terns fishing for minnows in Alaska. Four of us—Stan and Chuck Lee, Ken Kendall, and I—were looking for Alaskan brown bear along a small stream that flowed into Lake Iliamna. The salmon run had not yet begun, so the bear were still feeding on the hillsides. Minnows were plentiful in the stream and their surfacing stippled the water like patterns of rain. This activity attracted a noisy flock of terns. Some hovered like kingfishers, others dived, wheeled, ascended, and dived again, while still

Strong and beautiful flyers, arctic terns hold the record for long-distance migrations.

others plunged headfirst into the water. Minnows were being caught on the average of one fish for every three dives, a really remarkable proportion. After making their catches, a few of the birds swam on the surface, eating the minnows, but they did not try to catch any fish while swimming. As soon as the minnows were turned, so that they could be gulped down headfirst, and swallowed, the birds shot back into the air. It was much easier for the terns to see and to follow the movements of the fish from the air than it would have been from the water. All this activity was accompanied by the birds' high-pitched screaming.

Common Murre
(Uria aalge)

FIELD MARKS: *Black with white underparts, narrow wings.*
White line behind eyes during breeding season.
SIZE: *14–16 inches long with a wingspan of 28 inches.*
HABITS: *Achieve flight with difficulty, use wings and*
feet to swim underwater, lay a large egg.
HABITAT: *Winter in the open ocean, breed on the offshore islands.*
NEST: *Lay eggs directly on the ground.*
EGGS: *Color ranges from blue to brown to cream.*
Incubation 28–30 days.
FOOD: *Candlefish and hooligans.*
VOICE: *A loudly called Arr-r-r-r.*

The rise and fall of the boat in the choppy waters of Togiak Bay, Alaska, made photography difficult. To tell the truth, I was too awed by the scenery even to concentrate on photography. I felt as though I had entered a vast natural cathedral.

Parallel to the boat's course, sheer cliffs soaring to heights of more than a thousand feet jutted up out of the sea. The cliff faces, the water around me, and the air itself were literally filled with hundreds of thousands of birds, more than I had ever seen at any one time in my life. Although they included puffins, guillemots and auklets, about 99 percent were common murres, clouds of them.

The showy murre, fourteen to sixteen inches in length and with a wingspread of about twenty-eight inches, wears a contrasting black and white plumage, which resembles the formal attire of the penguin, to whom, however, it is not related. The murre's head, throat, back, upper parts of the wings and tail, and feet are jet black, while the underparts are pure white.

Once airborne, a murre flies with a strong, swift flight, its narrow wings beating rapidly. But it achieves flight only with difficulty. Before the murre can fly from the water, it must race along the surface for a considerable distance, wings beating frantically and feet splattering water wildly, to gain the momentum necessary to launch itself into the air. Sometimes even this desperate effort is inadequate, and the murre suddenly plops down and dives beneath the surface. When nesting or roosting on a cliff, the murre launches itself into the air by diving out into space and dropping as far as fifty feet down before it actually becomes airborne. With an elevation of less than fifty feet, the bird drops from its perch, hits the water, and, like a skipped stone, bounces back into the air to fly off.

The same narrow wings and awkward placement of the feet that handicap the murre in flight add immeasurably to its swimming and diving ability. Water is this bird's real element. It has no trouble outswimming the six- to eight-inch candlefish and hooligans on which it feeds. When swimming underwater, the bird utilizes its wings as well as its feet for propulsion. Capable of withstanding tremendous water pressure, the murre has been known to dive 180 feet beneath the surface.

Murres winter on the open ocean out of sight of land. In the spring they pair up and return to the offshore sea islands to nest. Every ledge, nook, cranny, and crevice, any spot that is reasonably flat, no matter how small, is utilized. There is no attempt to construct any kind of a nest, the single egg being laid on the bare ground or rock.

The murre lays the largest egg for its size of any bird I know. Measuring three and a quarter inches in length and two inches in diameter, the egg is

Common murres nest in large colonies on offshore islands and lay their eggs directly on the bare ground. Although the eggs are pointed and do not roll on flat surfaces, many are pushed off narrow cliff ledges into the sea.

sharply pointed and thus will not roll far on a flat surface even though it is unguarded by a nest. Many eggs, however, do get knocked off the narrow cliff ledges.

The eggs range in color from cream to brown to blue, and some may be heavily speckled. Those laid on the earth are soon soiled, as is the bird's white breast, by mud and excrement. The eggs are so close together that I cannot imagine how each female identifies her own. Studies in which the birds and their eggs have been marked prove that each murre knows her own egg or chick.

Birds usually lay sufficient eggs to compensate for predation and thus to assure continuation of the species. Although murres may lose some eggs and chicks to gulls, accidents, and storms, they really have no other enemies

Common murres lay one egg each breeding season and they incubate the egg for twenty-eight to thirty days. Both sexes share in the incubation process.

except man. Formerly, many colonies of murres were wiped out by eggers, who took the eggs by the boatload and either used them for food or sold them on the market. This practice has been outlawed, and the birds have been steadily gaining in numbers. If a murre loses her first egg, she lays a second.

Incubation is shared by both sexes and takes twenty-eight to thirty days. At first the young bird is fed regurgitated material; within a week or two small fish are substituted. By the time the chick is two weeks old, it has either fallen or been pushed from the ledge into the sea below. The young are as buoyant as corks and are more easily cared for by the parents on the water.

With the nesting season behind them, the murres' sole link to land is cut, and they return to the ocean vastness for the remainder of the year.

Tufted Puffin
(*Lunda cirrhata*)

FIELD MARKS:	*Summer: mainly black with white face, orange-red beak and feet, two blond plumes on either side of head. Winter: black wings and dusky sides, black face, less red on beak, no plumes. Chunky body, stubby wings, short tail.*
SIZE:	*12 inches long with a wingspan of 24 inches.*
HABITS:	*Steers while flying by dragging its feet. Strong swimmer. Found in large colonies. Drops for a landing.*
HABITAT:	*Ocean cliffs and rocky offshore islands.*
NEST:	*A hole beneath the rocks.*
EGGS:	*White, often spotted, one egg per year. Incubation 32–36 days.*
FOOD:	*Fish.*
VOICE:	*Usually silent, low growls in colonies.*

In describing the tufted puffin, one of my bird reference books stated that this bird was easy to identify because there simply wasn't anything else like it. That's true. Perhaps the puffin is best described by its nickname, "sea parrot."

The first time I saw a tufted puffin, I burst out laughing, and I still do each time I encounter one. In flight this laughable, lovable, ludicrous bird seems to break the laws of aerodynamics; it looks like a bullet with wings. Twelve inches long, the puffin's chunky body seems much too heavy for the stubby wings, which span twenty-four inches, and the bird must paddle frantically through the air. Its tail is short, and much of the steering control is accomplished by dragging its bright orange-red, webbed feet, which show up conspicuously against the puffin's jet black plumage. The feet have strong claws as an aid to climbing about on the rocks in which the puffin perches or under which it nests.

The puffin's large, bright red, triangular-shaped beak is a ridiculous adornment. Indeed, the outer segments fall off each winter, leaving the bird a much smaller, but just as efficient, beak. Male and female are look-alikes. The name "tufted puffin" derives from the two bleached blond, hairlike plumes that extend three or four inches in length on either side of the head, starting above the eye. In flight these tufts stream out backward, but when the puffin is perched on a rock, they are blown flower-child fashion all over its face. In winter the puffin sheds these plumes.

This bird is found from California north to Alaska, inhabiting the ocean cliffs and the rocky offshore islands. Gregarious by nature, it is usually found in large colonies. The breeding season extends from late May through July. A single lavender- or brownish-marked white egg is laid and incubated thirty-two to thirty-six days. Although most birds lay much larger clutches, a single offspring per year is enough to keep the puffin population stable. This is because living offshore and nesting in a hole beneath the rocks ensures the puffin a maximum of protection against its enemies, which include gulls, skuas, jaegers, and foxes.

The puffin feeds on fish and is a skillful swimmer, bobbing up and down on the water like a cork. After the puffin has fished for a while, it is not uncommon to see the bird fly back to its nest with five to six small fish dangling out of its mouth. What always puzzles me is this: How does it catch the fifth or sixth fish without dropping the first four? This is especially pertinent for a bird that appears to be as uncoordinated as does the puffin.

If you approach puffins too closely while they are on the water, they always seem undecided about what course of action to take. They may

During the breeding season, tufted puffins have long, curved, ivory-colored ear tufts and a large triangular red bill. The puffins shed the tufts and the outer segment of the bill in the winter.

lumber across the water, pounding it with their wings as if they were going to take off. Or they may suddenly dive to the safety of the depths. Or they may not even move at all, but merely look right back at you. When puffins manage to get up into the air, they buzz around in one or two large circles, then come back to land about where they had taken off. Unlike other birds, which plane in for a landing, puffins really drop in for one. They approach upwind, and, while still several feet above the water, bring their feet forward with toes widespread. Then they bring their bodies into a vertical position, with wings outspread, and just drop into the water with a loud "plop."

10 Columbiformes– Pigeons and Doves

Several hundred years ago there were three family groups in this order. Today there are only two, the dodos and the solitaries having become extinct. Only the Columbidae family is represented in North America, and of this group only 11 out of 209 species worldwide.

A unique feature of the order Columbiformes is that these birds drink water by suction. All other birds drink by gravity and must raise their heads to let their billful of water run down their throats.

The terms "pigeon" and "dove" are used interchangeably. The larger, chunkier bird is commonly referred to as a pigeon, a French word employed by the Norman invaders of England for the bird the Saxons called a dove. The smaller, slimmer bird is called a dove, from the Dutch word *duif*.

The common domestic pigeon is called a rock dove when it is feral, or wild. Pigeons have been domesticated for centuries. Often used for food, squab or fledgling birds are gourmet delicacies in luxury restaurants, but pigeons are most famous as message carriers. The carrier pigeon's ability to return to its home, or cote, is legendary.

At one time the passenger pigeons of North America may well have been the most abundant of all birds. These pigeons numbered into the billions and darkened the skies, but their need to nest in concentrated flocks caused their destruction. As the forests were cut down, the birds were deprived of food, but, even more important, they could not adapt to nesting in smaller numbers.

Doves are famed as symbols of peace, yet the males fight bloody battles during the breeding season. Perhaps the symbolism is based on the birds' soft cooing. The sound is indeed peaceful, albeit monotonous when kept up interminably. The mourning dove is the only native bird known to nest in every one of the forty-eight contiguous states.

Pigeon or Rock Dove
(Columba livia)

FIELD MARKS:	*Dark gray body, iridescent head, white rump, dark terminal tail band.*
SIZE:	*11–16 inches long with a wingspan of 24 inches.*
HABITS:	*Practices monogamy. Wing tips collide on takeoff.*
HABITAT:	*Throughout the country.*
NEST:	*A few twigs.*
EGGS:	*White, 4 in a clutch. Incubation 16–18 days.*
FOOD:	*Grain or whatever is available.*
VOICE:	*Cooing sound.*

The common pigeon, which infests most of our cities, is descended from the wild rock dove of Europe and Asia. This bird has been domesticated for more than three thousand years, and more than two hundred different varieties have been developed from the parent stock. Some breeds, such as certain of the "pouters," can hardly fly.

Widely distributed, the rock dove, or pigeon, is found throughout the continental United States and into Canada from the Maritime Provinces westward to British Columbia. It is a small-headed, short-legged, fan-tailed bird with an overall length of eleven to sixteen inches and a wingspread of twenty-four inches. The pigeon comes in many different colors and patterns, but the most common is variegated gray above with a white rump and a dark terminal tail band. Male and female have a similar appearance although the male is larger.

Pigeons are monogamous and very devoted. Pigeon fanciers who race these birds take advantage of these qualities by introducing a new male into a paired area just before the resident male is shipped off for a race. The fanciers claim that this brings out the male's best racing abilities as he flies home to fight for his mate.

During courtship the males put on a real display, bowing, strutting, puffing up, and cooing. The nest is composed of a few twigs, usually placed on one of the many window sills or cornices on city buildings and skyscrapers. Four white eggs, one and one-quarter inches long and one inch in diameter, are commonly laid. The male usually broods the eggs in the middle of the day, while the female broods the rest of the time. Incubation varies from sixteen to eighteen days.

The young hatch out as blind, naked, helpless, and homely little creatures. The knobs, or ceres, on the top of their beaks appear to be their most dominant characteristic. For the first week the young pigeons are fed "pigeon milk," a semi-fluid mass, resembling cottage cheese, which is regurgitated by the parents. On this fare the young grow rapidly. In one month's time they will have reached maximum size. Frequently, young birds of many species may weigh more than the adults before they leave the nest. Flying usually trims the rock doves down to about one pound each. They are capable of flying at speeds of up to sixty-eight miles per hour.

In the country pigeons feed mainly on weed seeds and spilled grain, but in the city they depend on man to feed them. Thousands of people daily buy feed for the pigeons and as many thousands share their lunches with them. In rural areas, pigeons have man as their chief enemy. They are also preyed upon by snakes, hawks, and owls. In the city by far the greatest hazard these birds encounter is flying into buildings and windows.

The pigeon or rock dove is a familiar sight to all city dwellers. Wild pigeons are increasing in numbers and are becoming a health hazard in many areas of the nation.

Pigeons were always an important part of my early life. My uncle, who raised racing homing pigeons, had one of his cotes in our backyard. When his birds participated in the 600-mile races, everyone watched to see and to clock the first arrivals. Some homing pigeons have flown accurately more than 2,500 miles, and some have even been trained to search for moving ships. The racing homers resemble the wild, or feral, pigeons and are often confused with them.

Today the common wild pigeons have become so numerous that they constitute a health hazard in many parts of the country, chiefly because their dried dung releases into the air organisms contagious to human beings. New York City alone has an estimated five million feral pigeons and countless numbers of pen-raised birds.

Owing to the magnitude of the health hazards, different control programs have been instituted. In rural areas control by shooting is possible; in the city live-trapping is the most common method. James Wafford, of Missouri's Wildlife Research Laboratory, has conducted successful research on New York's pigeons using an oral contraceptive in feed placed out for them. This has had no effect on the birds other than to limit the number of their offspring.

Mourning Dove
(*Zenaidura macroura*)

FIELD MARKS:	*Buffy brown with darker wings; long, pointed, white-edged tail; slim body.*
SIZE:	*11 inches long with a wingspan of 19 inches.*
HABITS:	*Nests singly and feeds in flocks. Wings produce a whistling sound. Male struts while courting the female.*
HABITAT:	*Suburbs and farmlands.*
NEST:	*Flimsy construction of twigs, leaves, or moss.*
EGGS:	*Pure white, 2 in a clutch. Incubation 15 days.*
FOOD:	*Weed seeds, grain.*
VOICE:	*Soft, fluttering call.*

The mourning dove, named for its sad call, is the most prevalent wild dove in the West. This reddish fawn dove has a pointed tail bordered with white edges.

The ancient myth-maker who first depicted the dove as the symbol of peace was sadly misinformed. In actuality, far from being a shy, retiring harbinger of universal good, the dove—particularly in the breeding season —is aggressive and quick to battle other males of his kind. The battles are often fierce and bloody.

The mourning dove is familiar to most of us. It is found from British Columbia south through the forty-eight contiguous states of the United States and into Panama. When full grown, the dove's slim body and tapered tail measure eleven inches in length. It has a wingspread of nineteen inches and weighs between four and six ounces. Upper parts are grayish blue and underparts reddish fawn. Male and female are indistinguishable, being as alike as two peas in a pod.

With the approach of spring, the winter flocks of doves begin to break up. The battles of the males for mates hasten the split. The male dove's courting posture closely resembles that of the common pigeon. He struts around the female on the ground, head bobbing back and forth, tail flared, or he may rub bills with the female and coo softly. The soft, fluttering *coo, coo, cooah, coo* gives the dove its name. Perhaps there is a touch of mourning in the call to remind one of somber occasions. To the bird, however, it is a song of love to its mate and a proclamation of territory to its rivals.

As soon as the doves have paired off, they begin to seek a nesting spot. I have found that they favor evergreen trees. Their nest, a frail contraption of twigs, leaves, or moss, is the flimsiest I have ever seen. It is a wonder that it manages to hold the two pure white eggs, measuring one inch long and one-half inch in diameter, that comprise the usual clutch. The nest is so poorly constructed that, on several occasions, I have been able to look up through the bottom and see the eggs through the gaps in the twigs. Frequently—and it is probably a good thing for the species—the dove builds its nest on top of one that has been abandoned by another bird. The male dove usually gathers all the nesting material and flies back to the nest site, where he presents it to the female. She, supposedly, builds the nest.

Both parents participate in incubating the eggs, which requires fifteen days. In the north the mourning dove commonly has two annual broods; in the southern states it has three.

When first hatched, doves are among the homeliest of baby birds. As they develop, their white natal down is replaced by brown feathers. After another molt, in the late fall, they acquire the basic gray coloration of the adults. The youngsters eat regurgitated "pigeon milk," a lumpy, cottage-cheese type of partially digested food, by inserting their beaks into a corner of the parent's beak. The parent accomplishes the transferal of food by considerable pumping with its beak. Before the young doves leave the nest, they are being fed seeds and insects. Grass, weed, and hay seeds are eaten as well as domesticated grains that have been spilled or lost on the ground by the farmer during harvesting operations.

The eggs and young of the dove are subject to attack by raccoons, opossums, black snakes, crows, and jays, but the adults are so swift in flight that only the pigeon hawks and duck hawks can catch them. Owls, however, often pick them off their perch at night.

Because the bulk of its diet is composed of weed seeds, the mourning dove is highly beneficial to man. In most of the southern and midwestern states the dove is considered a game species and a sporting one at that. In many of the northeastern states, on the other hand, it is considered a songbird and is afforded complete protection. Extensive studies have proved that about 60 percent of all doves perish each year, whether they are hunted or not.

11 Cuculiformes— Cuckoos and Their Allies

Of the 2 families in this order, Musophagidae and Cuculidae, only the latter is found in North America. We have 5 species of cuckoos, anis, and roadrunners out of 127 species worldwide.

Cuckoos from other parts of the world are parasitic; they lay their eggs in the nests of other birds, which then hatch them and raise the young. The cuckoos of North America do not have this habit. They are, in addition, particularly useful birds, because they consume large quantities of the hairy caterpillars that most birds shun. In general they have slender, rounded wings and long tails. Male and female are look-alikes.

The roadrunner of our Southwest, the only member of this order to be discussed, is a ground cuckoo whose legs have become longer and stronger for better adaptation to life on the ground. The leg development has been made at the expense of the wings, so although the roadrunner can fly, it does so only for short distances.

Roadrunner
(*Geococcyx californianus*)

FIELD MARKS:	*Mottled dark brown and white back, white belly, blue feet and legs, blue and orange piece of skin behind eye, dark brown crest on head. Long bill, neck, and tail.*
SIZE:	*22 inches long with a wingspan of 16–18 inches.*
HABITS:	*Runs at top speeds. Uses tail to show emotions. Creature of habit.*
HABITAT:	*Desert areas.*
NEST:	*Crude and bulky, twigs lined with grass or feathers.*
EGGS:	*Pale yellow, 4–6 in a clutch. Incubation 18 days.*
FOOD:	*Small lizards, horned toads, spiders, small mammals, small birds.*
VOICE:	*Dovelike coo, descending in pitch.*

Although it exists only in the southwestern desert areas, the roadrunner is a familiar household personality. This cuckoo that travels on the ground has become a symbol of the modern automobile.

If ever a bird has been well named, it is the roadrunner. This long-billed, long-necked, long-legged, long-tailed member of the cuckoo family spends the greater part of its time running up, down, or across the road at top speed. It was formerly found from Kansas, south to Mexico and west to the Pacific, but the encroachment of man has reduced its range. Nowadays it is commonly seen only in the desert areas of the Southwest.

I saw my first roadrunner when driving through southern Oklahoma on my way to Lubbock, Texas. Slamming on the brakes, I grabbed my camera and jumped from the truck, but the bird was gone. After this had happened on several more occasions, I finally learned this little secret: If a roadrunner dashes across the road in front of you and disappears in the brush, *don't* chase it. You can't possibly catch up with it, anyway, for it only thinks you want to race and so redoubles its effort. Instead, play it cool. Sit down in the shade, if you can find any, and wait. Nine times out of ten the roadrunner comes back to see what you are doing. Frequently it jumps up onto a low bush or cactus to get a better vantage point—*then* you snap your picture.

Can the roadrunner fly? It can, for short distances of perhaps several hundred feet. At least that's the longest distance I ever saw one fly. Usually they fly just to cross an arroyo, a canyon, or even a road, when a speeding car gets too close.

The roadrunner's wingspan is sixteen to eighteen inches, and it has a tail about twelve inches long, out of a total length of twenty-two inches. The long tail is a necessity; it acts as a counterbalance when the bird is running at top speed and has to turn at a sharp angle. The tail is also used to show emotions: It is raised almost vertically when the bird displays or is excited, and it is carried horizontally when the bird runs. When the roadrunner flies, the tail is widely fanned out and provides considerable lift. Some southwesterners believe that wearing a roadrunner tail feather in your hat will keep you from being bitten by a rattlesnake.

The bird's basic colors are a mixture of white, buff, dark brown, and blackish green. Legs and feet are blue. Behind the eye is a long, horizontal slip of bare skin, vivid orange and blue in color. When excited or disturbed, the bird displays this brightly colored skin, raises the dark crest on its head, and pops its bill mandibles together, making an audible clicking sound.

This bird is a creature of habit. Once it has adopted an area as its home territory, it can usually be found in the same place at the same time every day. When hunting for food, the roadrunner is so punctual in passing a certain spot in its area that it resembles a caretaker punching a time clock.

Small lizards that inhabit its area constitute this bird's staple food. Watching the lizards, you can easily understand why the roadrunner is so fast. It has to be, if it is going to be able to make a meal of those speedy lizards. Sometimes when fed a large lizard, the young roadrunner is unable to swallow all of it. Gulping and gulping until the lizard is down as far as possible, the young bird sits with the remainder of the lizard's body and tail dangling from its mouth. As the digestive processes proceed, the lizard gradually slips down the bird's throat.

Roadrunners are famed as snake killers. They can and do kill snakes but seldom bother with one that is too large to be eaten. They are interested in finding a meal, not in killing snakes. On occasion they kill rattlesnakes. The snake is fast, but the birds are faster. Also, by fluffing out their feathers and extending their wings, the birds present a large but false target for the snake to strike. When the snake finally is teased into striking, the roadrunner jumps backward. This is repeated until the snake tires and is reluctant to strike again. No longer does its large, flat head follow the bird's every movement as it circles its victim. Now the roadrunner dashes in and pecks at the snake's eyes. Once it has succeeded in blinding the tired snake, the bird beats it into submission with its powerful beak.

The big Texas grasshoppers and other insects also account for much of the roadrunner's diet. In the midst of its running, the bird suddenly jumps a foot or two into the air to catch a flying insect or snatch one from a bush. Horned toads, spiders, small mammals, occasionally small birds and eggs, and some seeds are eaten as well.

After pairing, the birds build a crude, bulky, grass- or feather-lined nest of twigs in a dense bush, thicket, or cactus, such as the cholla. The nests are so well hidden that they are extremely hard to locate. I managed to photograph one through the courtesy of Martha Whitson, who, with her husband Paul, was doing a study of the roadrunner's life history in Big Bend National Park, Texas.

Four to six pale yellow eggs, about one and one-half inches long and a little over one inch in diameter, comprise the usual clutch. The parents take turns incubating them. One bird relieves the other by literally pushing it off the eggs in order to get on with the job. The female does most of the brooding, while her mate busies himself catching food to bring back to her. Brooding, or incubation, begins as soon as the first egg is laid; eighteen days later it is hatched. Because eggs may be laid over a period of two weeks, the first nestling may be one to two weeks old by the time the last of its litter mates is hatched.

If danger threatens her eggs or young in the form of a cacomistle or a raccoon, the female tries to lure it away by pretending to be injured. By the time the young are three weeks old, they are ready to leave the nest and follow after the parents.

At one time the roadrunner was classified as a nuisance bird and was shot on sight. It was believed to be detrimental to natural quail production. This charge has never been substantiated, and, although it is probably true once in a while, the good this bird does for man by eating insects far outweighs the bad.

12 Strigiformes–
Owls

The highly adaptable members of this order are found under a variety of conditions, from the freezing Arctic wastes to the burning deserts. One hundred and thirty-four species of owls exist throughout the world. Some ornithologists group all owls into one family, but it is generally conceded that the eleven species of barn owls belong in the family Tytonidae, while the remainder—including the four species discussed—belong in the family Strigidae.

Because the hawks and the owls have similar hunting and prey affinities, they were once classified together. The hawk is a day-flying bird of prey and depends upon its keen eyesight. Although the owl has good eyesight, it is a largely nocturnal bird of prey and depends more upon its keen sense of hearing. The owl's ear openings are exceptionally large and partially covered with a flap of skin. Often the ears are of different sizes, making it easier for the owl to locate its prey by the variations in the volume of sound reaching each ear.

To facilitate seeing in the dark, the owl has a large facial disk that helps to reflect the small amount of available light into the eye. Most birds have eyes at either side of the head, but the owl's eyes are fixed in sockets on the front of its face. Because the owl cannot move its eyes, it must turn its head to watch a moving object. Sometimes one gets the impression that the bird has turned its head completely around. In reality, the owl turns its head over its shoulder as far as it can in one direction, then whips it around in the other direction almost 360 degrees, with a motion too quick to be seen. Most owls hunt at night, but a few hunt in the daylight hours.

Small prey is swallowed whole, and the undigested bones, fur, and feathers are regurgitated in pellet form. Larger prey is torn apart with the beak.

Screech Owl
(Otus asio)

FIELD MARKS:	*Brownish red or dark gray and white. Only small owl with ear tufts.*
SIZE:	*7–10 inches long with a wingspan of 24 inches.*
HABITS:	*Strictly nocturnal. Moves constantly. Catches its prey by sound rather than sight. Swallows mice whole and regurgitates the inedible portions in a pellet.*
HABITAT:	*Towns, orchards, small woodlots.*
NEST:	*Large hollows in old trees.*
EGGS:	*White, 3–5 in a clutch. Incubation 26–28 days.*
FOOD:	*Mice, moths, beetles, small birds, fish.*
VOICE:	*Tremulous whistle running down the scale.*

Because the screech owl frequents the haunts of man, more people probably are aware of this owl than of any other owl. Over most of its vast range—all of the United States and parts of Canada and Mexico—where one or another of its eighteen subspecies is found, the bird is called a screech owl. Yet this owl doesn't really screech; it whistles a tremolo call that has a soft, eerie slide down the scale. The western subspecies has a call that is just a one-tone note. In the southern states this little owl is called a "shivering owl," and that name seems most appropriate to me. Heard emanating from the darkness, the call can send delicious little shivers running up and down one's spine.

In the South the call used to send shivers of apprehension along the spines of all who heard it, because this owl was supposed to be a prophet of doom. To ward off the impending disaster foretold by the owl, certain rituals were observed, such as turning over the left shoe at night or pulling out the left-hand pocket of an unworn pair of pants. That such rituals were successful was proved by the absence of disasters befalling those who practiced them.

Anyone who can whistle can easily imitate the call of a screech owl. The tone and pitch do not have to be perfect to elicit a response from the bird. If the owl is anywhere within hearing, it will answer and, in many cases, will fly out to investigate. The screech owl calls most frequently in the springtime breeding season and is most responsive at that time.

One unusually warm evening in early April I was sitting on our darkened porch when a screech owl called. I whistled back. We kept up this communication as the owl came closer and closer. Finally I was rewarded by seeing his plump little form land on the banister encircling the porch. Like all his kind this owl was very alert and in almost constant motion, bowing and bobbing, turning his head from side to side as he searched for what could only be his competition or a prospective mate. Although I could imitate the main call that attracted the owl, I could not imitate the bill-snapping or soft cooing conversation needed to hold the bird after he had arrived. Finally realizing that he had been duped, the owl flew off. He didn't bother to hiss his displeasure, as he would have if sufficiently angered.

The screech owl is easy to recognize because of its small size—seven to ten inches long and with a wingspread of up to twenty-four inches. It also has conspicuous feathery ear tufts. A distinctive feature is its dichromatism, or tendency to develop two plumage color phases—a red phase and a gray phase; both colors may be found in a single brood. In the western subspecies, gray is the dominant color. These color phases help to explain why

The name "screech owl" is actually a misnomer, as the bird does not screech, but emits a tremulous whistle running down the scale. The screech owl's call can easily be imitated.

this owl is sometimes known locally as the "red owl" or the "gray owl."

During the daytime the screech owl sleeps inside a hollow tree or in a bird box, if a large enough one can be found. If forced to sleep out in the open, the owl perches on a tree limb situated as close as possible to the tree. If approached, but thinking itself undetected, the owl elongates its head and body, erects its ear tufts, and peers at the world through slitted eyes.

Three of the screech owl nests I have found were located in the large hollows of old apple trees. One cavity was used all year round; I had first discovered it in the wintertime, as one of the adult owls sat in the opening waiting for nightfall. This particular tree stood in an orchard about sixty feet from the road, and the owl was plainly visible as it sat upright in the opening. As I approached, the bird climbed back inside the hollow, but I

Excellent mousers, screech owls consume more white-footed mice than they do meadow mice because the meadow mice conceal themselves well in overhanging grasses.

proceeded to set up my camera and flashgun on a tripod, anticipating getting a photograph as the owl emerged after dark. But, as the sun sank, so did the temperature; I began to shiver with the cold. The photograph was never taken, because, instead of climbing back up to the opening, the owl shot from the hollow as though propelled by a catapult.

In general owls do not need nesting material, because the rotted wood of the hollows is sufficiently soft. Three to five white eggs, about one and one-quarter inches long and slightly narrower in diameter, comprise the usual clutch laid the latter part of April. Unlike most birds, which do not begin to brood until the entire clutch has been laid, hawks and owls begin brooding as soon as the first egg is laid. As the subsequent eggs may be laid over a week or two weeks, it is difficult to tell the exact incubation time, thought to be about twenty-six or twenty-eight days. The female does most of the brooding, but both parents provide food for the young.

In late spring and summer screech owls catch and eat large numbers of moths, beetles, and other insects. During the rest of the year they earn the title "flying mousetraps," owing to their expertise as mousers. Scientific tests have revealed that the majority of their prey is trapped by sound rather than by sight. These owls catch more white-footed mice than meadow mice, because the white-foot often runs across the top of the forest

Since the screech owl is a nocturnal bird of prey, it is seldom seen during the daylight hours. The bird uses this time to catch up on its sleep.

floor, while the meadow mouse may be concealed beneath the overhanging grass. On several occasions I have seen a screech owl catch small birds that were roosting in dense evergreens. Birds form a hefty part of their diet during the wintertime, when other foods are in short supply.

Most people are surprised to learn that the screech owl, like many of the larger owls, frequently catches fish and crayfish for food. This owl likes to bathe in water and doesn't hesitate to plunge into shallow water to catch fish. I have seen screech owls that had been drowned after being caught in muskrat traps set at least an inch or more underwater.

At first baby owlets eat regurgitated food provided by their parents. Later they eat bits of food torn for them by their parents or by themselves. Gradually the young owls become large enough to swallow a mouse whole; the inedible portions are regurgitated in a pellet. The young are cared for by the parents at the nest for about six weeks, but by midsummer they have left to make their own way in the world.

As the screech owl preys upon lesser creatures, it is taken in turn by the barred owl and the great horned owl. Of all owls the screech owl is the species most often killed by automobiles, perhaps because it frequents built-up areas more than the others, or perhaps because it is lured to the roadway by the insects that are attracted by automobile headlights.

Great Horned Owl
(Bubo virginianus)

FIELD MARKS:	*Mottled buffy brown and white, white throat collar, fine horizontal bars across belly.*
	Only large owl with ear tufts.
SIZE:	*20 inches long with a wingspan of 55 inches.*
HABITS:	*Roosts in evergreen trees. Starts courtship early in the year. Hunts at night.*
HABITAT:	*Common throughout the country.*
NEST:	*Usually an abandoned hawk's or crow's nest, occasionally in cavities.*
EGGS:	*Dull white, 3–5 in a clutch. Incubation about 28 days.*
FOOD:	*Game birds and animals, poultry, rats, mice.*
VOICE:	*Low hoots.*

Great horned owls swallow smaller prey whole, but they must tear large animals apart before eating them. The owls eat the entire prey and then regurgitate the undigestible material in a pellet.

Often referred to as the "tiger of the air," the great horned owl is one of our fiercest birds of prey. The only reason more people aren't attacked by one of these owls is that the bird seems to realize it would be unable to carry off its prize. Those who have been attacked were probably victims of mistaken identity—to an owl a fur cap or light-colored hat may look very much like a meal on the move.

One of the greatest thrills of the outdoors is to sit around a campfire late at night, listening to the conversation of a pair of great horned owls as their *hoo hoo hoooo, hoo hoo*s float in from the surrounding darkness. These largest of our "eared" owls measure approximately twenty inches in length and have a wingspread of fifty-five inches. They have conspicuous ear tufts and feathered toes. The upper parts are sooty brown with grayish white mottling, and the dark barred underparts accentuate the white throat.

Nearly two feet in length, the great horned owl gets its name from the feather tufts on its head.

The great horned owl is common throughout North and South America wherever suitable habitat conditions exist. Courtship begins early in the year, as love calls echo through the still January and February nights. Usually the abandoned nest of another bird, such as a crow, is taken over, and there the female lays her three to five dull white eggs, a little over two inches long and one and one-half inches in diameter. Often she is covered with the snow of late-season storms as she sits on the eggs. With such a beginning it is small wonder that young owls are hardy. Owls nest early, it is believed, so that the hatching of their young corresponds with the migration of the small birds that form a large part of the youngsters' diet. The incubation time is about twenty-eight days.

The owl can see well in the daytime but even better at night. Thanks to its loose, soft feathers, its flight is noiseless. Hunting at night is more rewarding, too, for that is when the rodents upon which the owl feeds are most active.

Unless a flock of crows discovers the owl's whereabouts and sets up the raucous cawing that helps draw you to its location, this bird is rarely seen in daytime. It prefers to roost in an evergreen, camouflaged by the heavy foliage and snuggled close to the trunk to further minimize detection. One way of locating the owl, however, is by its pellets. Mice, small rats, and similar small prey are eaten whole, if possible. Game birds, rabbits, squirrels, skunks, and other larger game must be torn apart, but are still swallowed in their entirety—bones, fur, feathers, and all. This mass goes down into the stomach, where body juices extract whatever nutrients are present. Anything left over is regurgitated as a large pellet, sometimes measuring four inches long by one inch in diameter. Many of the food habits of the owl have been ascertained by scientists studying the remains of the prey animals in the pellets.

That the owl is not a fussy eater is seen by the frequency with which it dines on skunks. The skunk's main defensive weapon is its powerful, nauseating scent. This weapon is enough to deter most attackers, but the fact that birds generally have a poor sense of smell nullifies the skunk's advantage in this case. Then, too, the owl's nictitating membrane protects its eyes from receiving the full impact of the skunk's spray.

The owls' young can find themselves in peril from the raccoon, but not when a parent owl is present.

There can be no denying that a single great horned owl is capable of destroying a tremendous number of game birds and animals as well as poultry. There is also no denying the tremendous amount of good done by this same owl when feeding on harmful rats and mice. Despite the inroads made on game, therefore, more states are realizing the beneficial services owls and hawks perform. Several states now give complete protection to birds of prey.

Short-eared Owl
(*Asio flammeus*)

FIELD MARKS:	*Tawny with white streaks above, brown stripes on buffy breast, dark patches about eyes, conspicuous facial disks.*
SIZE:	*13 inches long with a wingspan of 40–42 inches.*
HABITS:	*Often hunts in the daytime. Flight is irregular. Elaborate courtship ritual.*
HABITAT:	*Open, treeless areas.*
NEST:	*Slight depression in the ground lined with a few weeds and feathers.*
EGGS:	*Creamy white, 5–9 in a clutch. Incubation 21 days.*
FOOD:	*Mice, small birds, large insects.*
VOICE:	*Continuous monotone of sixteen or eighteen toots.*

Unlike most owls, the short-eared owl hunts in the daytime as well as in the evening and sleeps whenever it is tired.

The "short ears" that give this owl its name are actually short feather ear tufts, which are seldom, if ever, seen. The owl, on the other hand, *is* seen. That fact helps to identify it. Ordinarily owls are creatures of darkness, but the short-eared owl is often seen hunting for rodents in the daytime.

Intermittently active day and night, the short-ear sleeps whenever it is tired. In good weather it usually sleeps in a clump of high grass out in the marshes. When the weather turns bad, and the winds blow strongly enough to whip the tides into whitecaps, the owl forsakes its beach and marsh areas to seek shelter among the sturdier pines.

At a quick glance the short-eared owl might be mistaken for a marsh hawk, which frequents the same areas and has the same style of hunting. The marsh hawk, however, is slightly larger than the owl, has a longer tail and a conspicuous white rump band, or saddle. The owl has the typical large, rounded owl head and flaps about in flight like a giant butterfly buffeted by high winds, while the hawk flies with typical grace.

An adult short-ear is about thirteen inches long and has a wingspan of forty to forty-two inches. Its plumage is a mixture of buff, dark brown, and white. The breast and back are buff overlaid with dark brown stripes. The facial disks are fairly conspicuous, and the dark patch about each eye gives it the appearance of a burglar's mask. The voice is a continuous monotone of sixteen or eighteen toots.

A truly international bird, the short-eared owl is widely distributed over North and South America, Europe, Asia, and Africa. Its preferred habitat is the open, treeless expanse typified by the plains, steppes, pampas, veldt, marsh, and swamp areas of the world. In some areas, it is known as a "marsh owl" or "prairie owl." Although the wild areas of my home state of New Jersey are rapidly being destroyed by asphalt, concrete, and human beings, the short-ear still finds the remaining coastal areas to its liking and may even remain as a winter resident.

I saw my first short-ears at Brigantine National Wildlife Refuge, in southern New Jersey, while on a photographic trip with Betty Woodford. The day prior to our visit had been a stormy one in the area, and a higher than usual tide had inundated the marshes. Forced from their holes and tunnels by the encroaching water, meadow mice scurried about among the grasses and sedges seeking shelter. Taking advantage of this temporary confusion, the short-ears were particularly active. As many as eight to ten owls could be seen at one time flapping just above the high grasses, pausing here and there to hover while they searched the ground below. When a mouse was sighted, the owls immediately swooped upon it. If a mouse was caught, the owls remained on the ground, almost hidden in the vegetation as they gulped down their prey. If the plunge resulted in a miss, the owls bounced back into the air to continue their combing of the area. Occasionally one of the owls landed on a dead tree snag or post and watched intently for its prey to reveal itself.

The exceptionally large ear openings of the short-eared owl have convinced biologists that this bird locates more of its prey by sound than by sight. This is undoubtedly true, for the typical area frequented by this owl has such rank vegetative growth that a mouse's squeal or rustle in the dry grass is more readily heard than seen.

The short-ear winters in most of the lower three-fourths of the United States and heads north to its breeding grounds about April. The male performs a spectacular aerial courtship. From a height of two hundred to three hundred feet, he plunges toward the spot where the female lies hidden in the high grasses and claps his wing tips together in front of his body, producing a fluttering sound. Sometimes both birds fly together as the male goes through his performance.

The nest is a rudimentary affair, usually a slight depression in the ground garnished with fragments of dried weeds and an occasional feather. Much of the time the nest is in an exposed area, where its owners rely on the boggy, wet habitat to provide protection. Sometimes it is concealed beneath a natural tangle of vegetation; on rare occasions it is found in low bushes or in a hole in a riverbank.

The parents take turns incubating the five to nine creamy white eggs, one and one-quarter inches long and slightly narrower in diameter, for a period of about twenty-one days. The young at first are helpless, but even from the start they have the ravenous appetites that more than once have been the cause of cannibalism among them. Like the young of most of our birds of prey, little short-ears hatch out at different times over a period of as long as two weeks. The nestlings vary greatly in size, therefore, with the result that one of the large owlets may swallow one of its smaller litter-mates. Raccoons, too, eat the young owls, and also the eggs.

Mice, particularly the destructive meadow mouse, constitute the staple food of these grassland dwellers. Occasionally small birds of the ground-nesting variety—certain sparrows, meadowlarks, and red-winged blackbirds, for example—are eaten. Grasshoppers, crickets, and similar large insects are also favored. No mention of this owl feeding on game birds or animals appears in the records I have studied. Attacks on larger birds, such as hawks, herons, ducks, and even crows, have been cited, but these appear to have been instances of the owls either amusing themselves or, in some instances, defending their nesting territories.

On the other hand records show that plagues of mice and voles were routed by the intervention of congregations of these owls. Many studies have proved time and time again that the short-eared owl is a valuable ally of man and deserves protection.

Burrowing Owl
(Speotyto cunicularia)

FIELD MARKS:	*Mottled tawny and white. Long legs, sandy coloration, round head, stubby tail.*
SIZE:	*Eastern subspecies: 8–9 inches long with a wingspan of 22 inches. Western subspecies: 11 inches long with a wingspan of 25 inches.*
HABITS:	*Active both day and night. Lives in burrows. Flies with an undulating up and down pattern. Hovers when hunting insects.*
HABITAT:	*Open, treeless prairies.*
NEST:	*Fur, some vegetation, chips of manure, in underground burrow.*
EGGS:	*White, 6–10 in a clutch. Incubation 21 days.*
FOOD:	*Grasshoppers and other insects, mice, snakes, lizards.*
VOICE:	*Chirping sound.*

208

As the name implies, burrowing owls live in burrows, which they excavate with their long legs and sharp talons. However, the owls prefer to utilize the burrows made by such other creatures as prairie dogs and badgers.

Sitting on the wall surrounding the prairie dog village in Lubbock, Texas, I had a great time watching a group of solemn little burrowing owls. Unlike most owls, which are active only at night, burrowing owls are active both day and night. Whether standing atop a burrow mound or a fencepost, they are usually chirping and performing a bobbing little bow at the same time. They look for all the world like a group of Oriental potentates bowing to each other so formally and properly. For their size the burrowing owls have the longest legs of any members of the owl family, a feature further emphasized as they bob up and down.

Of the two subspecies of burrowing owls, the smaller is the eastern form, found in central Florida. I first saw this little owl, about eight to nine inches long and with a wingspread of twenty-two inches, in the Kissimmee palmetto prairie area. The western form, about eleven inches long and with a wingspread of twenty-five inches, can be found from southwestern Canada throughout most of the western and southwestern states. Both are sand colored, with buffy brown spots and white throat bands.

This owl owes its name to its custom of living in burrows, either in those made by another creature, such as the prairie dog, or in those it has excavated for itself. The fact that this owl can, and does, excavate its own burrows explains its long legs. These are more efficient for scratching dirt loose and kicking it backward than short legs would be. The eastern burrowing owl usually digs its own burrows in Florida's sandy soil. The western subspecies inhabits the abandoned burrows of prairie dogs, ground squirrels, badgers, or armadillos.

Many stories are told of the harmonious relationship that is supposed to exist between the burrowing owl, the prairie dog, and the rattlesnake. The truth is that all three creatures are often found together in the same area, but not in the same burrow; the liaison is less than cordial and is often strained. The rattlesnake frequents the prairie dog village for just two purposes: shelter and food. In spite of the tales one hears about snake burrows, most snakes are incapable of making a burrow and instead seek natural cavities or ready-made burrows to escape the heat or the cold, whichever it may be. In the case of a prairie dog's burrow, the snake seeks not only shelter but also the chance to eat the resident prairie dogs, the owls, and the owls' eggs. Even the association between the owl and the prairie dog is far from amicable. When danger threatens, in the form of a fox, badger, or hawk, both dive to safety in the burrows. If the owl happens to dive into a burrow that is already occupied, it is quickly evicted by the angry prairie dog. On several occasions a prairie dog has even killed and eaten the little owls.

The owl can strike back, too. Several times I have seen an owl swoop out of the air, talons outstretched, and strike at a prairie dog's head, causing it to duck and run. I don't believe that a burrowing owl could kill a prairie dog, simply because it is too large an animal.

This owl's breeding season occurs in April or May. The nest, located underground at least six feet from the entrance of the burrow, may be made of bits of fur, vegetation, or chips of dried horse or cow manure. The female usually lays six to ten white eggs, a little more than one inch in length and about one inch in diameter. The eggs are unseen in the dark burrow, so there is no need for them to be camouflaged. Both parents share in the task of incubating the eggs, a chore that requires at least twenty-one days. There is only one brood of young per year.

The largest number of young owls I ever saw at a single burrow was five. As it was late July when I photographed them, they had grown almost as large as their parents and could fly with ease. Some of the broods may already have started to split up. I had hoped to find some young owls unable to fly, so that I could get closer, to obtain better photos. But when I approached too closely, the owls either popped back underground or flapped away through the air. It was almost useless to follow after them, for each succeeding time they flushed at a greater distance. An undulating up-and-down flight pattern helps to identify these owls. They also hover like sparrow hawks when hunting insects in high grass.

If I disturbed the owls as they slept at the entrance to the burrows, they fixed me balefully with their great yellow eyes. Sometimes they only opened one eye to peer reproachfully at me. Although they appeared to be sleepy, they were always alert.

Burrowing owls are highly beneficial to man, since their staple food consists of grasshoppers or other insects. Once in a while a small rodent, such as a mouse or a snake or lizard, will also be taken as food.

Although the range of the western subspecies is large, this owl has steadily declined in numbers because its prairie dog host has been virtually wiped out by man. Then, too, the owl itself does not care for the encroachment of civilization. The burrowing owl is a lover of solitude, of wide-open, treeless prairies untouched by tractor or plow. Man's growing population is taking over more and more of this little owl's range all the time, to the detriment of the species.

13 Caprimulgiformes— Goatsuckers

The name Caprimulgiformes was given to the birds of this order because of the belief, prevalent in southern Europe at one time, that they sucked milk from goats at night. There is not, and never was, any basis for this superstition. Nevertheless, many other superstitions still surround these birds, arising from the fact that they are for the most part active at night.

Ornithologists disagree as to whether there are four or five families in this order. Only the family Caprimulgidae, consisting of six species, inhabits North America. All six species have a mottled gray or brown coloration that enables them to blend in with their surroundings. Most of these birds spend the daylight hours sleeping, resting, or nesting directly on the forest floor.

The members of this family are highly vocal, and their common names such as "poor will" and "chuck will's widow" derive from the sound of their calls. These calls are simple and easily imitated; the birds respond readily to the imitation.

Members of the Caprimulgidae family have weak feet, because they do little walking or perching. The wings are long, strong, and tapered, making these birds excellent fliers and highly mobile, qualities needed by birds that pursue flying insects.

In recent years it was rediscovered that the whip-poor-will, a member of this family, actually hibernates. It is the only bird I know of anywhere in the world to pass the winter in this manner, although many mammals, reptiles, amphibians, and insects do so. I say "rediscovered," because the Indians of Arizona, where this event takes place, had told about it for years, but no ornithologists would believe them.

Another peculiarity of this family is that some members move their eggs in their mouths to a safer spot if they feel the original nest site is threatened. Artist-naturalist John James Audubon first described this activity. Even though he was a bird expert, his description was always suspect, but it has now been substantiated by a sufficient number of correlating reports.

212

Whip-poor-will
(*Caprimulgus vociferous*)

FIELD MARKS: *Mottled tawny and white. Male has three white outer tail feathers, white collar, black lower face. Female has buffy collar.*

SIZE: *9 inches long with a wingspan of 21 inches.*

HABITS: *Seen only at dusk. Call is extremely repetitive. Eyes reflect a bright red. Hold their bodies horizontal to their perch.*

HABITAT: *Woods near fields.*

NEST: *Slight depression in the leaves.*

EGGS: *White with streakings, 2 in a clutch. Incubation 18–21 days.*

FOOD: *Flying insects.*

VOICE: Whip-poor-will, whip-poor-will, whip-poor-will.

The sound of a whip-poor-will calling in the soft spring twilight instantly takes me back to the farm where I was raised. At that time the call of the whip-poor-will was common throughout most of the rural areas of the eastern United States. Unfortunately, it is no longer heard over much of the bird's former range, and the night's silence remains unbroken by the staccato *whip-poor-will, whip-poor-will, whip-poor-will*. And we are all the poorer for its absence.

It is logical that the whip-poor-will should be named after its call. The call is stated and repeated with bell-tone clarity over and over again. Its Latin name *vociferous* means "strong voice."

Naturalist John Burroughs heard one bird make 1,088 consecutive calls. The greatest number of consecutive calls that I have personally recorded was 293, back in May 1950. At the time I was working as a ranger at Camp Pahaquarra, in northern New Jersey, living alone because the living quarters had not been completed. The camp is located on the site of copper mines originally opened by the Dutch in 1650, reworked in the early 1900's, and later abandoned. All that remained were large masonry retaining walls and concrete abutments. From one of these abutments the whip-poor-will called each evening, the valley walls causing the sound to reverberate and gain in intensity.

Ordinarily the bird showed up at its usual station between eight thirty and eight forty-five in the evening, so about eight fifteen I donned a heavier jacket against the evening chill that funneled down the narrow valley and secreted myself in a clump of honeysuckle vines, which covered part of the nearby wall. Within a few minutes the male whip-poor-will would show up. Its legs appeared stunted, and I never saw it walk; it always flew from one spot to another, even though the distance could be measured in inches.

The bird always turned until it faced out over the valley. Perhaps it felt safer with the wall behind it, or perhaps it just wanted to be in a better position to see. The first few calls were of a short run, perhaps five or six, or maybe a dozen. Then, as if assured that its tone was right, the calling began in earnest. The head was elevated and the gaping mouth open. I was so close that I could easily see the white feathers of the barred throat flutter with each call. The calling continued for about fifteen or twenty minutes, then the bird flew off to feed. At times the female flew by, and the male followed after her. At no time did I see the female join the male on the abutment. Off and on throughout the night the male returned, and again his call poured forth in a torrent, especially during the hours between two and five in the morning.

Adult whip-poor-wills are about nine inches long and have a wingspread

The whip-poor-will sleeps and nests directly on the forest floor, where its black, brown, and white coloration blends in with the dead leaves. If the bird is approached when resting, it will open its mouth and spread its wings and tail in a threat position.

of twenty-one inches. Their plumage is buffy brown, mottled with black, brown, and white spots, dots, and bars. The male has a white throat band and three white outer tail feathers; the female has a buff throat band and no white tail feathers.

The eastern half of the United States and the southern portion of Canada are home to the whip-poor-will. Some also breed in Arizona, New Mexico, and Western Texas.

Whip-poor-wills usually nest and rest directly on the forest floor. They need trees in sufficient numbers to provide shade for the ground, but they don't seek out dense thickets because they know how to use their mottled coloration to good advantage as camouflage. I have seen these birds resting on the cinders of a railroad track bed and along the gravel shoulder of a highway. When they flew up from the shoulder of the road at night, their eyes reflected a bright red.

If this bird is approached while resting in the forest in the daytime, it may spread its wings and tail in a threat posture and open wide its huge mouth. Actually the whip-poor-will is a gentle creature, and the threat is merely a bluff; as one approaches closer, it flies off.

No actual nest is constructed during the breeding season, although a slight depression forms in the leaves from the weight of the mother and her eggs. The two white eggs, about one inch long and one-half inch in diameter, are spotted and streaked with brown, gray, or even lavender. Apparently, only the female incubates the eggs, which require about eighteen to twenty-one days. Because so many of the whip-poor-will's activities are carried on under cover of darkness, its family life has been studied less thoroughly than that of the day-flying birds. At night you can't find the whip-poor-will, and during the daytime its coat of camouflage keeps it safe from prying eyes. Even when this bird perches in a tree or on a log instead of on the ground, it turns its body horizontally to its perch to minimize the chances of detection.

The chicks are precocial at birth, and like baby grouse or woodcock can disappear practically before your eyes. At an alarm note from the mother the young birds hide in or under the leaves on the forest floor. The mother may try to decoy danger away from the area by feigning injury. That danger lurks in the forms of snakes, raccoons, foxes, opossums, skunks, and hawks, among others.

All kinds of winged insects are eaten by the whip-poor-will. Unlike its cousin the nighthawk, which flies high in the sky after food, the whip-poor-will seldom flies higher than twenty to twenty-five feet and usually much lower. It often skims low over fields and through forests with its large mouth wide open, the stiff hairs on either side of the mouth serving to funnel the insects into the gaping maw.

When chasing moths the whip-poor-will dives, scoops, and turns in the air like a bat. With its strong, rounded wings, the bird is a skillful flier. Mosquitoes, locusts, grasshoppers, crickets, and flies are also taken. Occasionally, this bird feeds on the ground, savoring ants and beetles. Indeed, its food habits prove the whip-poor-will to be extremely beneficial to man, even though man's constant destruction of its habitat is steadily reducing its populations.

14 Apodiformes— Swifts and Hummingbirds

The swift and hummingbird families of the order Apodiformes differ so greatly in appearance that they were at one time thought to be two different orders. Nevertheless they share so many similar characteristics and differ so much from all other birds that they are now consolidated into a single order. They are thought to be distantly related to the order Caprimulgiformes, or goatsuckers.

Apodiformes means "footless ones." These birds are expert fliers and spend so much time in flight that their feet have degenerated to the point where they are no longer used for walking but only for perching. The swifts are among the fastest fliers in the world, with the Asian swift capable of flying at speeds of over two hundred miles per hour. The hummingbird can fly up, down, and backward as well as forward by being able to change the variable pitch of its wings, helicopter-fashion.

The hummingbirds of the family Trochilidae are found only in the New World. Among the 319 species are some of the smallest and most brightly colored birds in the world. Fifteen species of hummingbirds inhabit the United States, but only one species, the ruby-throated hummingbird, is found east of the Mississippi River.

The hummingbird's wing muscles, like the swift's, are larger in proportion to the rest of the bird than in any of the other species. These flight muscles represent between 25 and 30 percent of its total weight.

During migration the ruby-throat flies nonstop across the Gulf of Mexico, a distance of more than five hundred miles. Aerodynamacists have proved that, because of its weight, shape, and wing size, the bumblebee cannot fly, and an ornithologist has proved that the hummingbird is too small to make such long flights. The experts have proved their theories on paper but have yet to convince either of these two creatures of the impossibility of their accomplishments.

Ruby-throated Hummingbird
(*Archilochus colubris*)

FIELD MARKS:	*Metallic green back and top of head; white belly; brown tail and wing primaries; long, slender bill. Adult male has red throat.*
SIZE:	*3 inches long with a wingspan of 4¾ inches.*
HABITS:	*Moves wings at fantastic speeds. Hovers while feeding. Is attracted to bright flowers.*
HABITAT:	*Gardens, woods.*
NEST:	*Bud scales lined with plant down and covered with small pieces of lichens fastened into place with spider webbing.*
EGGS:	*Chalk white, 2 in a clutch. Incubation 14–15 days.*
FOOD:	*Flowers, tiny insects.*
VOICE:	*Rapid, squeaky chirping.*

The smallest eastern bird, the ruby-throated hummingbird lays two eggs about the size of a pea in a nest that is about one inch in diameter. The nest is constructed out of bud scales, lined with down, and covered with tiny pieces of lichens fastened into place with spider webbing.

The ruby-throated hummingbird is the easiest bird to identify in the eastern part of the United States, simply because no other hummingbirds are found there. That does not preclude the possibility of someone mistaking it for a moth or butterfly. It is, after all, the smallest eastern bird, three inches long and with a wingspread of four and three-quarters inches. Its tiny size sometimes results in freak accidents. Hummingbirds have been known to get caught in spider webs and on the prongs of a burdock bush.

The hummingbird is so named because its wings move at such fantastic speeds that they do indeed hum. When this tiny bird hovers while feeding at a flower, its body, head, and tail are clearly visible, but its wings are mere blurs. Taking photographs of a hummingbird without specialized equipment, I discovered that my fastest camera shutter speed of 1/1,000 of a second was nowhere near fast enough to stop the action. By using an electronic flash, I got a speed of 1/2,500 of a second. Still not fast enough. By using two lights on the same flash unit, I pushed the speed up to 1/5,000 of a second. That wasn't fast enough, either. Not until I got a custom electronic flash that worked at 1/40,000 of a second did I have success. I not only got sharp photographs of the bird and wings but even needle-sharp photographs of the feathers on the wings. When a hummingbird hovers, its wings vibrate about sixty times per second. When it flies at top speed, the wings move two hundred times per second and perhaps more. This bird is unique in that it can fly up, down, forward, or backward with ease.

Many people are disappointed to find that the ruby-throated hummingbird does not always have a ruby throat. The female never does; her throat and belly, like the male's belly, are white. Frequently, the male's throat appears black instead of red. The red is seen only when light is reflected from the throat at the proper angle, then it glows as brightly as a wind-blown ember. And just as suddenly the color may be lost. The hummingbird's back and the top of its head are a dark metallic green, the wing primaries and tail are brown.

Hummingbirds winter in the tropics as far south as Panama and follow the advent of spring northward as far as southern Canada. They gauge their trip to coincide with the blooming of the flowers on which they feed, such as lilacs, horse chestnuts, bee balm, scarlet salvias, and many more. In addition to sipping nectar, these birds also consume many such tiny insects as aphids, spiders, and mites. On dark, wet, or cold days, while flowers remain closed, hummingbirds become somnolent, thus reducing their metabolism and food requirements.

In migration, males and females travel in separate flocks, the males preceding the females by about ten days. By the time the females arrive, the males have selected their territories. Th male ardently woos the female with a preliminary courtship flight in a large arc of about ten feet, like that prescribed by a hard-swinging pendulum. The female joins in the prenuptial flight, both birds flying a vertical path up and down for a distance of about five feet. When the female is up, the male is down, and so it goes. Shortly thereafter they mate and begin the job of preparing for the forthcoming family.

Apparently the courtship flight proves too strenuous for the male, because he does not assist in either building the nest or incubating the eggs. The tiny nest, about one inch in diameter, is formed chiefly of bud scales, lined with plant down, and covered with small pieces of lichens fastened into place with spider webbing. Most of the hummingbirds have two annual broods. The two chalk white eggs are about the size of a pea, or roughly one-quarter inch long and slightly less in diameter. Incubation takes about fourteen or fifteen days. Although the male does not brood the eggs or help to feed the young, he usually remains in the area and helps to drive away intruders.

Despite its diminutive size, the ruby-throat is fearless. If it feels its nest is threatened, it will attack regardless of the size of the aggressor. Thanks to its small size and high speed, it easily outflies a larger bird and has been seen chasing crows, hawks, and even an eagle. Black snakes, raccoons, and opossums eat the young.

Hummingbirds seem to favor red flowers, particularly such large, deep, tubular flowers as the trumpet vine. Actually, what attracts them is the relative brightness of the flower. People who do not have the proper flowers, and who still would like to have hummingbirds in their yards, often put up sugar-syrup stations. I purchased a set of three of these from the National Audubon Society. A syrup approximating nectar, made of two parts water and one part sugar, is placed in a sealed test tube. To get the syrup, the bird pokes its beak through a red artificial flower near the base of the tube and drinks the liquid. In the course of a day, one bird may drink about two teaspoons of such syrup.

According to the instruction sheet accompanying the feeders, the first hummingbird to discover them would tell all its friends and relatives, and the rush would be on. The hummingbirds that came to my feeders must have been antisocial; a single pair, male and female, sampled one of the feeders, but no others were allowed near. The fighting between these feathered sprites was too fast for the eye to follow. But there was still no sharing of the feeder.

15 Piciformes— Woodpeckers

A distinctive feature of the order Piciformes is the position of the outside front toe. It is turned toward the rear, so that these birds have two toes in front and two in the rear of approximately equal length. Among the members of the species *picoides* this outside toe is missing, so that these birds have only three toes.

Of the 6 family groups in this order only the Picidae are found in North America, being represented by 22 out of 224 species. All these woodpeckers have the strong, chisel-shaped beaks that are their working tools. The birds also use their bills to "drum" on trees, poles, and even electric transformers as a means of communication and to make the excavations they utilize as nest sites. The stiff, pointed tails are used to brace their bodies while drilling for insects. Most Picidae have long, pointed, sticky tongues, which are employed to withdraw the insect from its hole. Woodpeckers usually work from the base of a tree up to the top, then fly off to the base of another tree and start over again.

These birds fly with an undulating flight, flapping their wings three or four times, then folding them against their bodies, dropping into a shallow arc, then flapping to get back to the top of the arc. Some species migrate, others are year-round residents. Woodpeckers are not gregarious and, when disturbed, hop around to the far side of the tree to hide in much the same way a gray squirrel does.

With the exception of the yellow-bellied sapsuckers, woodpeckers do not harm the trees they feed on. They never drill into a live, healthy tree. The only time woodpeckers bore into a tree is *after* an injurious insect has already dug or chewed its way under the bark. Woodpeckers are symptoms of something wrong with a tree; they are not the cause.

Yellow-shafted Flicker
(*Colaptes auratus*)

FIELD MARKS:	*Buffy brown back and wings, whitish underparts with black spots, black bib, black moustache except in adult female, golden undersurface on wing and tail feathers, long tongue with barbed tip.*
SIZE:	*10½ inches long with a wingspan of 21 inches.*
HABITS:	*Undulating flight pattern. Prolific egg producers. Drilling into power and light poles.*
HABITAT:	*Open country near large trees.*
NEST:	*In dead trees.*
EGGS:	*Glossy white, 6–8 in a clutch. Incubation 12–13 days.*
FOOD:	*Carpenter ants, black and red ants, insects, berries, fruit.*
VOICE:	Flick, flick, flick.

The yellow-shafted flicker is our only brown-backed woodpecker. When flying overhead, the flicker's yellow wing and tail linings flash brilliantly in the sunlight.

I have always had a special fondness for the flicker, because it was the first bird I studied enough to write about. My observations did little for the world of ornithology, but they got me started in the nature-writing field at the tender age of eight.

At the time I was living in Paterson, New Jersey. In our backyard stood a large elm tree that had been killed by the Dutch elm disease. Flickers were common in the area, and one male made his presence known during the breeding season by using a metal electric transformer case for his sounding board. All through the early spring he would make his call, then drill so furiously on the metal that the reverberations sounded as though a machine gun had opened fire. Evidently this unique approach soon won him a mate, for in a short time two flickers were looking for a nesting spot. The elm tree they selected had been dead long enough to be partially rotten on the inside. When the flicker drilled into the wood, the rotted pieces he pulled out with his beak drifted away like sawdust. The flicker, like the Seven Dwarfs, apparently believed that he should whistle or sing while he worked, because he gave a loud call each time before hammering out another rotted piece of wood.

Many woodpeckers, flickers included, like to drill into power and light poles. This may explain some of the flicker's local names, such as "yellow hammer" and "high-hole." One example of poetic justice I'll never forget occurred the time flickers were burrowing into a telephone pole near my home. They had just finished the excavation and were about to begin laying their eggs when they were set upon by starlings. The starlings harassed the flickers constantly from morning until night. At last the flickers abandoned the nest, and the starlings promptly moved in. The starlings had been in possession of the nest for just about two weeks when the pole was removed by the phone company because it was in such poor condition. The flickers didn't get to use the nest they had worked so hard to build, but at least the starlings didn't get the benefit of the flickers' labor.

Although the carpenter ants, which riddle dead trees, are their main food, flickers more than any other woodpeckers gather much of their food on the ground. The red or black ants that tunnel into the earth and make anthills are avidly sought and eaten by the flickers. All woodpeckers have long tongues with barbed tips; these they insert in drilled holes to remove the ants or grubs inside. The flickers' tongue is longer than most woodpeckers' and can be extended for almost three inches beyond the tip of their beaks. When feeding on ground ants, flickers make no attempt to spear their prey. They simply extend their tongue into the anthill, and when the ants run out to attack the tongue, the flickers slurp them up. Flickers also feed on most other insects, as well as occasional berries and fruit.

Male and female flickers have a similar coloration: brown with black dots and a black bib, a red spot on the back of the head, and yellow undersides to the wings, which give the birds their name. The adult male is identified by a dark moustache-marking. The young of most other birds are marked like the female. In the flickers the juvenile plumage is like the male's, because the young of both sexes have the black moustache-marking that the young female loses when she becomes adult. Full-grown flickers measure ten and one-half inches long and have a wingspread of twenty-one inches.

The yellow-shafted flicker is a migratory bird. It winters in the southeastern United States, moving northward and westward as far as Alaska for the breeding season.

Flickers are extremely prolific. Although the usual clutch consists of six to eight glossy white eggs, about one inch long and somewhat narrower in diameter, many experiments have been conducted to see how many eggs a flicker would lay before giving up. In one instance, when the newly laid egg was removed each day, the female laid seventy-one eggs in seventy-three days. The eggs are incubated for twelve to thirteen days, and both parents join in the task of incubation as well as in the care and feeding of the young. One annual brood is common, but occasionally there may be two.

Starlings compete with the flicker for nest sites. Black snakes will feed upon both the eggs and the young while the adults are preyed upon by hawks and falcons.

Hairy Woodpecker
(Dendrocopos villosus)

FIELD MARKS:	*White back and belly, black wings with white spots and bars, long bill. Male has red spot on back of head.*
SIZE:	*10 inches long with a wingspan of 17½ inches.*
HABITS:	*Wings make noise when flying. No migration flights. Nesting occurs in April.*
HABITAT:	*Forests and woodlands.*
NEST:	*Cavity in a tree.*
EGGS:	*White, 4–5 in a clutch. Incubation 14 days.*
FOOD:	*Insects.*
VOICE:	*Loud peek.*

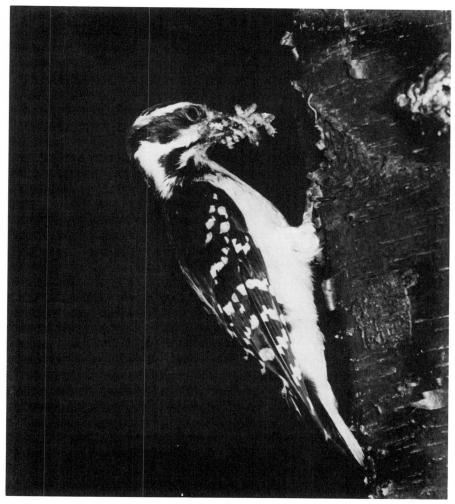

In order to protect their young, hairy woodpeckers drill very small entrance holes in the trees that hold the nests. The parents have a real struggle trying to squeeze into these holes when bringing food to the baby birds.

The hairy woodpecker is a forest dweller and much shyer than the smaller downy. Because our home is adjacent to, or perhaps I should say surrounded by, thousands of acres of woodland, the hairy woodpecker is a frequent visitor to my suet feeder. As it feeds, it keeps peering in our picture window to keep an eye on our activities. If anyone ventures out on the porch, the hairy takes off at the first click of the doorlatch, while the downy will continue to feed.

Both species have practically identical white and black, barred and spotted coloration, with a red patch at the back of the males' head. The hairy is larger, about ten inches long and with a wingspread of seventeen and one-half inches, and has a larger, heavier beak.

Some birds, the owls, for example, have soft pinions that make their flight noiseless; other birds, such as the doves, have such stiff pinions that their wings whistle when they fly. I first became aware of the stiffness of the woodpecker's pinions while working on my deer book. To gather data on the deer's movements and activities in our orchard, I used to stand among the upper limbs of one of the old apple trees. One evening in October I heard a *swish, swish, swish* sound. At first I couldn't locate the sound, but the next time it occurred, I noticed a hairy woodpecker fly by beneath me. It flew past, then back, then around again, its strong pinions making a highly audible sound. I couldn't imagine what the bird was trying to do; I hadn't moved, but the hairy was undoubtedly alarmed by my presence. At last, apparently satisfied that I didn't represent danger, it flew into a hollow limb jutting out from the main branch on which I was standing— I was standing on its residence. Once inside the hollow, the woodpecker settled down for the night and didn't fly out when I climbed off the tree a short time later.

The hairy woodpecker is found throughout the entire continental United States and in all the forested regions of Canada.

As the hairy woodpeckers are year-round residents, there are no main flights nor any great show of mating activities. The males call, but as a rule they do not make their presence known until they start excavating a nest site, generally in a dead tree. Both male and female share in the actual drilling operation, which usually occurs in April. Four to five white eggs, one-half inch in length and one-quarter inch in diameter, are laid, and incubation takes about fourteen days.

The parents are good foragers, and, as the woodlands usually abound with insects and caterpillars at this time, food gathering is no great problem. You can have few doubts about the great benefit of the hairy woodpeckers to the forest when you sit by, as I have, and see the multitudes and variety of insects for which these birds search. For about the first week the parent birds must climb into the nest cavity to feed the young. This always entails a struggle, because the entrance hole is smaller than the woodpecker's body.

When one of the parents returned with food, it clung to the outside of the tree for a considerable time. At last, prompted by the cries of the young, the parent inserted its head in the hole and went through violent, struggling motions before being able to squeeze inside. After the young were fed, the same battle ensued to get back out.

Watching all this, I wondered why the woodpeckers hadn't simply enlarged the entrance hole. It then dawned on me that birds don't have doors, and the small entrance hole was the only means the parents had of protecting the young. Within a week's time the young hairies were large enough to climb up inside the cavity and stick their heads out to be fed.

Tree-climbing snakes, such as the various black snakes, are the young's greatest enemies. Raccoons and opossums also try to feed on them. Because the adults usually sleep in hollows at night, owls are not important as enemies, but the Cooper's hawk and the goshawks are.

Man can be considered an enemy, not from direct persecution of the bird, but because he alters the bird's habitat. By cutting down entire forests and constantly removing dead or dying trees, man does the woodpecker great harm. He not only destroys the bird's potential nesting sites but its food larders as well.

Downy Woodpecker
(*Dendrocopos pubescens*)

FIELD MARKS:	*White back and belly; black wings with white bars; pointed, stiff tail feathers. Male has red spot on back of head. Distinguished from hairy woodpecker by smaller size and smaller bill.*
SIZE:	*7 inches long with a wingspan of 12 inches.*
HABITS:	*Frequently seen around human habitations. Stay in pairs all year around.*
HABITAT:	*Suburbs, orchards, woods.*
NEST:	*Hole in a dead tree.*
EGGS:	*White, 4–6 in a clutch. Incubation 12 days.*
FOOD:	*Insects and vegetable matter.*
VOICE:	*Rapid rattle descending in pitch.*

Our only white-backed woodpeckers, the downy and hairy woodpeckers have almost identical coloration. The downy woodpecker is the smaller of the two and has a much shorter bill.

The downy woodpecker is probably the best-known member of this family because it is the friendliest. Anyone who takes a few minutes to tie up a small piece of suet and attach it to a tree is sure to be rewarded with this bird's company. During the winter, when insects are scarce and the weather is cold, the suet gives real heat-building energy.

I play host to large numbers of birds at my feeding station in wintertime. One day, when feeding chickadees, I had my hand and arm outstretched. A downy woodpecker flew out of the tree and landed on my leg. He then proceeded to hop up until he had climbed into the large sleeve of my wool mackinaw, where he poked about for several seconds. Not finding anything to interest a woodpecker there, he flew out.

The downy is often confused with the hairy woodpecker because they are identical in appearance, except that the downy is slightly smaller, about seven inches in length and with a wingspan of twelve inches, and has a smaller bill. Their white and black, barred and spotted coloration is similar, and the males of both species have a patch of bloodred feathers on the back of the head. The stiff, sharply pointed tail feathers are used to brace their bodies against trees as they do their drilling.

Downies are found all over the country, and no place can lay a special claim to them. They inhabit as far north as Alaska all the way down to the Gulf Coast, but they shun the higher elevations and are seldom found in places with altitudes of more than three thousand feet.

My observations lead me to believe that the downies stay paired over most of the year. I see the same pairs feeding at my stations all year long. The only difference that I notice in their actions is that in the fall and wintertime the male insists on feeding first, even driving the female away should she be at the feeder ahead of him. During the breeding season, he allows the female to feed first. His gallantry at this time evidently atones for his past rudeness, and the female soon accepts his advances.

Most new nest sites are chosen and worked on in April. The downy seeks out a dead tree and excavates a hole inside up to ten inches deep and whatever diameter the width of the tree allows. The entrance hole is about one and one-quarter inches across. I have noted that dead birch trees are favored nesting locations for the downy, because these trees rot fast, and digging a hole in them is easy. The birch usually falls down within a year, but one season is all the bird needs.

Because the four to six eggs, little more than one-inch long and slightly narrower in diameter, are hidden in a cavity and will not be seen, they are white instead of having a camouflage pattern. Both male and female take turns incubating the eggs, which take about twelve days to hatch. One brood is raised per year. Two to three weeks must elapse before the little ones are large enough to fly. Again the parents share the job of feeding the young. Even after the youngsters have left the nest, they stay with the parents for a short time and are still fed by them.

During the period when the young are being reared, the food-gathering activity becomes frantic as the parents attempt to satisfy their youngs' incessant demand. The food of the downy consists primarily of insects gleaned by carefully searching the bark of trees and by excavating wood riddled by worms and other harmful insects. Occasionally the downy eats such vegetable matter as berries and seeds. Once in a while it imitates the sapsucker and eats part of the cambium layer of a living tree. This slight damage is more than offset by the tremendous good the bird does in consuming vast numbers of insects.

A little-known facet of this bird's diet is its large consumption of corn borers. Many times in the winter I have been out in fields from which the corn had been harvested but in which the stalks were still standing. The loudest sound in the cold air was the dry rasping of the old cornhusks rubbing against the dead stalks. Then, if you listened carefully, you could hear a faint *rat-tat-tat-tat*. Walking cautiously toward the sound, I soon discovered the downy woodpecker busily pounding away at the cornstalk. Most of the holes it drilled were directly above the joint of the stalk, because the downy knew this was a favorite spot to find the grub of the corn borer.

When a species of bird has only one brood a year, it is a good sign that this is enough for the species to keep its population stable. If predators took a large number of the species, it would raise more than one brood. The Cooper's hawk, sharp-shinned hawk, and goshawk are the main birds to prey on the downy, yet I seldom find the feathers of a downy scattered about in the woods to show where one has been killed.

16 Passeriformes—
Perching Birds

The order Passeriformes is the largest order of birds, containing 5,100 species, or about three-fifths of all the living birds of the world. These birds are considered last, because they represent the highest development in the evolution of birds. They also represent the greatest conflict among ornithologists and taxonomists, who cannot agree on the number of families—between 50 and 70—or the number of species—between 450 and 700—belonging to this order. North America has roughly 22 families, 14 of which are discussed, and 77 species, 23 of which are discussed.

The feet of these land birds are specially adapted to perching, with three short toes in front and an extra-long toe in the rear. It is this long rear toe that makes perching possible. The bird bends its leg when perching; this shortens a tendon in the rear toe so that it is locked into a closed position around the perch.

Many of these birds migrate south in winter, not because they can't stand the cold, but because insects are in short supply in the north at that time of year. On the other hand, many seedeaters among them do not migrate.

More than four thousand species of perching birds are classified as songbirds, because they have the syrinx muscles needed to make singing possible. There is a tremendous variation in the singing ability of the various species.

The family Tyrannidae consists of the tyrant flycatchers, so called because some of the species, such as the kingbird, are absolutely fearless and will attack any bird or mammal that may threaten them or their territory. The eastern phoebe is a member of this family.

The family Hirundinidae is made up of the martins and swallows. The name *swallow* comes from the Old Norwegian word *svalva*. These birds are always welcome around homes and outbuildings, and the birds respond by building their nests close to man or in the special homes man makes for them. Long before the coming of the white man, the American Indians put up clusters of gourds to establish martin colonies. Although the swallows do not fly as fast as the swifts, they spend more time in flight and are more agile, because their tail feathers can be used for steering.

Ranking as the most intelligent of all birds are the crows and jays, members of the family Corvidae. For this reason some ornithologists place them last on the list of birds: most experts today, however, place the seedeaters last. The seedeaters may be of more recent origin, but they do not compare to the Corvidae in intelligence. The crow is one of the few birds able to count. Although these birds are classified as songbirds, anyone who has heard their raucous cawing or shrill calls may wonder why.

The titmice and chickadees, among the friendliest little birds of the woodlands, comprise the family Paridae. The name titmouse is a conjunction of two old Anglo-Saxon words: *tit,* meaning "small," and *mouse,* the Anglicized version of *mase,* a common name for several small birds.

The only birds to spend more time climbing upside down than right side up are the nuthatches, of the family Sittidae. While hanging upside down, the nuthatch bends its head backward so that its bill is horizontal or raised above the level of the ground. Its name is a corruption of the word *nuthack,* because this bird hacks open the different types of nuts on which it feeds.

The wrens, of the family Troglodytidae, are little busybodies. So prolific and effusive is their song it doesn't seem possible that such an outpouring can emanate from a bird so small. The wrens hold several distinctions. One species has the most restricted range of any bird of North America. The Zapata wren is found only in a five-mile-square swamp in Cuba; it never leaves that area. Many North American birds have come from other continents. The wren is one of the few American birds to reverse the trend and to spread from this continent to Asia and Europe.

The mockingbirds, catbirds, and thrashers are all mimics and form the family Mimidae. They are related to, but scientifically distinct from, the wrens and thrushes. Although they are much larger and have much longer tails, the mimics are wrenlike in their friendliness and inquisitiveness. None of the other mimics can compete in song with the mockingbird, which is unsurpassed as the finest songster in the bird world.

Birds that are obviously thrushes and some that aren't immediately recognizable as thrushes make up the family Turdidae. Not until we compare the spotted breasts of the young robins and bluebirds does the relationship become apparent. The food of most of the thrushes is about evenly divided between animal and vegetable matter. Unfortunately their fondness for certain fruits and berries sometimes classifies several members of this family as nuisance birds. The majority, however, are beneficial.

The common starling belongs in the Old World family of Sturnidae and was deliberately introduced into North America. Other introductions have resulted in this bird being established almost everywhere except South America. Many of the birds of this order hop while on the ground, but the starling walks. These noisy, gregarious birds sometimes get together in flocks, which may number in the tens of thousands, and create a thunderous racket. It is only fitting that the myna bird, probably the most adaptive talking bird in the world, is a starling.

The vireos, members of the family Vireonidae, are birds of somewhat subdued coloring and habits. Not noted for the quality of their song, they are permitted by their quiet coloring and unobtrusive ways to inhabit an area unbeknownst to most people. Vireos feed primarily on insect life and are valuable additions to any woodland.

The family Parulidae, or wood warblers, is one of the most numerous bird families in North America, with fifty-three species. These birds are among the smallest and most confusing of our birds. As their name implies, they are woods-dwellers and perch at the top of the tallest trees in the area. During migration they appear in wave after wave to settle in the treetops.

No members of the subfamily Ploceidae are native to North America, for while we have many native sparrows, none is colonial. The two members of the sparrow weavers found on this continent have both been introduced by man. Today the house sparrow is the most widespread and most commonly known small bird in the world.

The name Icteridae comes from the Latin *icter,* meaning "yellow." While applicable to the orioles, the meadowlarks, and the bobolink, this name falls short for the grackles, the cowbird, and most of the blackbirds. These birds have widely varied food requirements, in the fulfillment of which some have become either allies of man or his greatest avian enemies. To make matters worse, the beneficial birds are not gregarious, while the nuisance birds are.

The Fringillidae family group is characterized by strong, short, conical bills, which are designed to crack the seeds that make up the bulk of its diet. These birds are strikingly dissimilar in coloration, some being exceedingly bright and gaudy, while the majority dress in somber tones and hues. They are for the most part gregarious, at least during the period of migration, in which the majority participate.

Eastern Phoebe
(*Sayornis phoebe*)

FIELD MARKS: *Dark gray above, whitish below, no conspicuous wing bars.*

SIZE: *5½–6½ inches long with a wingspan of 9–11 inches.*

HABITS: *Persistent tail wagging. Solitary by nature. Quiet courtship. Flycatcher. Nests under cover. Raises two broods of young in the same nest in the same year.*

HABITAT: *Around the haunts of man.*

NEST: *Mainly mud and moss.*

EGGS: *Pure white, 5 in a clutch. Incubation 15–17 days.*

FOOD: *Flys, mosquitoes, moths, spiders, caterpillars, and beetles.*

VOICE: *Fee-be, fee-be, fee-be.*

As the gradually waxing March sun slowly pushes daily temperatures higher, scores of insects creep out of crevices, cracks, and crannies to flutter about. Although representing only a fraction of the hordes that will follow, they are conspicuous after their absence during the winter months. Of only passing interest to the casual human observer, these flying insects provide nourishment to certain small, bright-eyed, tail-wagging birds that seem to appear almost simultaneously. The identity of these dark-headed birds with gray-brown upper parts, whitish under parts, and black bills, is seldom withheld. In muted tones they proclaim their name over and over again—*fee-be, fee-be, fee-be*.

The phoebe winters in our southeastern states from the Carolinas west to Oklahoma and Texas and south to the Gulf of Mexico. Its northward migration is governed by the advance of the warm weather that stirs from dormancy the insects on which it feeds. Other birds may symbolize spring's advance guard; the phoebe is spring's guarantee.

During much of the year the phoebe is solitary, but through preference, for it is not entirely antisocial. It displays belligerency only when a competing male tries to usurp an ancestral or a favored nesting site. About ten days after the males have selected their respective territories, the females arrive, and mates are soon chosen. Courtship is a quiet affair, unaccompanied by posturing or display, although the male is in almost constant attendance upon the female.

Before Europeans settled the North American continent, the phoebe used to build its nest on the sides of cliffs. Today this bird is almost always found around the haunts of man. The favored nesting sites are located under cover —under bridges and inside, on, or around farm buildings or house porches. Most of my life I have had phoebes build nests on the porches of the various homes where I have lived. In all my years of observing and photographing birds, I have found but two phoebe nests sited in the original manner and one of these, used year after year, is within an enclosed, sloping, abandoned mine shaft.

Although the phoebe's nest may have a liner of grass, plant fibers, or hair, it is constructed principally of mud and moss. Small gobs of mud are used rather than the mud pellets utilized by the barn swallow in its nest construction. The nest may be located on the top of a beam, if possible, or plastered directly on its smooth face. The female attends to the work of nest building, which is a leisurely procedure, often extending over a two-week period.

The usual clutch of five pure-white eggs, measuring about three-quarters of an inch in length and one-half inch in diameter, is laid during the week

Eastern phoebes usually lay five pure white eggs in a nest constructed mainly of mud and moss. The birds build their nests slowly and lay the eggs during the week following the completion of the nest.

following completion of the nest. Incubation is performed by the female and requires fifteen to seventeen days.

Phoebes are flycatchers, gathering most of their food while in flight. Unlike swallows and swifts, which sweep back and forth in catching their prey, phoebes sit on a favorite perch and make short forays to snap up a hapless insect as it flies past. Marvelously adroit on the wing, phoebes frequently hover in the air to snatch a spider or inchworm dangling on its gossamer thread.

Records describe phoebes feeding occasionally on small berries, yet I have never seen them do so. On the other hand, I have watched them by the hour as they snapped up flies, mosquitoes, moths, spiders, caterpillars, and beetles. Such feeding habits make the phoebes highly beneficial to man.

Both parent phoebes do yeoman work cramming food into the gaping mouths of their young, toiling from daylight to dark and sometimes beyond. Many an evening I have watched them snare the insects attracted to my porch light. Perched on top of the light, the phoebes have no need to fly; they simply snap up the insects as they hover about the light.

On their rich, high-protein diet, young phoebes grow rapidly. In about fifteen or sixteen days they are as large as their parents, measuring five and one-half to six and one-half inches in length and having a wingspread of nine to eleven inches. Although phoebes are preyed upon by woods hawks, black snakes, and an occasional marauding raccoon, their greatest enemies are parasites. While all birds have lice and mites, and the nests of all birds are infested with parasites, the phoebe is the only bird I know of that attempts to raise two broods of young in the same year in the same nest.

When a phoebe builds a new nest, some of the parasites from its body infest the nest, feed on the young as they hatch out, and, thus nourished, have a population explosion of their own. Young phoebes and parasites continue to grow apace, although the birds leave the nest before the parasites become much more than a nuisance. By the time a second brood of phoebes is hatched, however, the parasitic hordes almost smother and literally consume the young.

Barn Swallow
(*Hirundo rustica*)

FIELD MARKS: *Cobalt back, tawny underparts, deeply forked tail with white spots.*
SIZE: *6 inches long with a wingspan of 13½ inches.*
HABITS: *Strong, swift flight.*
HABITAT: *Near farms.*
NEST: *Mud and grass or straw.*
EGGS: *White with brown splotches, 4–5 in a clutch. Incubation 14 days.*
FOOD: *Insects.*
VOICE: *Twittering.*

In mid-August 1968 I was photographing the hordes of lesser flamingos at Kenya's Lake Nakuru when the air was suddenly filled with a loud twittering. Dozens of barn swallows appeared, their wings flashing as they darted through the air scooping up a good share of the myriad insects. According to well-known ornithologist Don Turner, the birds had just arrived on their wintering grounds after having flown thousands of miles from Europe. He assured me that these were the same type of barn swallows that I knew back home in New Jersey, which winter mainly in South America and breed in North America.

During the late fall or winter, while on their wintering grounds in South America, the swallows molt their feathers, and the young then appear identical to the parents in their buff and blue coats. When full grown, they measure about six inches long, have a wingspread of thirteen and one-half inches, and a forked tail.

The barn swallow does not arrive on its northern breeding grounds until long after most of the other migrants. A too-early arrival may coincide with a cold snap that would prevent the movement of insects, thus shutting off the swallow's food supply. A prolonged cold spell could cause the hungry birds to perish.

Whenever possible this swallow prefers to use the same nest it occupied the previous year. To renovate an old nest is easier than building a new one. Sometimes an old phoebe's nest is appropriated and put to use. Most barn swallow nests are built on the vertical surface of an exposed beam or ledge. If a nail or spike protrudes from the beam, the swallow is sure to incorporate it into the base of the nest as an anchor. A good source of mud and grass or straw is a must for nest construction. The mud must be rather "soupy," neither too firm nor too liquid. This the bird gouges out by the mouthful from a pond's edge or from puddles. The mud is then made into a pellet about the size of a small bean and made to adhere tightly to the beam and to each succeeding pellet, perhaps by the mucilaginous property of the bird's saliva. As a binder, small bits of grass, straw, and sometimes rootlets are mixed in the mud.

A disk of pellets is first cemented to the beam, then the bowl-shaped outward construction begins. It is comparatively easy to build vertically, because the top piece rests directly on the one beneath it. However, the swallow has to build not only up but also out, with the top pellet projecting beyond the one below. The bird builds the nest higher while sitting in the nest, thus making certain that the nest will accommodate its body. Ordinarily it takes a week or more for a pair of barn swallows to complete their nest, but I watched one pair complete a nest on a cabin porch at the Orange

Barn swallows are buff below and blue above and are our only swallows that are truly swallow tailed. As their name implies, the birds nest in barns on exposed ledges or beams.

Y.M.C.A. Camp on Fairview Lake, New Jersey, in just four days. The birds added as much as two inches of complete construction per day. At this same camp three barn swallows' nests were built inside overturned canoes stored across the rafters in the boathouse.

Except in the northernmost reaches of its range, the barn swallow raises two annual broods. A clutch of four to five brown-splotched white eggs, about three-quarters of an inch long and one-half inch in diameter, is common for this swallow. Both parents take turns incubating the eggs, with frequent changes so that both have ample opportunity to feed and exercise. Most clutches hatch in fourteen days, although some may take a little longer. At about the same time, the number of insects reaches its peak.

The parents feed the young constantly and in the course of a day harvest thousands of insects. Swallows are incessantly flying about catching insects over a much larger area than is covered by the phoebes, which catch insects that fly near their perch. Because swallows spend so much more time in

Barn swallows are swift and graceful flyers and can easily be identified by their flight. These birds often fly for sheer pleasure and like to play games in the air.

flight than the phoebes do, their metabolism is correspondingly higher and so is their food requirement. On their protein-rich diet, young swallows grow rapidly and within two weeks are able to leave the nest. Their dependency upon their parents lasts for another week, and then they are on their own.

In flight the swallow is without peer. It flies strongly, swiftly, and with great agility, revealing its true mastery of its ethereal element. After its food requirements have been met, the swallow is often so reluctant to sit quietly that it plays games. Many times I have watched a group of swallows, or even a single bird, carry a small, white chicken feather aloft, drop it, then dive and catch it, only to release it and repeat the performance again and again. Apparently this was done for sheer pleasure, although it can also provide excellent training for the younger birds.

As a boy I was raised on a farm, which means that I was raised with barn swallows. The swallows' appearance each spring was as much an accepted part of my life as the new growth of crops or the summer vacation from school. The birds' name, too, was particularly apt, because the barn was where the swallows lived. Their constant comings and goings were watched with great interest, and I could study their family life, carried on right above my head, as I milked the cows.

Today, unfortunately, barn swallow populations are declining, because modern farming methods are denying them the use of the traditional nesting sites. Before the coming of the white man, these swallows used to build their nests on the sides of sheer cliffs, in caves, or in rock fissures. Gradually they began to build in barns, wagon houses, under the eaves of buildings, or under bridges. Our modern sanitation laws prohibit exposed beams in cow barns, and farmers build enclosed garages instead of open wagon houses. Where a few years ago a dozen barn swallows might nest on one farm, today only two or three, or perhaps none at all, nest there.

Blue Jay
(*Cyanocitta cristata*)

FIELD MARKS: *Turquoise-cobalt wings and tail, white belly and white bar and spots on wings, gray-blue above, conspicuous crest. Only crested blue bird in the East.*

SIZE: *12 inches long with a wingspan of 17 inches.*

HABITS: *Stores away food for the future. Extremely noisy. Eats the eggs of other birds. Erects its crest when alarmed or excited.*

HABITAT: *Oak and pine woods.*

NEST: *Twigs with a lining of rootlets.*

EGGS: *Greenish, 3–6 in a clutch. Incubation 16–17 days.*

FOOD: *Insects, berries, fruit, grain, acorns.*

VOICE: *Loud* cant, cant *or shrill tweetling whistle.*

246

Blue above and whitish below, the blue jay is one of our most attractive birds. The jay's crested head and black neck band further enhance its beauty.

With its bright plumage, cocky, pointed beak, and crested head, the blue jay is one of our most attractive birds, yet it is often condemned for its actions. Cited is the fact that in the springtime it eats the eggs of other birds and, occasionally, even eats baby birds. Furthermore the blue jay is noisy, arrogant, and a bully around bird-feeding stations. These allegations are all true. Still it seems unfair to criticize the blue jay for behaving in the way that is natural to it.

When this jay is alarmed or excited, which seems to be most of the time, it raises its blue crest. Its back and rounded, black-barred wings and tail are bright blue. The face and underparts are white, and white also marks the wings and tail. Being larger than most of the other birds, about twelve inches in length and with a seventeen-inch wingspread, the blue jay automatically enjoys a decided advantage over most of its competitors.

The old-fashioned term "common scold" perfectly describes this jay. Nothing passes through the area it inhabits without an expression of opinion or comment. Its shrill call ringing through the forest alerts other creatures and puts them on their guard, thus inadvertently making the jay an ally of every wild creature in the vicinity.

Its strident call, together with its brilliant coloration, not only calls attention to everything that moves but also to the jay itself, an ultimately disastrous procedure. Woods hawks, such as the Cooper's and the sharp-shinned, take a large toll of these birds. I find the feathers and remains of more jays than I do of all other birds combined.

The blue jay ranges from Newfoundland and Quebec to Alberta, south to Colorado and Virginia. Large numbers may migrate farther south each winter. Every spring an odd drama is enacted at Sandy Hook, New Jersey. The jays flying north along the coast follow the sandy spit out to its terminus, then, fearful of continuing over water to New York, many turn south and fly along the western shore until they reach the mainland. They

Blue jays construct their bulky nests in heavy cover close to the trunks of trees. The nests are made of twigs and rootlets and are supported by several branches.

Insects, particularly grasshoppers, are the primary elements in a young blue jay's diet, but the immature birds will also take berries, fruits, and grain.

then turn east, fly north again along the coast, and repeat the entire performance. Some of the jays spend weeks engaging in this fruitless flight. Other birds make the short overwater flight with no difficulty.

Jays like to nest in heavy cover, preferably in evergreen trees. They tend to place the nest close to the tree trunk, supported by several branches. Bulky, though neat, the nest is made out of twigs and has a lining of fine rootlets. Three to six greenish eggs, about one inch long and one-half inch in diameter, comprise a clutch. Both of the parent birds incubate the eggs for a period of sixteen to seventeen days.

After the young hatch, they are fed all types of food, with insects, caterpillars, and other animal matter heading the list. As the birds grow older, some berries, fruits, and perhaps grain, are added to the menu. During this period, when the blue jay has its own young to care for, it makes its greatest depredations against other birds; this, however, is true of all creatures with young.

The blue jay has one characteristic which is not too well known. It is one of the few birds with enough foresight to store away food for the future. During the early fall, when the oaks are divesting themselves of acorns, the jay busily gathers them. This activity puts the bird into direct competition with the squirrel. Both creatures go through the same process of gathering the fallen nuts and then burying them in the forest floor for future use. Those that are dug up later are used for food. The surplus nuts, or those that are forgotten or missed, eventually sprout, take root, and may become trees. Obviously both squirrel and blue jay deserve the credit for many of our beautiful hardwood forests.

Steller's Jay
(Cyanocitta stelleri)

FIELD MARKS:	*Cobalt blue with dark crest and shoulders. Only crested blue bird in the West.*
SIZE:	*11–13 inches long with a wingspan of 18–19 inches.*
HABITS:	*Robs other birds' nests. Noisy when curious or displeased. Extremely bold.*
HABITAT:	*Coniferous forests.*
NEST:	*Bulky twigs, mud, and rootlets.*
EGGS:	*Greenish blue, 3–4 in a clutch. Incubation 14–16 days.*
FOOD:	*Nuts, fruits, berries, insects.*
VOICE:	*Raucous and varied calls.*

Bluer than the blue jay, the Steller's jay is our only western crested jay. The bird erects its crest when excited or frightened.

Jays everywhere are bold, brazen, brassy, and beautiful. The Steller's jay, the only western crested jay and the counterpart of the eastern blue jay, has even more blue than its eastern cousin. The blue is deeper and richer, and there is practically no white on the body. Head, crest, and upper neck are sooty black; wings and tail are barred with black. The largest jay in the country, this bird measures about eleven to thirteen inches in length and has a wingspread of eighteen and nineteen inches. Various subspecies of Steller's jays are found from Baja California north to Alaska, where the first specimen was collected by German naturalist Georg Wilhelm Steller, who accompanied Vitus Bering on his voyage of discovery to Alaska in 1741.

It is not unusual for these jays, as inhabitants of predominantly coniferous forests, to prefer conifers as nesting sites. Their preference seems to be based on the fact that evergreen needles provide greater concealment than do leafless deciduous trees. When the birds raise a second brood, a deciduous tree is often chosen, because by that time the leaves are out and the protection factor is equalized.

Usually the nest is situated at a moderate height between eight and sixteen feet. It appears to be a slapdash construction, but close examination proves otherwise. The base is composed of bulky twigs that the bird either picks up from the ground or snaps off a tree. A thick layer of mud cements the sticks in place. Rootlets are then placed in the mud and are woven together.

When the nest construction is finished, the female lays three or four greenish blue eggs, about one and one-quarter inches long and seven-eighths of an inch in diameter. The parents take turns incubating the clutch; in fourteen to sixteen days the job is done. In two more weeks the young birds are fledged. Even though they can fly from the nest, young jays continue to be dependent upon the parents for at least another week.

Like all jays the Steller's jay has no compunction about robbing other birds' nests, but they are quick to put up a good defense when their own nest is threatened by their chief enemy, the hawk. In an area where there are orchards or gardens, the jay is often considered a nuisance, because it shows a decided preference for nuts, fruits, and berries of many different kinds. The fact that it also consumes a great many harmful insects is a plus mark on the other side of the ledger. This type of diet makes the wilderness jay a tremendous asset.

The Steller's jay has a varied repertoire of calls. These may differ in tone but are similar in volume; all are loud. The jay's habit of scolding anything about which it is curious or displeased does not endear it to hunters. For a hunter to be discovered by a jay while attempting a stealthy stalk is a disaster. The clamor set up by these birds alarms everything in the countryside. As the hunter moves along, the jays keep pace, effectively pinpointing his location.

I met my first Steller's jay in California's Yosemite National Park. We didn't have a formal introduction; the jay simply invited itself to my picnic lunch. The only reason I got anything to eat is that I was bigger than the jay.

The day was hot, so instead of eating lunch in my camper, I made up a couple of sandwiches and sat at a picnic table under a fir tree, enjoying the soft breeze. In a matter of minutes I had company as the jays arrived. One, bolder than the rest, landed on the table and hopped my way, crest fully erected, tail twitching nervously. Closer and still closer it hopped. Anxious to see what it would do, I didn't move. When it reached my plate, the jay made a hasty stab at my sandwich, but the butter had bonded the bread to the meat and cheese. Although the jay's spirit was willing, it just couldn't carry the load but managed to tear out a strip of the soft bread, and with this prize retreated to a nearby tree to feed. Emboldened, the other jays flew down and closed in. Hungry myself, I made a compromise: I ate the meat and cheese and tore the bread to shreds for the jays. Thinking always of photographs, I retrieved my cameras as well as more bread from my camper and was rewarded with the photographs that appear here.

Common Crow
(*Corvus brachyrhynchos*)

FIELD MARKS:	*Completely black. Most commonly seen black bird.*
SIZE:	*21 inches long with a wingspan of 39 inches.*
HABITS:	*Posts a sentinel while feeding. Travels in large flocks. Roosts in communities.*
HABITAT:	*Woodlands, farmlands, river groves, shores.*
NEST:	*Well-made bowl of sticks, lined with cedar bark and deer hair.*
EGGS:	*Greenish with spots, 3–5 in a clutch. Incubation 15–18 days.*
FOOD:	*Corn, baby birds, eggs, berries, fruit, melons, insects, carrion.*
VOICE:	*Distinctive caw.*

Although smaller than the raven, the crow is larger than most other black birds, measuring twenty-one inches in length with a wingspan of up to thirty-nine inches.

The solid black crow and its raucous cawing are familiar in practically every part of the United States. It is not easy to get a really good look at a crow, for man spells danger, and all crows respond accordingly. Also, because the crow may well be our most intelligent bird, it has no trouble staying out of man's way. It is able not only to hold its own but even to increase its numbers.

In a well-made nest situated high in the top of a tree forty to sixty feet from the ground, the female lays her three to five brown-splotched greenish eggs, measuring slightly less than one and one-half inches long and slightly more than one inch in diameter. The incubation period is fifteen to eighteen days. Every crow's nest I have seen has been lined with deer hair to make it softer for the young.

The parent crows are good food gatherers and keep their offspring from going hungry. Pinfeathers sprout and are worn off as the baby crows gradually obtain their black plumage. The young are able to leave the nest in about three weeks. When full grown, a crow measures about twenty-one inches in length, has a wingspread of up to thirty-nine inches, and weighs up to twenty ounces.

Crows eat almost everything, and where they follow the dictates of their appetites, their interests clash with man's. They are best known for attacks on newly planted corn. Crows become busy as the first sprouts of corn thrust up through the earth. At this time the dried kernel of corn has absorbed moisture and becomes soft and edible. Baby birds of all types, eggs, berries, fruit, and melons are also listed on the crows' menu. Carrion and animals killed on the highway provide the bulk of their diet through the winter months.

As the nesting period draws to a close, the crows start to band together in flocks numbering into the hundreds. When the flock feeds, sentinels are posted on the perimeter, so that it is almost impossible to approach the flock undetected. At the first call of alarm from the sentry, the entire flock takes wing.

The flock appears to take pleasure in heckling and molesting every owl or hawk it can find in its travels, diving at the victim and pestering it relentlessly. In the case of the owl, particularly, the crows do their best to drive the bird right out of the country; they well know that at night the owl is not above killing a sleeping crow and using it as a meal. The raccoon, too, is a threat.

As cold weather approaches, the flocks grow larger, and many crows migrate to a warmer climate. Some of the flocks that remain behind may number between ten and twenty thousand birds. These flocks scatter over the countryside every day to feed, but return at night to a central location to roost together. Some crow roosts become well known and are used year after year. At other times the location of the roost is moved from one area to another, if the crows are molested.

The crows usually gather in fields adjacent to their roost from about three to five in the afternoon. Then, just as darkness descends, the entire flock lifts like a dark cloud and flies into the woods to the roost, where they settle down for the long winter's night.

In spite of their depredations against cultivated crops, it must be recorded that crows do a great deal of good by consuming tons and tons of insect pests. Crows also frequent garbage dumps, where, by their competition for the available food, they help keep down the number of rats.

Crows are very intelligent birds and are extremely wary of danger. They always post sentinels to protect the flock when they are feeding.

Black-capped Chickadee
(Parus atricapillus)

FIELD MARKS:	*Black patch on head and beneath throat, light gray back and wings, white cheek patches and belly.*
SIZE:	*5¾ inches long with a wingspan of 8½ inches.*
HABITS:	*Undulating flight pattern. Extremely friendly. Roosts in tree cavities.*
HABITAT:	*Woodlands.*
NEST:	*Natural tree cavities.*
EGGS:	*White with brown spots, 4–12 in a clutch. Incubation 12 days.*
FOOD:	*Insects and their eggs.*
VOICE:	*Whistle* chick-a-dee-dee-dee-dee.

The chickadee is a small bird with a black head and throat, and white cheek patches. The black-capped chickadee is about five and three-quarter inches long with a wingspan of eight and one half inches.

If a bird popularity contest were ever held, I am sure the black-capped chickadee would win hands down. No other bird family is as universally friendly and beloved as that to which the chickadee belongs.

In the wintertime, when most other birds have forsaken the greater part of the eastern United States for sunnier climes, the black-capped chickadee comes down from the north to enliven our woodlands and our lives. The rougher the weather, the more frigid the wintry blasts, the more cheerful the chickadee becomes, or at least its cheerfulness becomes more evident when contrasted with its surroundings. Hanging onto a wind-tossed birch or aspen tree, the chickadee, with feathers fluffed out, searches for food and keeps the woodland alive with its *chick-a-dee-dee-dee-dee.*

A black-capped chickadee takes sunflower seeds from between the author's lips. These tame birds are very friendly and may be trained to take food from humans.

The chickadee is one of our smaller birds, measuring about five and three-quarters inches long, of which two and one-half inches represent its tail. It has a wingspread of eight and one-half inches and an undulating flight pattern. The reason for its common name is instantly apparent: The top of its head and its throat are jet black, as are its tiny eyes, which would be almost impossible to see if they were not so bright. Cheek patches and belly are white, back and wings slate gray. As both sexes are similarly colored, they are indistinguishable at just a cursory examination.

A cavity-nesting bird, the chickadee seeks out such a spot in which to roost. I can always tell which of the chickadees using my bird feeder is sleeping in a small cavity: Its tail usually is badly bent. When the breeding season draws near, the bird seeks out natural hollows in trees or nests that have been abandoned by woodpeckers. Birdhouses, too, are frequently utilized. If a suitable cavity cannot be found, the chickadee soon remedies this situation by excavating a nest of its own in a dead birch tree. There may be two annual broods.

Nesting takes place from April until July. Four to twelve eggs may be laid in one clutch. The eggs, slightly less than one-half inch long and one-quarter inch in diameter, are predominantly white with a scattering of brown spots. Both male and female help with the incubation, which takes about twelve days. They are most devoted parents.

Insects and their eggs form the bulk of the chickadee's diet. Most of the insects are sought in their hiding place beneath the bark and in the crevices of trees. In searching for their food, the birds hop right on around the limb so that almost half of the time they are hanging upside down. Many types of plant and weed seeds are also eaten. Peanuts are the most favored food at bird feeders, with sunflower seeds a close second. A piece of suet will be visited daily and helps the chickadees to gain the fat needed to combat the cold weather.

With a little patience these birds can be coaxed to feed on your outstretched hand. I have the birds in my area trained to land on my chin and take sunflower seeds from between my lips. Guests arriving at my house are often startled by chickadees flying down and alighting on their heads and shoulders as they walk up onto the porch. The birds are merely looking for a handout, as they know I always carry seeds in the pockets of my jackets. They must think everyone else does too.

Chickadees are so small they are seldom bothered by the larger predators. Then, too, they are usually near dense cover into which they slip at the first sign of a hawk. These little birds more frequently do damage to themselves by flying into such objects as tree branches and limbs. Quite often chickadees fly against the glass windows of houses, yet their survival rate is high on the whole.

Being so small and leading such active lives, chickadees have a high metabolism rate and seldom live for more than three or four years. That the same groups of birds return to my area each year can be proved, for I can always walk out and call them down out of the trees to welcome them back each fall.

Tufted Titmouse
(Parus bicolor)

FIELD MARKS:	*Medium gray back and tail; white throat, breast, and belly; dark crest; black patch above bill; rufous patch on flanks; tufts. Only tufted gray bird found east of the Mississippi River.*
SIZE:	*5½–6 inches long with a wingspan of 10 inches.*
HABITS:	*Carries food to a tree limb to eat. Stores away surplus food. Travels in mixed flocks.*
HABITAT:	*Forests and woodlands. sticks, hair, and fur.*
NEST:	*Tree cavities lined with bark, moss, leaves, sticks, hair, and fur.*
EGGS:	*White with brown dots, 5–6 in a clutch. Incubation 12 days.*
FOOD:	*Insects, berries, nuts.*
VOICE:	*Clear whistled* peto, peto.

Tufted titmice are very sociable birds and often travel in mixed flocks. They usually associate with chickadees and juncos.

Its crest makes the tufted titmouse one of the easiest birds to recognize. Other birds with upstanding, visible crests—such as the blue jay, the cardinal, and the kingfisher—are much larger, more brightly colored, and better known. The tufted titmouse can easily be distinguished from its own close relatives, the three other titmice, because their ranges do not overlap. The tufted titmouse is the only species found east of the Mississippi River.

Five and one-half to six inches in length, this little bird has a wingspan of about ten inches, and a soft, dove gray back and tail. The crest is slightly darker, and there is a black patch above the bill. The face, throat, breast, and belly are white. A conspicuous rufous patch adorns the flanks, and the tail is slightly notched.

Many people seem to think that the tufted titmouse is a bird of the northern forests and that it comes down to their feeders in the wintertime. Actually, it is primarily a bird of the southeastern forests, having a range that extends from Florida north to Massachusetts, west to Iowa, and south again to Texas. It is not migratory but subject to seasonal, localized movements. While showing a definite preference for the woodlands, the titmouse moves into marginal and suburban areas in the wintertime because of the food made available to it at bird feeders. In these areas the titmouse is usually the most common bird at the feeders.

Such delicacies as sunflower seeds, raisins, peanuts, peanut butter, and suet easily lure the titmouse to a feeder. In the forest the bird feeds mainly on caterpillars, wasps, beetles, ants, spiders, and moths. When the adults of these insects become scarce, the bird seeks out and eats the egg cases, or larvae. In season it also consumes wild raspberries, strawberries, hackberries, blueberries, and elderberries. Chinquapins, beechnuts, and acorns are also taken. The titmouse does not like to feed on the ground, much preferring to carry its food to a tree limb, where it is sheltered by branches. As the bird cannot open its mouth far enough to pick up an acorn, it solves the problem by simply impaling the acorn with its beak. Its prize thus secured, the titmouse can then fly to a safe perch.

The bird opens sunflower seeds and acorns in the same manner. Perching on a small branch, it holds the acorn or seed firmly between its toes and against the solid limb as though it were an anvil. With its short, strong, chisel-shaped beak, the bird hammers at the shell or husk. A few sharp blows pierce the outer covering, which is removed, and the food is then broken into pieces small enough to be eaten.

When more food is available than can be eaten at the moment, the titmouse stores the surplus away in a nook or cranny in the rough tree bark. This bird feeds before storing the surplus; the nuthatch stores everything, then feeds.

The tufted titmouse is a cavity-nesting bird. For nesting, it uses such natural cavities as it can find in trees with rotted hearts or where limbs have fallen off. Lacking these, it uses abandoned nest sites of the flicker, the downy, and the hairy woodpeckers. I have seen the titmouse use a birdhouse and believe this to be a widespread practice. It also uses cavities for shelter, particularly in winter. I can almost tell the size of the hole a bird sleeps in by the way its tail feathers are bent in the morning. A hole with a diameter of from three to four inches puts quite a kink in feathers. Sometimes a tail is bent so far to one side, it is a miracle the bird can fly in a straight line.

Titmice have paired up and are nesting in April. After locating a suitable cavity, they haul in shredded bark, moss, leaves, sticks, hair, and fur. A lining of hair or fur seems to be a must for their nest, and they go to great lengths to obtain it—pulling hair from dogs, squirrels, horses, and even woodchucks. Actually, most of the hair or fur is obtained from carcasses of animals that have been killed or have died in the forests. During the courting season, the birds have several songs, the most common one sounding like *peto, peto.*

When the nest has been completed, the five or six eggs, about one-half inch long and one-quarter inch in diameter, are laid. The white eggs have small dots of various shadings of brown sprinkled liberally all over but concentrated on the large end. Both parents incubate the eggs, which take twelve days to hatch. The young are fed in the nest for fifteen to sixteen days before they are large enough to leave it. Even for a week or so after leaving, some of the young may return to the nest at night. In the northern part of their range, tufted titmice have one brood annually; in the southern part, two.

Although less trusting than black-capped chickadees, titmice are sociable birds and like the company not only of their own kind but also of chickadees and juncos. Mixed flocks are often seen traveling together in the wintertime. The family groups usually do not split up until the following spring, when the courtship period approaches.

The titmouse's principal enemy is the hawk.

If they have sufficient food, tufted titmice can brave the severest winter storms. It seems odd that birds whose main range is the deep south prefer to stay in an area where temperatures may drop below zero—which only serves to prove the theory that lack of food brought about by cold weather, not the cold weather itself, drives birds south. When the temperature plummets, the titmice simply eat more. After feeding, they retire to a cavity or sit in a shaft of sunlight, fluffing out their feathers until they resemble little balls. The air trapped between the fluffed feathers provides excellent insulation. A bird's body temperature usually ranges above 104° to 110° F. However, in cold weather the flow of blood to the legs is restricted, and the temperature of their extremities drops to about 38° F. This cold blood is not allowed to circulate freely through the bird's body, as it would have a tremendous cooling effect upon its whole system. To warm its feet while perched, the bird raises one foot at a time and tucks it in among its feathers.

The titmouse is a valuable ally to every forest because its food habits are entirely beneficial to man. In addition its bright, cheerful, friendly ways make winter seem less severe.

White-breasted Nuthatch
(Sitta carolinensis)

FIELD MARKS:	*Blue-gray upper parts, white breast and face, black cap on male, rounded tail tip. Only black-capped nuthatch with white cheeks.*
SIZE:	*5 inches long with a wingspan of 11½ inches.*
HABITS:	*Stores food before eating it. Usually travel in pairs.*
HABITAT:	*Deciduous woodlands.*
NEST:	*Cavity lined with bark, twigs, hair, fur, and feathers.*
EGGS:	*Light with dark brown blotches and spots, 7–9 in a clutch. Incubation 12 days.*
FOOD:	*Insects and vegetable matter.*
VOICE:	*Call* yank *repeatedly.*

White-breasted nuthatches are very acrobatic and are often seen running down the trunk of a tree headfirst. Nuthatches are the only tree-climbing birds to perform this feat.

The white-breasted nuthatch is a veritable dynamo, a real powerhouse of energy, on the go from morning to night. I know of no other bird so constantly and gainfully employed.

This bird is a sort of tree doctor. With its rapierlike bill, the nuthatch probes in, around, and under the bark and crevices of trees to seek out the insect life that may be hidden or hibernating there, in the process ridding the trees of many of the insects that may do them harm. The nuthatch cannot bore into a tree, woodpeckers do that; instead, the nuthatch concentrates on such insects as spiders, ants, moths, beetles, and caterpillars, which have not or do not bore into trees. Because it does not have to hammer at hard wood with its beak, this bird has no need to brace its body against the tree with its tail as the woodpeckers do, and consequently it has a rounded tail tip in place of the woodpecker's pointed one. Freed from the necessity of bracing its body against the tree for support, the nuthatch is more acrobatic and spends as much of its time climbing about upside down as it does right side up.

Slightly larger than the juncos and chickadees, the nuthatch is about five inches in length and has a wingspread of eleven and one-half inches. Males and females are look-alikes, with bluish gray upper parts and white under-parts, except that the female has a grayish cap and the male's is jet black.

Five subspecies of the white-breasted nuthatch blanket the United States, with the exception of the Great Plains areas. These birds prefer a deciduous forest to a coniferous one. Because they come so readily to bird feeders, they are among our best-known birds. Many people think of the nuthatch as strictly a winter visitor, but this is not so. The white-breasted nuthatch undertakes little seasonal movement; it usually breeds in the same area where it is found in the winter. The bird is seen more frequently in winter because food shortages concentrate birds in areas where feeders are located, and because most people do not feed birds in the summertime.

White-breasted nuthatches do not migrate and usually appear in pairs during the winter as well as during the rest of the year. In wintertime the male feeds first, but in the spring he presents food to the female. Although no virtuoso, the male frequently sings for the female at this time.

In early April the nuthatches seek a nest cavity. Because natural cavities are scarce, an abandoned flicker nesting hole is usually chosen. Once a site has been selected, shreds of bark and small twigs are gathered, and, when available, pieces of wool, hair, fur, and even feathers are also utilized. Both birds may gather the material, but the female does most of the nest-making.

Although the white-breasted nuthatch has only one annual brood, it is large. Seven to nine dark brown splotched and spotted, light eggs, a little more than one-half inch long and one-quarter inch in diameter, are commonly laid. The male may or may not participate in the task of incubation, which takes twelve days, but he is an industrious helper when it comes to feeding the young.

After the young have left the nest, the family may stay together until early winter. Some of the young appear reluctant to come to a bird feeder at first, but they soon overcome such reticence.

Although insects represent the bulk of its diet, the nuthatch also eats such vegetable matter as acorns, beechnuts, spilled grain, and seeds. In spite of its name, the nuthatch cannot crack the heavy shells of walnuts. It cracks other nuts, seeds, or kernels by forcing them into a tight spot in the rough tree bark, which forms a natural vise, then hammering away with its beak until pieces small enough to be swallowed break off. If a piece of food falls toward the ground, the nuthatch dashes after it, sometimes actually catching it before it lands. Then the bird hops back up the tree and goes to work again.

When this bird comes into a feeder, it selects the peanuts first and makes off with them. The sunflower seeds are next on the agenda, followed by the dried corn, either whole or cracked. It is also extremely fond of suet, and a large chunk will be visited steadily after the seeds are consumed. To a large extent the suet supplements the bird's diet of insects and is also a rich fuel for its internal furnace, allowing the bird to easily withstand the coldest temperatures. Peanut butter is another favorite food of the nuthatch.

For years I have been playing with the birds that come to my feeders each winter. I can go out on the porch, hold sunflower seeds in my hand or between my lips, and give a high-pitched whistle. This sound attracts all the birds in the area. Although the chickadees swarm down to feed, the nuthatches do not. They are driven almost frantic by this burst of feeding activity, which they are wary of joining. They fly into the fir tree, hop along the branches, climb up and down the trunk, flutter about and make passing dives down toward my hand, and give their *yank* call repeatedly. In all the time I have worked with them, only one nuthatch has ever responded. These birds simply can't force themselves to come in to feed from my hand, but as soon as I fill up the feeder and walk away five or six feet, they fly right in with the other birds.

When several birds land at the feeder at one time, there is very little actual conflict or contact but a great deal of bluffing and intimidation. The white-breasted nuthatches usually do more threatening, bluffing, and blustering than any of the other birds. While so engaged, they flare out their tails and wings and rock back and forth sideways with the bill wide open, presenting a frightening appearance. The other birds do not appear to be unduly alarmed, recognizing it as a meaningless threat. At other times nuthatches, while not particularly gregarious, can be sociable and appear to enjoy the company of chickadees.

Nuthatches spend little time in actual feeding at the bird feeder. They fly in, snatch the food, and fly off to secrete the nut, seed, or kernel in a safe storage space. Most of the storage spaces are no more than one hundred feet from the feeder. In my yard nuthatches tuck the seeds beneath the bark of the giant fir trees, under the overlapping metal sheets on the front porch roof, under the eaves of the new house addition, behind the furring laths on the old barn, and in the splits of the old apple tree stumps.

The nuthatch may fluff out its feathers and doze for a while in the weak sunlight of a winter's day, a siesta that apparently has a completely revitalizing effect. The rest of the afternoon is spent probing for insects or pilfering some of the stores of the other nuthatches. There is no great animosity between the nuthatches over this activity, because each seems to be continuously "borrowing" from its neighbor.

Principal among the predators of the nuthatch are small hawks, which eat the adults, and black snakes, which devour the young.

House Wren
(*Troglodytes aedon*)

FIELD MARKS:	*Sepia above, lighter underparts, indistinct eye stripe, lightly cross-barred. Grayest of the wrens.*
SIZE:	*4½ inches long with a wingspan of 7 inches.*
HABITS:	*Very aggressive and energetic. Cocks its tail over its back. Responds to birdhouses. May attack other birds' nests.*
HABITAT:	*Shrubbery and brush.*
NEST:	*Twigs.*
EGGS:	*White with brown spots, 10–12 in a clutch. Incubation 11–13 days.*
FOOD:	*Insects.*
VOICE:	*Buzzy song.*

The plainest wrens, house wrens have grayish brown coats and an indistinct eye stripe. They may be distinguished from other wrens by their lack of a dark belly.

Without a doubt, more birdhouses are built every year for house wrens than for any other species of birds. The word *birdhouse* seems to be almost synonymous with house wren. With the possible exception of the English, or house, sparrow, this wren responds to birdhouses more readily than do any other birds. Some people are carried away with the birdhouse idea and have dozens in their yards, with no regard for a bird's personal territory requirements. A bird requires this personal territory to ensure possession of an area large enough to supply its food needs and those of its brood. Too many birds of one species packed into the same area would result in a shortage of food and eventual starvation.

Most birds only drive out birds of their own species, but the house wren tries to drive out all other birds as well. Even though different species usually have different food habits, and so are not directly competitive, the wren tries to reign supreme over its territory. This little bird can be extremely aggressive and actually attacks other birds' nests, puncturing their eggs or killing the young. I once watched in amazement—and finally stopped—a wren as it dragged baby bluebirds from a birdhouse and attempted to throw them to the ground below.

Both sexes look alike in their grayish brown coats and with their narrow, rounded tails, but the male is a little darker hued. Adults are four and one-quarter inches long and have a wingspread of seven inches.

The "buzzy" song with which the wren fills the air from morning to night is enjoyed by some persons and detested by others. I happen to like

When unable to find a suitable birdhouse, house wrens display a tremendous amount of ingenuity in locating nesting sites. Wrens will nest almost anywhere and are often found in the most amazing and unlikely places.

to hear a wren singing. It is considered impolite for anyone to sing or talk, or to attempt to sing or talk, with one's mouth full of food. Knowing nothing about etiquette, the wren proceeds to sing full blast regardless of whether it has food in its mouth or not. And if the wren is gathering food for its young, its mouth is usually full.

One thing is certain: No one can call the wren a sluggard. It is one of the most dynamic and energetic bits of fluff alive. Sometime in April it arrives on its nesting ground, which extends all across the United States from the Atlantic to the Pacific north of Kentucky and Colorado, and immediately starts searching for a nest site. Every knothole, crevice, abandoned woodpecker's hole, and birdhouse is scrutinized as the fussy little bird acts out its Latin description, *troglodytes*, "cave-dweller." The wren always seems to be suffering from a housing shortage or else displays amazing ingenuity in adapting to odd nesting situations. I have discovered wrens' nests in such unlikely places as a mailbox, the bow of an overturned canoe, the pocket of an apron hung up on a line, a police call box, and under the cover of an electric meter.

If the wren settles on a birdhouse, a spring housecleaning is the first order of business. Every twig, blade of grass, or scrap of material of the old nest is first thrown out. This is a good health practice, as it also helps to rid the birdhouse of lice and mites with which almost every such structure is infested. Then comes the chore of rebuilding the nest. Both birds join in gathering the material, although much of the time the male brings it to the female, and then she builds the nest.

Occasionally the male brings his mate a twig that she rejects and throws out. He may have considered it a particularly fine twig, even though a bit too long and having a fork in it, or he may have become attached to this twig, only to have it spurned by the female. So the fun begins. The male takes the twig, twists it, turns it, tries it this way and that in his efforts to place it in the nest, even dropping it half a dozen times. But give up? Never. He continues working at it until at last the twig is inside and placed in the nest. The female returns and promptly throws the twig outside. The male returns it, his mate rejects it, and so it goes until one or the other finally gives in, and the pair get on with the job of nest building.

To compound his problems, the male wren is often polygamous and maintains several females and their nests. Wrens lay large clutches. Often there may be as many as ten or twelve brown-spotted white eggs, not quite one-half inch in length and a little narrower in diameter, to a clutch. The incubation period is eleven to thirteen days. With all these mouths to feed, the parents have to be energetic. By actual count, one pair of wrens made more than one thousand trips in one day bringing food to their young. Wrens are most helpful to man, because 98 percent of their diet is composed of insects, but they are at the mercy of black snakes, which feed upon their young.

Mockingbird
(*Mimus polyglottos*)

FIELD MARKS: *Dark gray cap, neck, and back, white throat, off-white belly, black wing primaries and central tail feathers, white wing coverlets and outer tail. Very long tail.*

SIZE: *9–10 inches with a wingspan of 15 inches.*

HABITS: *Imitates other bird songs. Sings at night. Molts in the fall. Very aggressive.*

HABITAT: *Towns and rural country.*

NEST: *Small twigs, grass, rootlets.*

EGGS: *Blue-green with dark brown spots, 4–5 in a clutch. Incubation 12 days.*

FOOD: *Insects, fruits, and vegetable matter.*

VOICE: *Mimics other birds. In addition to its vast repertoire of songs it also has a harsh, guttural call.*

Few birds sing at night, but mockingbirds sing loudly from conspicuous perches. The mockingbird not only has a beautiful song of its own, but it is an excellent mimic and can imitate perfectly the song of any other bird.

In the mockingbird's Latin name, *mimus* means "mimic," *poly* means "many," and *glottos* means "tongue," all adding up to "many-tongued mimic." No one could improve on that description.

The mockingbird is America's most famous songster; no other bird can compare with it. Not only can it perfectly imitate the song of any other songbird, but it often improves upon the original score with its own superior arrangement. In addition, the mocker has a beautiful song of its own. Ornithologist William L. Dawson said he once heard a mockingbird change its tune eighty-seven times in seven minutes, and he was able to recognize fifty-eight different bird songs being imitated.

When I was in Big Bend National Park, in Texas, I heard a mockingbird sing in what was to me a foreign language. As I was totally unfamiliar with any of the park's local bird calls, the mocker was, of course, singing in an unknown language—it was imitating the songs of the birds of the park. Like most mockingbirds, this one preferred to sing from an elevated perch and chose the top of a tall agave for this purpose.

One of our few birds to sing at night, the mockingbird, in this respect, has often been compared to the European nightingale. Both birds perform well on warm summer nights, brilliantly on bright moonlit nights. To enhance Florida's famous Singing Tower at Lake Wales, nightingales were imported from Europe. Everyone was delighted when the birds had adapted to their cages and began to sing. In a short time the area around the tower resounded with the songs of the nightingales. Then they stopped singing, yet the songs continued to be heard. The mockingbirds of the area had added the nightingales' song to their repertoire; in the face of such competition, the nightingales fell silent. Unlike its songs, however, the mockers' calls are hoarse, rather guttural *chucks*.

The two subspecies of mockingbird have extended their range until they are now found throughout the United States and even occasionally in southern Canada. Long celebrated as a bird of the Deep South, the mockingbird still claims that region as its main bastion. That we are in a global warming trend is self-evident to anyone who observes nature. Many species of birds, animals, and even plants are gradually inching their way northward from what was always considered their general range. One of the most conspicuous of these "pioneers" is the mockingbird.

In my home state of New Jersey, the mocker was a permanent resident only in the southernmost portion in 1955. It was seen occasionally in the summer in the central part of the state but did not breed there. About 1960 the bird began to be seen in my northwestern county. For the past six years or so, it has been a resident of Sussex County to the north of me and is now well-established farther north in New York State.

The mockingbird is not always greeted with open arms, despite its vocal artistry. It is larger than most of the other songbirds in its area, being about nine to ten inches in length, of which more than half is taken up by its exceptionally long tail, and it has a wingspread of about fifteen inches. Its size, natural aggressiveness, and strong sense of territoriality sometimes get the mocker into trouble with bird lovers. Many people complain that the mockingbird drives other birds away from bird feeders, even though it may not be feeding at the station itself. It simply doesn't want the other birds trespassing on what it considers its own territory. Most birds that exhibit strong territoriality not only fight others of their own species at all times but often fight what they think are others of their own species, in other words, their own reflections.

The mockingbirds' diet is often highly beneficial to man, sometimes of dubious benefit, and occasionally destructive. The birds frequently feed on the ground and, during the time of insect activity, eat large numbers of caterpillars, grasshoppers, crickets, beetles, spiders, and weevils. The bulk of their diet is composed of vegetable materials and wild fruits, such as holly, dogwood, smilax, blackberry, raspberry, multiflora rose, elderberry, poison ivy, red cedar, wax myrtle, mulberry, and the fruits of the prickly pear.

It is when the bird feeds on cultivated fruits that it becomes a nuisance. In Florida I have seen mockingbirds feeding on the pulp of oranges. It also develops a great fondness for grapes, cherries, and cultivated blueberries and strawberries. However, the good these birds do as a species far outweighs the depredations of a few individuals.

The mockingbird now is more a bird of civilization than of the wilderness and seems to enjoy the proximity of man. Perhaps it needs an appreciative audience for its vocalizing. This bird prefers heavy tangles and thickets as a nesting site, and these it can often find in rural and even suburban areas. In my area of New Jersey, the mocker favors the multiflora rose hedges that have been planted for wildlife and are now common and widespread. Nest building usually begins in April.

Both male and female gather material and join in the construction of the nest. Usually bulky, the nest is well built of small twigs, grass, and rootlets about four to eight feet off the ground. Four or five dark-spotted bluish green eggs, a little more than one-half inch long and slightly narrower in diameter, comprise a standard clutch. The female does most of the incubating, which takes about twelve days. Both parents feed the young, which are large enough to leave the nest when they are two weeks old.

When the young birds first leave the nest, their plumage is brown instead of gray, but, following another molt in the fall, they look like their parents. The adults also molt in the fall and, unlike most other birds, are actually in their brightest colors over the wintertime. Adults have a gray cap, neck, and back. The throat is white and the belly is off-white. Wing primaries and central tail feathers are jet black, while wing coverlets and outer tail feathers are white. The white wing coverlets are very conspicuous when the birds are in flight and constitute the best field identification marks.

As soon as the young mockers are capable of fending for themselves, they seek territory of their own. In the north this bird raises two annual broods; in the south it raises three.

Thanks to its aggressiveness, the mockingbird has few natural enemies. Like the kingbird, the mocker attacks hawks, cats, dogs, and snakes with impunity. Such enemies occasionally make off with young mockingbirds or even with the adults themselves, but not very often. They usually recognize the mockingbird for the fighter it is and stay clear. In its continuous fight with cats and dogs, the mockingbird frequently lands on the animals' heads and pounds away savagely with its long, sharp beak. In some instances the harassment is so constant, especially when these pets have easy-going natures, that the animals refuse to go out in the yard where the birds are residents.

Perhaps the mockingbird's fecundity, coupled with its adaptability, aggressiveness, and territorialism, accounts for its rapidly expanding range. Like man, it feels the pressures of a population explosion. The high regard in which the mockingbird is held is evidenced by its selection by the states of Arkansas, Florida, Mississippi, Tennessee, and Texas as their official state bird.

Robin
(Turdus migratorius)

FIELD MARKS:	*Blackish gray back, brownish red breast, yellow bill; female lighter in color.*
SIZE:	*8½ inches with a wingspan of 15 inches.*
HABITS:	*Often builds more than one nest.* *Rises early to catch worms.*
HABITAT:	*Towns, suburbs, clearings, deep forests.*
NEST:	*Grasses and twigs, with mud liner.*
EGGS:	*Deep blue, usually 4 in a clutch. Incubation 12–13 days.*
FOOD:	*Earthworms, nightcrawlers, caterpillars, moths, spiders, ants, grubs, berries, fruit.*
VOICE:	*Wide repertoire of clear, whistled songs.*

Robins frequently build many nests in one breeding season and then select one nest where they will deposit their clutch of four blue eggs. The young birds hatch in twelve or thirteen days.

The largest member of the thrush family, the robin is probably the best-known bird in the United States. It is found in every state from the Atlantic Ocean to the Pacific, and its friendliness makes it a neighbor to all. We tend to think of it as a bird of the dooryard, because that is where most of us find it, hopping about on our lawns. Yet it is just as much at home in the deep forests.

For years I was amazed at how many robins I constantly saw on my trips into the Canadian wilderness. A further surprise was the discovery that the robin was the most frequently seen bird encountered on my first trip to Alaska. Despite the flotillas of puffins and flocks of gulls, the robin was the species I saw in greater numbers than any other. This does not mean that the robin exists in greater numbers than any other bird, because it does not. It is simply the bird that is encountered most frequently by most people.

The fact that the robin is found over most of the North American continent has inspired the common belief that it is the first bird to migrate north in the spring. Robins in my area of New Jersey migrate south, but many of the Canadian robins come to New Jersey for the winter. This is true of most states south of the Canadian border. Consequently, there are always a few robins in most areas, and these can be seen in the middle of winter; when they are, they are frequently taken to be harbingers of spring.

When the real migration starts, the males arrive first. They locate the territory they wish to claim as their own and battle for it if the need arises. The females follow about two weeks later. A short time afterward, breeding takes place, and the construction of a nest is begun. Both birds gather the grasses, twigs, and mud with which the nest is built. The female shapes the final mud liner by pressing with her breast and stamping with her feet.

I have seen some robins working on as many as six nests at one time. Occasionally other birds build surplus nests, but the robins do this frequently. Not all the nests will be in the same stage of construction, and as the egg-laying time approaches, a final decision is made, and just one nest is finished and utilized.

One psychotic robin started six nests on my front porch at one time, each nest between a different set of rafters. She completed three nests and laid eggs in two of them but finally narrowed her choice down to one. Another robin built its nest between the antlers of a mounted deer head that hung on my neighbor's back porch. She paid little attention to the constant comings and goings or to the slamming of the screen door. The spot was really ideal, for there the robin was safe from predation, had a roof over her head, and was only a few feet from a large lawn. Yet another robin, which has nested for the past two years in the ivy over my barn door, refuses to tolerate people and goes screaming out of her nest whenever anyone walks by.

Four blue-green eggs, a little more than one inch long and one-half inch in diameter, make up the usual clutch and are incubated by both parents. I have often watched the "changing of the guard," as one bird relieves the other at the nest, which is performed with almost clockwork regularity. The female spends much more time at this chore than does the male. The

Robins often choose unusual sites for their nests. Here a robin has constructed its nest between the antlers of a mounted deer head.

Young robins lack the red breasts of the adults, but they can be identified as robins by their rust-colored underparts and their gray backs.

eggs are hatched in twelve or thirteen days. Most robins raise two and sometimes three broods of young per year.

Young robins leave the nest about two weeks after they hatch. Most seem to venture out just a little too soon, because they fly poorly, if at all, at this time. Once upon the ground, their mortality rate is high. House cats are probably the robins' number one enemy, with hawks next in line.

Like other members of the thrush family, young robins have speckled breasts, which turn to the orangey red color of the adults as they mature. Both sexes have grayish brown plumage, but the female's is paler and she also lacks the male's black head. A full-grown robin is about eight and one-half inches in length and has a wingspread of fifteen inches.

The old saying about the early bird catching the worm is true in the case of the robin. This early riser gathers up many earthworms and night-crawlers before they are driven back to their underground burrows by daylight. Caterpillars, moths, spiders, ants, and grubs are also taken. Many types of fruit, both wild and cultivated, comprise the vegetable portion of the diet. This fondness for fruit is the cause of the robin's single conflict with man. Orchard owners, particularly those raising cherries, often suffer heavy losses when this bird attacks their trees with its voracious appetite.

The robin has a wide repertoire of songs and calls. My favorite is the soft, tweedling one it sings in the evening.

Wood Thrush
(Hylocichla mustelina)

FIELD MARKS: *Mainly brownish olive; brownish red head and back; white throat, breast, and underparts with black spots.*

SIZE: *7 inches long with a wingspan of 13½ inches.*

HABITS: *Males do all the singing. Flick the feathers on the back of the crown when alarmed.*

HABITAT: *Deciduous forests and suburbs.*

NEST: *Lined with mud and rootlets.*

EGGS: *Blue or blue-green, 4 in a clutch. Incubation 13–14 days.*

FOOD: *Insects and wild fruit.*

VOICE: *Bell-like notes.*

The wood thrush is an eastern bird and it may be found from Minnesota to the East Coast and from Quebec to Panama. It may be distinguished from other thrushes by its plumpness, its russet head, and the large number of prominent spots on its breast.

Through the center of the scout camp where I lived for many years ran a deeply cleft gorge, whose hillsides were mantled in tall hemlocks and interlaced rhododendrons. At the bottom ran one of the purest little mountain streams I have ever seen. In this cathedrallike setting the wood thrushes would sing. After a hard shower, when the leaves still dripped and the air was freighted with moisture, the thrushes tried to outdo themselves and one another with melodies so sweet they still echo in my mind's ear.

The wood thrush is a handsome bird, being mainly brownish olive but with a brownish red head and back and white throat and breast with large black spots. Unlike robins and bluebirds, which lose their spots upon reaching maturity, the wood thrush retains its spots. Both sexes are identical in appearance, measure about seven inches long, and have a wingspread of thirteen and one-half inches.

Wood thrushes are eastern birds, ranging from Minnesota to the Atlantic Ocean and from Quebec south to Panama, where they spend the winter. Males usually arrive in the north about three days before the females and are readily distinguishable because they do all the singing. The female makes the choice of nest location, usually selecting a hardwood shrub. Most nests I have found have been located about twenty feet off the ground, in large dogwood bushes. There are reports of the thrush nesting in evergreen trees, but I have never seen this.

The wood thrush's nest is usually in the fork of a branch or occasionally is saddled on the top of a fair-sized limb. Like that of its cousin, the robin, this thrush's nest has an inner mud liner, but, while the robin builds the innermost liner of dead grass, the thrush uses fine rootlets.

This bird's four blue or bluish green eggs are about one inch long and one-half inch in diameter. Incubation takes thirteen to fourteen days, with the female often starting the brooding period before the clutch is completed. This actually makes little difference, because all the eggs hatch the same day. The female alone does the incubating, although her mate helps to guard the nest after the young are hatched. He also helps with the feeding. There may be two broods in one year.

Although the wood thrush's diet is primarily composed of insects, it includes a fair amount of wild fruit as well. Caterpillars, inchworms, cankerworms, spiders, ants, and moths are the main insect staples.

The brooding female and the young birds in the nest point their beaks skyward if alarmed. It is thought that they do this to expose the white throat and so blend better with the nest, which always has considerable white-colored material built into it. When the adult birds are alarmed away from the nest, they flick their feathers on the back of the crown as though they were crested.

The sharp-shinned hawk and the Cooper's hawk are the two most feared enemies. Other hawks and owls, as well as raccoons, opposums, and snakes also take their toll. Man does little to harm the wood thrush. Often, when woods are cut down to make way for residential buildings, thrushes make themselves at home in the new plantings and shrubbery. At times the thrush becomes almost as tame as the robin and searches for earthworms and other food out on the open lawns.

The wood thrushes leave my area of New Jersey rather early for their warmer winter home. By the middle of September the local woods have been forsaken by them. I always hate to see them go and welcome their return. With their silvery, bell-like notes, they can sing their way into anyone's heart.

Eastern Bluebird
(*Sialia sialis*)

FIELD MARKS:	*Cobalt back, wings, and tail; brownish red breast.*
	Female is paler and duller on top.
SIZE:	*6½–7½ inches with a wingspan of 12½ inches.*
HABITS:	*Not aggressive in defending nest or in competing with*
	sparrows or starlings. Builds nests inside cavity.
HABITAT:	*Woodlands and rural areas around farms and orchards.*
NEST:	*Grasses laid in cavity of old trees, nesting boxes,*
	old woodpecker or bank swallow cavities.
EGGS:	*Pale blue, 4–6 in a clutch. Incubation 12–14 days.*
FOOD:	*Insects, wild berries, and fruit.*
VOICE:	*Musical, warbling song.*

The bluebird has probably been the subject of more songs than any other bird. It is supposed to denote peace and tranquility. Bluebird weather is perfect, clear, and balmy. And the bird's character and temperament seem to be in accord. No wonder the bluebird is so popular, and the decline in its population alarms so many people. Many factors have brought about this situation.

In the 1800's many family farms had orchards containing trees that were old enough and large enough to have rotted centers and limbs. The bluebird is a cavity-nesting species; it will not build its nest out in the open. In modern orchards, such old trees are removed.

To take the place of the hollowed-out trees, many people built bird-nesting boxes. The bluebird took to these houses readily, and at first, it looked as if all would be well. The importation into the United States of the English house sparrow and the starling, both also cavity-nesting species, created great competition for the available houses. As both the sparrow and the starling are extremely aggressive, the bluebird lost out to its competitors.

Another factor in its decline is that, although the bluebird is an early migrant, it is not a hardy bird and is often killed by cold weather. Nor does the bluebird migrate as far south as most of the other birds do. In recent times thousands of bluebirds have been killed when extreme cold penetrated the southern states. The eastern bluebird is the only bluebird found east of the Great Plains region.

At the first hint of warm weather, the male bluebirds head north for their summer range, which extends into Canada as far as Hudson Bay. The females follow about a week later. In the interim the male selects his territory and locates a nesting site. The nests I have observed were either in birdhouses or in decayed apple trees. The bluebird also utilizes old woodpecker cavities and, on occasion, bank swallow nests. The nest itself is composed mainly of grasses and lacks the mud liner common to other thrush nests.

The bluebird's four to six pale blue eggs measure about seven-eighths inch in length and just over two-thirds inch in diameter. Incubation is twelve to fourteen days, with the female performing most of the work. Both parents feed and care for the young but do little to protect their brood from predators.

One nest I had under observation was invaded by a house wren. When the wren entered the birdhouse, both parent bluebirds flew around outside, uttering calls of alarm but not actually attempting to defend the nest. The wren grabbed a baby bluebird by the wing, dragged it to the entrance hole,

Bluebirds are the only birds with a blue back and a russet breast. Like many other species, female bluebirds are less colorful than the males.

and threw it to the ground below. I chased the wren away, retrieved the young bird, and placed it back in the birdhouse. If I hadn't been there, the week-old baby would have died, because it needed more protection than could be given it out in the open.

Young bluebirds have very little blue coloration. Their underparts are white with typical thrushlike mottling of gray. Adult males have light blue upper parts and rusty red throat and breast. Females have blue on the wings and tail; throat and breast are dull brown. These birds measure about five and one-half inches in length and have a wingspread of twelve and one-half inches. The western species have a blue throat and rusty patch on the back.

This bluebird's natural enemies include house cats, hawks, raccoons, opossum, snakes, and red squirrels. Flying squirrels often occupy birdhouses in the wintertime, gnawing the entrance hole large enough so they can enter easily. Any enlargement of the hole over one and one-half inches permits a starling to enter, and the bluebird can't stand up to a starling.

Insects, such as grasshoppers, crickets, wasps, bees, beetles, and spiders, along with wild fruit and berries, are all gathered for food. Very little cultivated produce is taken. From the point of view of its dietary inclinations, the bluebird is considered to be one of our most beneficial bird species. It is now often encouraged by man.

In the last few years a concentrated effort has been undertaken to construct bluebird trails. These are sections of rural road with bluebird houses spaced along them for miles. Many such trails are in existence now. The Grand Rapids Audubon Club has put countless thousands of these bluebird houses along roads in Kent County, Michigan, as part of their Bluebirds Unlimited project. The birdhouses are also generously peppered around Louisville, Kentucky, and many other American cities today.

I can't think of a more worthwhile project nor a more worthy bird.

Starling
(*Sturnus vulgaris*)

FIELD MARKS: *Iridescent black. Bright yellow beak and green-purple breast in summer. Heavily speckled winter plumage. Short tail.*

SIZE: *6 inches long with a wingspan of 15 inches.*

HABITS: *Does not migrate. Spends the night in large communal roosts. Deprives other birds of nesting cavities.*

HABITAT: *Cities, farms, suburbs.*

NEST: *Twigs in cavities.*

EGGS: *White, 4–6 in a clutch. Incubation 2 weeks.*

FOOD: *Insects, fruit, grain.*

VOICE: *Rasping, whistling chirp.*

Starlings were first successfully introduced in New York in 1890. Rapidly increasing in numbers, the birds soon spread across the country and are now becoming a health hazard in many areas.

Few birds are as thoroughly detested as is the starling. Dirty, noisy, and destructive, it is even despised by dedicated bird lovers, and with good reason. The hundred million or more starlings in the United States represent a living and growing monument to man's ignorance and to his ability to spoil his surroundings.

The starling is not native to North America but an immigrant. Several abortive attempts to introduce the starling were carried out in the 1870's and 1880's. In 1890 a Mr. Eugene Scheifflin released sixty starlings in New York City's Central Park. A year later he released forty more. Why? Because Shakespeare mentioned starlings in his play *Henry the Fourth*. Mr. Scheifflin thought it would be a good idea to have every bird mentioned in Shakespeare's plays represented in the United States. No attempt was made until years later to study the bird thoroughly and to determine what effect it would have on our native species. Now it is too late for studies. We can't begin to control the starling, let alone eradicate it.

By 1896 starlings were firmly established in all New York City's boroughs; by 1898 they were entrenched in New Jersey and Connecticut; by

1940 they had traversed the width of the continent and settled in California. Starlings also spread northward. The first to arrive in Vancouver, British Columbia, was seen in 1946; by 1954 the number had grown to 500; by 1958 to 25,000. Today starlings are found in all forty-eight contiguous states and are pushing even farther north into Canada and Alaska as well as south into Mexico.

Most of our native birds migrate each spring and fall; the starling does not. It may shift its feeding grounds as its food supply increases or diminishes in any given area, but it does not migrate. In the wintertime starlings forsake the fields and woodlands to move into the cities with their bright lights. Not that the starlings care for bright lights particularly; they take advantage of the heat the lights give off. The birds seek to snuggle up against all sorts of electric signs, nooks and crannies of houses, chimneys and smokestacks, and any other spot radiating heat. Even if no heat is being produced, by roosting in the eaves, copings, and belfries of houses and churches the starlings are out of the wind and much warmer than they would be roosting out in the thickets in the countryside. Then, too, they pack together so tightly that they share a lot of mutual body warmth. Before Congress spent $29,500 to install electronic bird-shocking devices on the Supreme Court Building, it was estimated that 35,000 starlings roosted there every night.

In winter the starling's head, back, wings, and beak are dark; its throat, breast, and belly are heavily spotted with white. As the breeding season approaches, the spots disappear, the breast turns a bright, metallic purple-green, and the bill becomes bright yellow. When it soars in for a landing, the bird's sharply tapered wings resemble in silhouette that of the famed British Spitfire fighter of World War II. A strong flier, the starling can reach speeds of about fifty miles per hour.

During the breeding season, starlings call to each other continually with a rasping, whistling chirp, and a large flock of these birds can make a most offensive racket. Although their own calls are not melodious, starlings often imitate the whistles and calls of other birds and can even master the "wolf" whistles common to teen-age humans.

When the birds pair off, they build a bulky nest of twigs in whatever suitable cavity or cranny they have chosen. The female lays four to six almost white eggs, which lack mottled camouflage patterns and measure about one inch long and one-half inch in diameter. The parents take turns incubating the eggs. After two weeks or so, the young are hatched.

The plump, short-tailed starling is about one-third smaller than a robin, measuring approximately six inches in length and having a wingspread of fifteen inches. Highly intelligent, it is quick to seize every opportunity. Living with, and competing against, man successfully in Europe for centuries has given this bird a big advantage over our native birds. The starling is also hardy, tenacious, muscular, and aggressive. It quickly learns which of our native birds it cannot dominate and to tyrannize all the others. Occasionally the starling engages in actual conflict with our smaller birds.

The greatest cause of strife between the starling and our native birds is the increasing competition for nesting sites. The starling is a cavity nester like our native bluebirds, tufted titmice, tree swallows, chickadees, purple martins, flickers, and other woodpeckers. Since the starling does not migrate, it has usually occupied all the available nest cavities long before the other birds return from the south. Going through my personal records, I find instances where starlings had paired up and were checking nesting sites as early as January 22 one year and February 6 another year.

Starlings watch with interest as flickers start excavating a new nest cavity soon after pairing up each year. Directly the cavity is completed, one pair of starlings will move in and usually succeed in forcing the flickers to move out. This entire performance may be repeated several times until all the starlings' housing requirements have been satisfied.

Man also compounds the problem by refusing to allow dead trees to remain standing even in areas where they can do no damage when they fall. By getting rid of such trees, we inadvertently destroy many potential nesting sites. More importantly, we fail to deprive the starlings, for they get first crack at whatever is available anyway. As the starling population grows, so does the problem. Most pairs of starlings have two broods of young per year, and many have three. It is estimated that there may be as many as 100 million starlings in North America, thus making this bird one of the most populous species.

To feed so many starlings takes a tremendous amount of food. Clouds of starlings feed at municipal dumps, while many more snatch up the feed put out for other birds. Farmers who raise grapes, cherries, and sweet corn are often deprived of an entire crop when visited by a horde of starlings just prior to picking time. A commercial farmer in Caldwell, Iowa, who was fattening beef cattle with scrub potatoes, figured that the multitudes of starlings in his feed lots were consuming as much as twenty tons of potatoes per day. Conservative estimates place the agricultural loss in the United States to starlings in excess of $28 million per year. Some cities have even gone so far as to cut down their shade trees in an effort to deny these birds a roosting place. Fireworks, sticky repellents, odorous spray repellents, mechanical owls, live owls, and recordings of starling distress calls have been used in attempts to disperse the huge flocks that congregate in the cities. Such flocks of starlings deface public buildings with their excrement, make walking on the pavements below hazardous, and may prove to be dangerous to health.

Starlings have already been indirectly responsible for causing death to the human population. Federal Aviation Agency investigators found that a flock of starlings had been sucked into the engines of a huge jetliner at Boston's airport, causing it to crash into the harbor killing sixty-two

White spots cover the starling's breast, throat, and belly in the wintertime, but these spots disappear during the breeding season. The bird's breast becomes glossed with purple and green at this time, and its bill turns yellow.

persons. Bushes, trees, and weeds surrounding airports throughout the country were cut, repellents were sprayed everywhere, noise-making cannons were installed, and in some cases trained falcons were employed in an effort to keep starlings out of the areas.

All these devices are only temporary measures, for when a flock of starlings is driven from one spot, it simply congregates in another. In many large cities starlings are now being live-trapped and disposed of by carbon monoxide gas asphyxiation. In a single winter control agents in Syracuse, New York, disposed of 55,000 starlings. Because this is merely a control program, not a solution, it will have to be continued indefinitely.

The starling can be given credit for consuming a vast number of such insect pests as inchworms, caterpillars, Japanese beetles, bean beetles, potato beetles, and cutworms. Many of these insects, however, would have been eaten by our native species, if the starling hadn't driven them from the area. So the good the starling does is often a negative gain.

The only help man gets in his struggle with the starling comes from the hawk and falcon, which take the adult bird, and the black snake, which eats the young. But this assist does not go far. Starlings apparently do not take to heart the biblical saying "The meek shall inherit the earth." They certainly **are doing** their best to take over the earth.

Red-eyed Vireo
(Vireo olivaceus)

FIELD MARKS:	*Brownish olive above, white below, bright red eyes,*
	prominent white eye stripe, blue-gray cap.
SIZE:	*6 inches long with a wingspan of 10 inches.*
HABITS:	*Persistent singers. Has two annual broods.*
	Often hatches young of cowbirds.
HABITAT:	*Woodlands.*
NEST:	*White, teacup shaped.*
EGGS:	*White with brown spots, 4 in a clutch.*
	Incubation 12–14 days.
FOOD:	*Insects.*
VOICE:	*A monotonous tweedling.*

The red-eyed vireo lays her eggs in a white teacup-shaped nest, which can easily be identified. There are four eggs, white with brown spots, in a clutch.

If you were to ask the average person which bird is the most abundant, individuals living west of the Mississippi River would probably say the prairie horned lark; and they would be right. Individuals living east of the Mississippi would probably say the robin; and they would be wrong.

Surprising as it may seem, the red-eyed vireo is the most abundant bird in the east. Most people have never heard of this bird, let alone seen one. This situation is understandable, for the red-eye is a bird of the woodlands. Both male and female have the same drab, grayish green coloration, red iris, white eye stripe, and dark gray cap; they are only about six inches long, have a wingspread of ten inches, and are not noted for their song.

A parasite by nature, the cowbird will frequently lay an egg in a red-eyed vireo nest and let the vireo incubate it along with its own eggs. Here a red-eyed vireo is feeding a baby cowbird.

The best way to discover how many vireos have been in your area is to go out in the autumn right after the leaves have dropped from the trees. At that time the vireo's white, teacup-shaped nest can readily be seen, usually in the fork of a branch about six to eight feet above the ground. You will be amazed to discover how many nests you can find.

Because we can locate the nests easily, other creatures can too, the cowbird in particular. The cowbird never hatches out its own young but takes over the nests of other birds. From personal observation, I would say the cowbird takes advantage of the red-eyed vireo more than it does of any other bird, perhaps because there are so many red-eyes. Ordinarily the vireo lays just four brown-spotted white eggs, about one-half inch long and one-quarter inch in diameter. The cowbird seldom lays more than one egg in a single bird's nest, but she tries to get an egg in as many nests as possible.

Although the cowbird's egg is much larger than the vireo's, the vireo apparently cannot tell the difference and incubates it along with her own. In addition to being larger, the cowbird's egg usually hatches sooner, so that all the advantages are with the cowbird baby.

Many naturalists suspect that, as soon as the cowbird baby hatches, it shoves the other eggs out of the nest. The European cuckoo, which has habits similar to the cowbird, has been seen doing this. Although I have never seen this occur, I know that in many vireo nests containing a full clutch of eggs in addition to the cowbird egg, no baby vireos were raised, and the eggs disappeared after the cowbird hatched.

The red-eyed vireo usually has two annual broods. The parents share in incubating the eggs and rearing the young. The young birds hatch in twelve to fourteen days. In another two weeks or so, they leave the nest.

Vireos feed on a great variety of forest insects, such as spiders, caterpillars, and moths. A favorite food is the green inchworm, of the type that abounds in the forests near my home. The red-eye's feeding habits, therefore, are highly beneficial to man.

Wood hawks, raccoons, red squirrels, and black snakes prey upon the red-eyed vireo.

American Redstart
(Setophaga ruticilla)

FIELD MARKS: *Male: Mainly black with scarlet-orange patches on the wings and tail, white belly. Female: olive brown above, white below, with large yellow patches on wings and tail.*

SIZE: *4½ inches long with a wingspan of 8½–9 inches.*

HABITS: *Nest at considerable heights in trees. Some females sit tightly on the nest and can be approached.*

HABITAT: *Deciduous forests.*

NEST: *Bark, rootlets, and grass, lined with feathers or deer hair or both.*

EGGS: *Greenish white with small brown specks, 4 in a clutch. Incubation 12 days.*

FOOD: *Insects.*

VOICE: *Series of similar high notes with or without a characteristic lower terminal note.*

Female redstarts hide their nests by constructing them at considerable heights in trees. They further camouflage the nests by gluing lichens on the outsides with spider webs.

The American redstart is one of the most common and best known of the smaller warblers, being about four and one-half inches long and with a wingspread of eight and one-half to nine inches. Owing to its fragile beauty, it is often referred to as the "butterfly of the warblers." The common name *redstart* is a corruption of the English word *redstert*, meaning "red-tailed." The early English settlers in North America mistakenly named this bird after the common redstart of Europe, which actually had a red tail. The two birds are not related, however; our bird is a warbler, while the European bird is a member of the thrush family. The Cubans call our redstart *candelita*, meaning "little torch," because the bird brightens up their dark forests in the winter months.

Luckily, the redstart's colors set it apart so that it can be readily identified, unlike the many confusing warblers. Our redstart isn't really red at all but a rich salmon orange and black. The male is jet black with a white stomach. His lesser and greater wing coverts and a portion of the outside tail feathers are orange. The female has a white belly and throat, grayish head, and mousy brown back, wings, and tail. Where the male is bright orange, the female is pale yellow. In *The Birds' Calendar*, ornithologist Howard Elmore Parkhurst described these differences eloquently. "If the male redstart is a fiery coal, the female is a trail of ashes in his wake."

The birds leave their winter home in Central and South America and the West Indies about the end of March. They arrive in northern New Jersey about May 1. Unlike many of the other warblers, which pass right on through, the redstarts stay and nest in the area. Their breeding range extends from South Carolina to Tennessee, northwest to Canada's Yukon, and east to Newfoundland.

The males usually arrive on the breeding grounds first, and by the time the females join them, have staked out their territories, defining the boundaries both by song and battle. Redstarts are arboreal, usually nesting at considerable heights in the trees. My area has second-growth timber, a mixture of birch, oak, maple, tulip, ash, elm, and basswood, which seems to suit the birds perfectly.

While the male is busy defending his territory, the female devotes herself to construction of the nest. Although various locations are utilized, the nests I have found have been saddled on the tops of horizontal limbs. In most cases the nest was built against, or between, smaller vertical branches. About three inches in diameter and one and one-half to two inches in depth, the nest is composed of bark, rootlets, and grass. The outer surface is often camouflaged with lichens glued on with spider webs, while the interior is softened with a few feathers or deer hair, or both.

Occasionally redstart nests five to six inches deep are found. Close examination generally reveals them to be composed of several layers, the additional layers having been created to floor over the original clutch of eggs that had been taken over by a cowbird.

Both the redstart and the yellow warbler are frequent victims of the cowbird, which lays her eggs in other birds' nests rather than raise her own young. Although both warblers often hatch and raise young cowbirds, they just as often recognize the strange egg among their own and sacrifice the entire clutch by rebuilding another nest on top of the first one. One yellow warbler nest had five layers of eggs; the cowbird's persistence was matched by the warbler's.

Ordinarily the redstart's nest is well hidden. One nest I was planning to photograph rested on a limb of a sycamore tree. I had discovered it only by watching the male flutter about the tree as the female worked. A short time after the nest was completed, an infestation of caterpillars defoliated the entire tree. The exposed nest was destroyed by a predator, and I never got my photos.

Four brown-specked white or greenish white eggs, about one-half inch long and slightly narrower in diameter, make up the usual set. The job of incubation is performed solely by the female over the required twelve-day period. While incubating, the female sits tightly on the nest and can easily be approached.

The redstart nest pictured here was located in an elm tree that stood about twenty-five feet from my home. To take the photograph, I used a remote-control release. Fastening my camera and flashgun to a limb, I ran the air hose to the ground, removed the ladder, and hid under some camouflaged material.

It wasn't long before the female returned to brood. I allowed her plenty of time to become settled and to warm the eggs. When all was in readiness, I squeezed the air bulb. At such times the usual sequence would be: Camera goes off, flashbulb goes off, bird goes off. Then I would have to reinstall the ladder, climb up and rewind the camera, replace the flashbulb, and wait for the bird to come back. However, in my years of working with wildlife at close quarters, I have found that most creatures find assurance in a soft-toned human voice. So now I talk as I work. It doesn't matter what the subject is—perhaps even a recital of the alphabet or Lincoln's Gettysburg Address—the important thing is the low, steady tone.

As the redstart sat upon her eggs, I talked to her, busily snapping pictures all the while. When I had all the photographs I wanted, I thanked the bird and quietly withdrew. Not until some time later did it occur to me that it was a good thing no one had been around to observe me sitting up in a tree chatting to a bird.

During the weekend that the eggs should have hatched, I had to be away from home. The first thing I did on my return was check the eggs—they were gone, the bird was gone, and the nest was torn apart. I doubted that a hawk, crow, or raccoon would have come so close to the house and assumed that the damage had been the work of a pilot black snake. This snake is common in the area and is often seen up in the trees, where it feeds on young squirrels and birds.

Both parents feed the young, but, unfortunately, I never got any pictures of the male. The redstart's diet is not only beneficial to the bird but also to man, in that it consists almost entirely of insects. All types of harmful beetles, spiders, caterpillars, harvestmen, plant lice, and leaf and tree hoppers are eaten. The bird divides its time between climbing all over the tree searching diligently for its prey and functioning as a flycatcher in active pursuit of its prey through the air. I have often watched the redstart fly about, hover for a moment, then gobble down an inchworm descending on its silken cable.

The young are fed in the nest for eight to ten days and then are soon capable of catching their own food. There is only one annual brood, and the young resemble the female when they leave the nest. The redstarts remain on their breeding grounds until the end of August, then head south.

House Sparrow
(Passer domesticus)

FIELD MARKS: *Male: mottled tawny and dark brown above, grayish underparts, black bib, white cheeks, chestnut nape. Female: whitish underparts, whitish line above eye is only distinctive marking.*

SIZE: *5½ inches long with a wingspan of 9½ inches.*

HABITS: *Extremely prolific. Usually found in large flocks, very pugnacious. Builds nest in or under shelter.*

HABITAT: *Cities, towns, farms.*

NEST: *Large and bulky.*

EGGS: *Gray with red-brown spots, 4–8 in a clutch. Incubation 12–15 days.*

FOOD: *Grain, fruits, berries, vegetables, insects.*

VOICE: *Long series of monotonous musical chirps.*

House sparrows become so sooty in the city that many people fail to recognize the clean bird when they come across it in the country. The male house sparrow has a white cheek, black throat, and chestnut nape; the female is dull brown and buff and has no distinguishing features.

Like a basket of leaves tumbled about by a "dust-devil," a flock of noisy house sparrows arrive. They whirl about, land, take off again, all the while keeping up an incessant chirping and quarreling. Among the most pugnacious and troublesome of all birds, these sparrows—erroneously called English—have no champions. Their introduction into the New World was a mistake, one for which we are still paying.

In 1850 green inchworms were defoliating the trees in New York City's Central Park. The local birds evidently couldn't keep the hordes of worms under control. Someone, who has safely remained anonymous, came up with the bright idea that the house sparrow was the ideal bird to clean up the situation; so importation from England began. Several attempts failed, but the states adjacent to New York all helped out by passing laws giving the house sparrow complete protection.

Eventually the sparrow established itself and began reproducing. In a short time it was so well established that it rapidly expanded its range. Today it is found everywhere on the continent except in the far north and in southern Mexico. Not only did the sparrow fail to eat any inchworms, but it proved to be such a pest itself that within fourteen years the adjacent states had repealed their protection laws. By then it wasn't the sparrow that needed protection, it was the native bird population that needed it.

The main fault found with the house sparrow is that it cannot build its large, bulky nest out in the open. It must build in or under shelter. A spot up under the rafters, behind a loose weatherboard, in a hollow tree, or in a birdhouse is an ideal location. By using hollow trees and birdhouses, the sparrow is in direct competition with many of our more desirable native birds, such as the bluebird, the chickadee, and the titmouse. Even if one of these birds is already using such a location when the sparrow discovers it, the sparrow soon drives the occupant out. In fact, the decline of our bluebird population is in direct proportion to the increase in the numbers of house sparrows.

These sparrows are extremely prolific and appear to breed promiscuously. Four or five broods each year are not uncommon. On the farm in northern New Jersey where I was raised, I often found house sparrows nesting as early as February. Four to eight grayish eggs, usually heavily spotted and blotched with reddish brown and measuring about one-half inch in length, slightly less in diameter, comprise a clutch. The female incubates the eggs for twelve to fifteen days while the male helps in gathering food to feed the young.

When full grown, sparrows measure about five and one-half inches long, have a wingspread of nine and one-half inches and brown upperparts. The male has a gray cap, black throat and bill, white cheeks, dull brown back and white underparts, while the female has a broad buff eye line and buffy underparts.

Grain is the staple of the sparrows' diet. They gather it in fields or in barns when it is stored, or eat it directly out of the feed troughs of cattle and chickens. They also pick out undigested kernels from manure. Fruits, berries, and vegetables are avidly eaten. The sparrows' one saving grace is that they also eat insects. Japanese beetles as well as cutworms, moths, and caterpillars are often held in check by these birds. On the other hand, many of these insects would have been eaten by the native birds that the house sparrows dispossessed.

Being exceedingly gregarious, these sparrows enjoy and seek out their own kind to the extent that they are usually found in large flocks. Their habit of nesting in, on, or near man-made structures makes it possible for their droppings to be unsightly or even cause a great deal of damage.

The house sparrow is extremely hardy, and adversity only seems to strengthen it. Quick to take advantage of every opportunity, it is, to the disgust of most people, probably the greatest beneficiary at bird feeders. Virtually the only control on the sparrow population is provided by cats, hawks, and snakes.

Most male birds are intensely jealous and fight to defend their mate and their territory. Many, too, fight their own reflections in windows or other

Although they breed indiscriminately, male house sparrows are extremely jealous and will become very aggressive in defense of their mates. The birds will even fight their own reflections in windows or other shiny surfaces.

shiny surfaces. Ornithologists are often able to determine the exact limits of a bird's territory by moving around small upright mirrors, which the bird attacks until they are moved beyond the limits of his "yard."

Robins and cardinals are noted for fighting their own reflections, but I had never heard of house sparrows doing this until one chose to attack my kitchen window. Because I live in a wooded area away from town, there are few sparrow visitors. This particular sparrow, however, thought his own reflection was one sparrow too many, and the battle was joined.

Outside the window stood a large rhododendron bush, where the sparrow perched and from which he launched his attack. *Thump, thump, thump,* he went all day long from dawn to dusk. *Thump, thump, thump,* he continued, week after week and month after month. Breeding season passed, and still the obsession remained. Through most of the winter the attack persisted. When the bird ate, I don't know. With the coming of spring, the pace was stepped up. When I moved from the house the sparrow was still going strong. Probably only old age could stop him.

Red-winged Blackbird
(*Agelaius phoeniceus*)

Field marks:	*Male: black with scarlet shoulder epaulets, fringed with a whitish yellow band. Female: dull brown above, heavily brown-streaked white breast and throat.*
Size:	*8 inches long with a wingspan of 12–13 inches.*
Habits:	*Feeds, flies, and roosts in flocks. Male performs courtship ritual. Frequently nests in hay fields.*
Habitat:	*Marshes and fields.*
Nest:	*Tight little cups.*
Eggs:	*Blue-green streaked with dark brown, 4 in a clutch. Incubation 11–12 days.*
Food:	*Insects, fruits, berries, grain, corn.*
Voice:	*A squeaky* konkareeee.

306

When male red-winged blackbirds migrate, they eat, roost, and travel in a flock. Three to four days after they arrive at the breeding grounds, the flock breaks up and the birds begin the process of selecting their own personal territories.

It is estimated that blackbirds are responsible for an annual loss to agriculture in the United States of about $100 million. In North America grackles and cowbirds are grouped with the other blackbirds, but the chief culprit is the red-wing.

The red-winged blackbird's population, like our human population, is exploding. Records and bird counts reveal that the red-wing's is doubling and redoubling—up 300 percent in three years in Ohio, where most of the studies have been conducted and so much of the damage done by this bird has been concentrated.

In those nonfarming areas where the red-wing is not looked upon as a menace, it has always been most welcome. Many a year by early March I have despaired of the weather ever improving in my area of New Jersey. Then, suddenly, from an ice-locked marsh that had appeared lifeless all winter, whose reeds and cattail stalks had been rustled noisily by the cold, biting wind, came an old familiar sound—*konkareeee*—the first call of a male red-wing proclaiming to all that spring had officially arrived.

The male red-wing is a strikingly handsome bird, about eight inches in length with a wingspan of twelve to thirteen inches. Its bright jet black plumage is broken by brilliant scarlet shoulders, fringed on the lower edge with a whitish yellow band. Although many people are aware of the red shoulder patch, they have never noticed the band of yellow. The female looks like a large sparrow, with her dull brown upper parts and heavily brown-streaked white breast and throat.

The red-wings winter in the southern United States from the Atlantic Ocean to the Pacific, wherever there are areas of open water in marshes and swamps. Early March finds them in New Jersey, and by the end of the month they are on their breeding grounds in Canada. The males arrive about ten to fifteen days before the females and immature males. For the first couple of days the males remain together as a flock, feeding, roosting, and traveling together. In flight they perform the most precise evolutions, puzzling scientists and naturalists who have attempted to determine the nature of the communication between each individual that manipulates the flock so precisely as an entity.

Three or four days after their arrival the males select their personal territory, and their calling fills the air. When the females arrive, each male tries to convince a potential mate that the territory he has selected is the finest and that he is superior to all the others. He bows and scrapes, teeters forward on a branch until it looks as if he will lose his balance, flares his wings and tail. Perched in front of the male, the female is thus treated to the display of the male's bright red and yellow wing patches every time he bows. Within a few days most of the birds are paired. In areas where the females outnumber the males, polygamy is common. In some cases, however, the opposite is true, as one female has been seen accepting two or more males.

Formerly red-wings built their nests among the reeds, cattails, bullrushes, and tules or in bushes found in swamps and marshes. Today they have proved their adaptability by nesting in ever larger numbers out in hay fields, particularly in alfalfa fields. We do not know for certain whether the

Formerly red-winged blackbirds usually suspended their nests about two feet above the ground, but lately they have also been nesting in hay fields. The females lay four eggs and incubate them for eleven to twelve days.

Young male and female red-winged blackbirds are similar and both resemble the adult female, with her dusky brown coloration. However, the young males have the beginnings of the scarlet shoulder patches of the adult males.

birds' increased population forced them to nest in the hay fields or whether nesting in the hay fields allowed their population to increase. The transition has taken place within the last thirty years and accelerated in the late 1950's and early 1960's. The birds still utilize those of their ancestral swamps and marshes that man has not drained or filled. Back on the family farm I never saw red-wings nesting in our hay fields; now they are common in hay fields.

Most red-wing nests are tight little cups, neatly woven and suspended above the ground or water at various heights up to, but seldom exceeding, two feet. Here again another transition is taking place; the birds nesting in hay fields are with increasing frequency building their nests directly on the ground.

A clutch of four eggs is most usual with these birds. The bluish green eggs, heavily streaked with dark brown, particularly on the larger end, measure about one inch long and one-half inch in diameter. The female performs the job of incubation alone, a chore that takes eleven to twelve days. All the time the female sits on the eggs, her mate remains perched nearby, often singing and posturing.

Both parents feed the young when they hatch. Frequently the male captures the food but then presents it to the female to feed to the youngsters, almost as though he didn't quite trust himself to do the job properly. The male also cleans the nest, but infrequently, leaving the removal of the fecal sacs to the female.

During the rearing season, the red-winged blackbird is particularly beneficial to man, its diet at that time being composed almost exclusively of insects. The parents make hundreds of trips per day with food, which they cram forcefully down the youngsters' gaping maws. The young bird that reaches the farthest, gapes the widest, and squawks the loudest gets fed most frequently. If it does not instantly swallow the food placed in its mouth, however, the parent is likely to remove it and feed it to one of the other youngsters.

Although all types of insects are taken as food, some of the better known are grasshoppers, crickets, mayflies, green inchworms, moths, spiders, cutworms, wireworms, and flies of assorted types. The young are fed in the nest for about two weeks and for about one week after they leave it. Then the first brood is abandoned to shift for itself, as the parents start their second brood. Occasionally red-wings may even have three annual broods. When the young leave the nest, both sexes are superficially alike, having the sparrowlike appearance of their mother. Closer examination discloses that the young males have a dark brown band on the spot where they will sport their red epaulets in the adult plumage.

It is about the time the young birds are leaving the nest that the red-wings begin to get into trouble. Many berries and fruits are ripening, and the multitudes of birds frequently cause such widespread depredation that they literally wipe out the entire crop. Their forays against such crops can bring economic ruin to the farmer. But it is when the red-wings invade the corn fields as the kernels are filling out with milk that they are most destructive. In Ohio alone it is estimated that these birds are responsible for a yearly loss to farmers of more than $15 million. In the southern rice-growing states, the losses are comparable. Farming can be a hazardous undertaking, and the red-winged blackbirds are making it a disaster in some areas.

As yet, man has not found the answer to this problem. The most common protection is the use of scaring devices, such as gas cannons, but these do not represent a permanent remedy. The Ohio Agricultural Research and Development Center had some success with sorghum grains that are bird resistant. The principal problem here was that, when the birds did not like the grains of the special hybrids, they merely congregated and concentrated in the fields having grains they would eat. Trapping and shooting the birds has had negligible results. Hawks, cats, foxes, raccoons, opossums, and skunks all prey on the red-wing, but not enough to make a dent in their ever-growing population.

Under study now is the use of sterilizing agents, and these, perhaps, hold the greatest hope. Although the birds themselves cannot be sterilized, sterility can be induced by getting them to ingest the sterilizing factor with baited feed. No one wants to see the red-winged blackbird wiped out, but we realize that control of their numbers is imperative, and physiological control seems to be the most acceptable method.

Baltimore Oriole
(Icterus galbula)

FIELD MARKS:	*Male: scarlet-orange with black head, back, wings, and tail center. Female: brownish olive above, yellow below.*
SIZE:	*6½–7½ inches long with a wingspan of 12 inches.*
HABITS:	*Builds nest on the top of tall trees. Very brave and pugnacious. Voice carries long distances. Starts north much later in the springtime than most birds.*
HABITAT:	*Grove trees and shade trees.*
NEST:	*Long, pendant nest of milkweed, dandelion, and horsehair fibers.*
EGGS:	*Grayish white with brown streaks and blotches, 4–6 in a clutch. Incubation 14 days.*
FOOD:	*Insects, fruits, berries, garden peas.*
VOICE:	*Rich, piping whistled notes.*

311

With its fiery orange and jet black plumage, the male Baltimore oriole is one of the most colorful birds on the North American continent. The bird's bright coloration attracts predators, but it is extremely pugnacious and well able to protect itself.

The Baltimore oriole is one of the most brightly colored birds in North America. The male's bright orange breast, belly, back, and outer tail feathers contrast sharply with his black head and throat, upper back, and center tail feathers. The female is a subdued yellow and black. About six and one-half to seven and one-half inches in length, the oriole has a wingspread of twelve inches. Although not considered a songster, it has one of the loudest and clearest calls of all of our birds, its pure notes carrying for an amazingly long distance.

When Cecil Calvert, second baron of Baltimore, settled the territory of Maryland with his colonists in 1634, the settlement was named Baltimore in his honor. To show the people back home in England what some of the New World creatures looked like, skins of various birds and animals were sent to London. Among them was the skin of a beautiful orange and black bird they mistakenly called an oriole after the European oriole. In 1776, when the great Swedish naturalist Linnaeus was preparing his scientific nomenclature, he called the bird the Baltimore oriole in honor of Lord Baltimore, whose family colors matched the bird's orange and black.

The Baltimore oriole spends the winter in Mexico or Central America, where its startling beauty rivals the color of the gaudiest of the native tropical birds. In the springtime the oriole starts north much later than most birds, arriving on its breeding grounds about May 1. Found all over most of the eastern United States, it is extending its range farther north into Canada. The Bullock's oriole (*I. bullockii*) is found in our western states, while the orchard oriole (*I. spurius*) is most common in the southern states.

Although the Baltimore oriole is well known by sight and sound, it is most famous for its nest, which cannot be confused with that of any other bird. It is usually constructed in a location where it can swing and sway with every passing breeze. Tall, stately American elms are favored trees, as are maples and basswood. I have also found oriole nests in weeping willow trees that bend even more than other types of trees. The willow is chosen not only for its flexibility but also for the protection afforded by the long, silvery gray undersides of the willow leaves which help to hide and camouflage the nest.

The long, pendant nest of the Baltimore oriole, which has given the bird such local names as "hang-bird" and "hammock-bird," is a masterpiece of construction. The natural fibers of milkweed, dandelion, and horsehair are carefully woven into a clothlike material. Both male and female gather the material, but the female does all the actual weaving. Using her beak principally, but her feet as well, she deftly shuttles each thread or fiber in, out, and around, and the nest progresses rapidly. To make sure that the nest is the correct size, the female does much of the construction while sitting inside. She also bounces around a lot to help give the nest the proper form. In four to six days it is completed.

Orioles are highly adaptable and quick to take advantage of man-made material. I have watched these birds sit on a cotton clothesline and unravel the loose ends to salvage the threads for use in their nest construction. Many people aid the birds as I do by placing strands of light-colored wool or cotton thread and string where they can be easily gathered. I have also seen orioles incorporate pieces of cloth and paper into their nests. All the nests I have seen have been a soft white or faded gray.

When the oriole builds around a fork of a twig, the nest is open at the top. Most of the nests are constructed in this fashion. The remainder of the nests, particularly those in willow trees, have the opening on the side. When a willow tree is used, three or four of the long, supple branches are tied together in a cluster in such a manner that the opening has to be on the side.

The oriole's nest is amazingly strong. An ornithologist tested its strength by cutting down a nest that had been used and abandoned and had also been hanging out all winter. To a scale he fastened the branch to which the nest was attached and poured lead shot into the nest to see how much weight it would require to tear the nest loose from the branch. Although

The female Baltimore oriole is a subdued yellow and black and has two bars on its wings. The female orioles use both their beaks and feet to weave the nests out of the natural fibers that are available.

the entire bird family only weighed six to eight ounces, and the nest had been exposed to the ravages of the weather for almost a year, eighteen pounds of lead were required to tear the nest loose from its fastenings. Despite this strength, the oriole seldom, if ever, reuses a nest it has built, although it frequently returns to the same tree the following year to build a new nest.

The female lays four to six grayish white eggs, streaked and blotched

The male Baltimore oriole pictured here has brought food for his young back to the nest.

with brown, which are a little more than one-half inch long and slightly narrower in diameter. She does all the incubating and hatches the young in about fourteen days. Only one brood is raised each year. Both parents are diligent about feeding the young.

When photographing an oriole's nest that hung over the canal paralleling the Delaware River a few miles above Trenton, New Jersey, I noticed one of the hungry young birds had crawled up to the edge of the nest. Evidently it wasn't getting fed as fast as it desired, so it clutched the edge of the nest, fluttered its stumpy wings, and kept up a continuous whimpering. Because this was the only young bird visible, both parents stuffed food into its gaping mouth. Finally, either exhausted from holding on or too full of food to do so, the young oriole lost its footing and started to fall out of the nest. Luckily one foot became entangled in threads of the nest, and there the young bird hung, squawking its head off. Both parents immediately answered its distress call, but they could do nothing but fly about or perch nearby and add their own calls to the din. Maneuvering my canoe into position beneath the tree, and pulling down the supple willow branches, I was able to lower the nest sufficiently to pop the little one back inside.

Orioles are well known for their bravery in defense of their nest and young, and this pair was no exception. They dived at my head, screeching mightily, as other birds in the neighborhood joined in the clamor. Instead of being able to retire a hero, I was driven off as though I were a routed predator. At that I was lucky not to have been stabbed in the eye.

Without question, the courage of the Baltimore orioles is a tremendous advantage to the species. They have been seen disputing territory with even the redoubtable kingbird, a bird that is absolutely fearless. Orioles have been known to attack cats, crows, and hawks. Many such brightly colored birds as the scarlet tanager and the blue jay are killed and eaten by the goshawk, the Cooper's, and the sharp-shinned hawks. I have never found the scattered feathers of an oriole that had been taken by these birds. Although the orioles' brilliant coats attract attention, their pugnaciousness stands them in good stead.

The Baltimore oriole is highly beneficial to man, because 85 percent of its diet is made up of insects, mostly pests. It is one of the few birds that eats the large, hairy caterpillars, such as the tussock moth caterpillar. A heavy infestation of tent caterpillars is welcomed by orioles. Most of the insects and caterpillars this bird feeds on are gleaned from the treetops, as the oriole seldom feeds on the ground. No insect is too small for the oriole, which diligently seeks out aphids and plant lice.

Occasionally the oriole eats fruits and berries. When feeding on cherries, it does not gobble down the whole fruit as the greedy robin does, but deftly skewers each piece of fruit with its long, thin beak, then drinks the juice and eats some of the pulp. This oriole also has a fondness for garden peas, splitting the ripe pods to get them. These few depredations can be forgiven the oriole in the light of all the good the species does, protecting shade, forest, and fruit trees.

No longer a bird of the wilderness, the Baltimore oriole has become a bird that frequents our dooryards. In these days, when the whole world is in flux, the creature capable of adapting to change is the one able to survive. This colorful and versatile bird has been chosen as the state bird of Maryland.

Cardinal
(Richmondena cardinalis)

FIELD MARKS:	*Male: scarlet with black throat; only scarlet bird with crest. Female: yellow-brown with scarlet tinge on wings, tail, and crest. Both have scarlet beaks.*
SIZE:	*7¾–8¼ inches long with a wingspan of 12 inches.*
HABITS:	*Raises two broods a year. Erects crest at the sign of danger. Nonmigratory.*
HABITAT:	*Hedgerows, wood margins, suburbs.*
NEST:	*Usually built in thick copse or vine.*
EGGS:	*White or greenish, 4 in a clutch. Incubation 12 days.*
FOOD:	*Sunflower seeds, weed seeds, grain, wild fruits, insects.*
VOICE:	*Repetition of loud slurred whistles.*

The only all-red bird with a crest, the cardinal is sometimes called the cardinal grosbeak bcause of its large, thick beak. The cardinal uses this strong beak to crack open sunflower and weed seeds.

Sometimes called the "Christmas bird," the cardinal is our only crested red bird. In his bright scarlet feathers the cheerful and industrious cardinal brightens the landscape whenever he is seen. In wintertime, particularly, when most people are happy not to have to venture outdoors, and the sleet rattles against the windowpane, just a glimpse of this bird flashing across the snowy scene is enough to lift the spirits.

Although not as handsomely attired as he will be in the breeding season, the male is still a riot of color compared to the drabness of his winter surroundings. One of the cardinal's most conspicuous characteristics is the crest, which lies flat under ordinary circumstances but springs erect at the slightest hint of danger. This plumed headpiece gives the bird a charmingly jaunty appearance. A black face and throat distinguish the male, while both sexes have heavy, conical beaks. The female, too, is crested. Although she lacks the scarlet coloration of the male, her yellow and green coloring, tinted with red, makes her a beauty. The young resemble the female in coloration. Full-grown adults measure about seven and three-quarters to eight and one-quarter inches in length and have a wingspan of twelve inches.

A daily ration of sunflower seeds is good insurance that the cardinal will call at your home every day during the winter months. His heavy beak is ideally constructed to crack seeds, and he shells out the kernels with almost machinelike precision. At this time of the year he is most ungentlemanly, driving his mate away so that he can feed first.

February ushers in a change of attitude. Although the weather is still bitter and the wind is keen as a knife, the male cardinal starts to sing. Seeking out the highest treetop, he pours fourth his plaintive call, the sound tumbling down to please all who hear it. His aggressive actions toward the female now cease, and he begins to court her.

Like any lovesick swain delivering a box of candy to his beloved, the male nows seeks out the choicest sunflower seeds, cracks them, and places the kernel carefully in the female's mouth. To show that she appreciates all this attention, the female flutters her wings and feigns helplessness.

The nest is usually built in the thickest copse or vine that can be found. Honeysuckle vines are choice spots. The four white or greenish eggs, about one inch long and one-half inch in diameter, generally take about twelve days to hatch.

The little ones' incessant demands for food keep both parents busy throughout the daylight hours. In addition to sunflower seeds, cardinals feed on weed seeds, some grain, wild fruits, and insects, including such pests as caterpillars, cutworms, codling moths, and boll weevils. Busy as he is, the male occasionally seeks out an elevated perch to sing. If everything goes as it should, cardinals raise two broods per year.

Their chief predators are hawks, cats, and black snakes.

Originally a resident of the Deep South, the cardinal has increased its ranges and now can be found in most of the eastern states up to the Canadian border. It is beloved wherever it is found and has been chosen the state bird by Kentucky, Delaware, Illinois, and Indiana. Because of its diet the cardinal is of economic importance to man as well as being an object of beauty.

Evening Grosbeak
(*Hesperiphona vespertina*)

FIELD MARKS: *Male: orange-yellow forehead, belly, and back; black wings with white patches; black top of head; sooty throat and lower face. Female: silvery gray with yellow on nape and sides. Largest yellow bird with heavy beak.*

SIZE: *7½–8 inches long with a wingspan of 12–13 inches.*

HABITS: *Very friendly and allows a close approach. Bill varies from white in winter to pale green in spring. Flies in loose flocks and with an undulating pattern.*

HABITAT: *Abundant in conifers.*

NEST: *Twigs lined with lichens.*

EGGS: *Bluish green spotted on the larger end with olive brown, 3–4 in a clutch. Incubation 12–14 days.*

FOOD: *Seeds of the ashleaf maple, fruits, berries, plant and tree seeds.*

VOICE: *Short uneven warble suggestive of the house sparrow.*

The evening grosbeak eats many varieties of seeds and consumes tremendous amounts of sunflower seeds at feeding stations. The bird holds the seed at the back of its beak, exerts pressure to crack it, and then extracts the meat with its tongue.

Unpredictable is the word for the evening grosbeak, particularly in the eastern portion of its range. You can never be sure when this bird will appear, or if it does appear, how long it will stay. Try as you may to woo the grosbeak with goodies at a feeding station, it condescends to stay only so long as staying suits its purpose. It is a real "here-today-gone-tomorrow" bird.

The designation "evening," *vespertina* in its Latin name, was applied to the grosbeak in 1825 by William Cooper, who took the word of a Major Delafield that the bird was heard only in the evening when it bestirred itself to start its nocturnal activities. On the contrary, the bird is usually very active early in the morning. Its characteristic beak is described by the French *gros*, meaning "big." *Hesperiphona* derives from the Hesperides of Greek mythology, nymphs who dwelled in the western region where the sun went down. Although his name originally described the grosbeak's western mountain range accurately, it no longer does.

This bird has steadily expanded its range eastward. Since first reaching the East Coast in the winter of 1889–1890, it has appeared sporadically but in ever increasing numbers. The winter of 1968–1969 will undoubtedly go down as a record-shattering year for wintering evening grosbeaks on the East Coast. They were seen almost everywhere and in unprecedented numbers. And in the spring of 1969 the first nesting record of this grosbeak in New Jersey was established.

Of the three subspecies of evening grosbeak, the eastern variety, which we are discussing, has the largest range. A western variety is found from the Rocky Mountains to the Pacific Ocean, and the Mexican variety is found in the southwestern states and in Mexico.

The male is a chunky seven and one-half to eight inches in length, has a wingspan of twelve to thirteen inches, and a bright yellow forehead, belly, and back. The top of the head is black, and the throat and lower face are sooty. The wings have black primaries and white secondaries, while the tail is jet black. The slightly smaller female resembles a well-laundered version of the male. The large, heavy beak, white in winter but becoming greenish during the breeding season, is utilized to crack the seeds of the fruits on which this bird feeds.

The efficiency of the birds' large beaks is clearly demonstrated as you watch the grosbeaks shuck out sunflower seeds. They put the seed in the back of the beak, where more pressure can be exerted, using only one side of the beak at a time. The seed is held flat and pressure is applied, splitting the seed at the seams. With quick motions of tongue and beak the seed is then extracted and the empty hull allowed to drop.

In winter these birds scoop up beaksful of snow to alleviate their thirst. They are extremely fond of maple sap and drink the fluid as it drips from cuts in the maple tree in the early spring. I have seen many birds drink from a melting snow icicle but only an evening grosbeak drink from a maple-sap icicle.

Nests of the evening grosbeak have been found most frequently in evergreen trees at an average height of twenty-five to thirty feet above the ground. Usually located on top of one of the main branches but among the protective foliage, the nest is rather flat, having a cup of about two to two and one-half inches and a diameter of five and one-half to six inches. It is constructed of twigs, usually the dry "squaw" wood of the various spruce trees, and rootlets and is frequently lined with usnea lichens.

The male does not help the female build the nest, but he stays close to her as it is still the courtship period. During the courtship ritual the birds sit facing each other, bowing ceremoniously, extending their wings horizontally and making them quiver. The male does this to display his beautifully marked black and white wings and yellow body. The female's posturing is in imitation of the motions a young bird makes when it begs for food. If food is available at the time, the male feeds the female.

For the twelve to fourteen days required to hatch them, the female incubates the three to four bluish-green eggs, spotted with olive brown on the larger end and measuring a little more than one-half inch in length and a

A large, chunky finch, the male evening grosbeak is seven and a half to eight inches long and has a wingspan of twelve to thirteen inches. The bird is primarily yellow, but its wings are black and white and its tail and the top of its head are black.

little less in diameter. Although the male does not brood the eggs, he is solicitous of his mate and brings her food. The parents share the job of feeding the young.

When the young are first hatched, the parents feed them a pulp of thoroughly chewed insects and earthworms. Within three or four days the little grosbeaks are large enough to be fed whole caterpillars and other insects. The parents also start feeding them the soft green seeds of some of the maple trees or whatever berries happen to be ripening in the area.

By the time they are twelve days old, most of the youngsters are ready to leave the nest; all are gone by the time they are fourteen days old. For about another week the parents remain in close attendance, then the fledglings must forage for themselves. The evening grosbeak usually starts to nest so late in June or July that only one brood per year is raised.

The seeds of the ashleaf maple, or box elder, the favored wild food of the evening grosbeak, usually hang on the tree in clusters all winter, providing a

Slightly smaller than the male, the female evening grosbeak is a silvery gray and has yellow on the nape of its neck and the sides of its body.

source of food that is not buried beneath the snow. The seeds of all the maples are avidly eaten when they are green and even after they have fallen to the ground and have dried. Almost all kinds of fruits, berries, and plant and tree seeds are consumed.

In New Jersey grosbeaks swarm all over the dogwood bushes to gather whatever fruits have been missed by the robin migrations. At Amackassin School, near Blairstown, the ornamental Japanese cherry trees are burdened with fruits each fall. The grosbeaks love these fruits and make the trees their headquarters as long as the fruit lasts. The tiny pits are usually cracked with the beak, but the pits, pulp and all, are swallowed.

Everybody welcomes the appearance of evening grosbeaks at their feeders. The birds are extremely friendly and allow a close approach before flying off, usually returning as soon as the person withdraws. Welcome as the grosbeaks are, one could wish they didn't eat so much at one time. Eight or ten birds will consume a pint of sunflower seeds in about fifteen to twenty minutes. A flock of thirty to forty empties a feeder in half that time. Grosbeaks threaten and display among themselves, but there is little actual fighting among the birds at the feeders or elsewhere. Their principal enemy is the hawk.

Slate-colored Junco
(Junco hyemalis)

FIELD MARKS:	*Dark gray head, back, and breast; white belly and outer tail feathers; short beak.*
SIZE:	*5½–6 inches with a wingspan of 10 inches.*
HABITS:	*Flares tail when flying or landing. Flails wings against weeds to shake the seeds free. Raises two broods per year.*
HABITAT:	*Brush woodlands and overgrown fencerows in winter, brushy clearings and borders of coniferous forests in summer.*
NEST:	*Moss, twigs, dry grasses, and hair.*
EGGS:	*Blue with brown splotches, 3–5 in a clutch. Incubation 12–13 days.*
FOOD:	*Weed seeds, insects, wild berries.*
VOICE:	*Loose quavering trill.*

Most rural people know that the snowbirds appear just before the arrival of snow. Scientists, ornithologists, and taxonomists recognize these same birds as juncos, among the most numerous and widespread members of the sparrow family. Five different species of junco, and three subspecies of the slate-colored junco, inhabit North America.

The slate-colored junco is five and one-half to six inches in length and has a wingspan of about ten inches. The head, back, and breast are a uniform slatey gray. The belly and the two outer feathers on each side of the tail are white. These white tail feathers show up conspicuously as the bird flares its tail when flying and landing. Male and female are almost identical, the latter being a duller slate color. The adult's bill is bone white, while the immature bird's bill may be pinkish. Short, but triangular-shaped and strong, the beak is used for cracking open the hull of small seeds so they can be eaten. In fact, this bird's name derives from the Latin *junco*, or "seed."

This bird winters throughout the United States, except for the desert regions of Arizona, New Mexico, Texas, and southern Florida. In summer it is found in the Appalachian Mountains, the New England states, most of Canada and Alaska to the tree line, with the exception of the Hudson Bay drainage area. It occasionally crosses the Bering Strait to nest in Siberia.

Juncos are among the first small birds to arrive in the far north on their breeding grounds. At my home there are always several dozen birds, which travel in two or three small flocks. Almost all day long they are in the yard scratching about. Suddenly, one day in mid-March, they are gone. Just like that. I know then that the juncos will not be back until snow-time next November.

In western North Carolina many of the juncos don't bother to migrate a thousand miles or more to northern Canada; they simply fly to the top of the Great Smoky Mountains. This vertical migration, as it is called, allows the birds to nest in a Hudsonian life zone having the same damp coniferous type of forest that they would find in Canada.

The males usually arrive on the breeding grounds before the females and fight for the territory they have selected. To impress the female with his attractiveness, the male displays by drooping his wings and flaring his tail widely, revealing his prominent white outer tail feathers. If there is no response, he hops in little circles about her, displaying continuously. When the female has decided to accept him, she learns the limit of his one- or two-acre territory, and thereafter the two are inseparable inside it.

The favorite spot for a junco's nest is against or under a bank or a rock face, which serves as a natural roof over the nest. If such a location is lack-

The slate-colored junco is largely a dark slate gray, but has a white belly and white outer tail feathers. The male prominently displays these feathers when trying to attract a mate.

ing, the bird will also build under a heavy thicket, bush, or tangle, or against a tree stump. Both birds gather the moss, twigs, dry grasses, and hair, but the female does most of the actual construction.

The slate-colored junco commonly raises two broods per year, the first in mid-April, the second in mid-July. Three to five brown-splotched bluish eggs, one inch long and slightly less than one-half inch in diameter, comprise a clutch. Incubation, occupying twelve to thirteen days, is performed by the female, but both parents feed the young and remove the fecal sacs for nest sanitation.

The young are fed high-protein insects in regurgitated form at first; later they are fed whole insects. In twelve to fourteen days the young juncos are able to leave the nest. Three or four days later they are capable of fending for themselves.

Weed seeds constitute the bulk of the junco's diet, thus making this bird an exceptionally valuable ally of the farmer. Its winter habitat is the border of brushy woodlands or overgrown fencerows, which provide shelter from storms and from attack by its enemies, the Cooper's and the sharp-shinned hawks. From these sheltered places, too, the bird can readily forage over the fields for food.

Before the advent of modern harvesting combines and threshers, such grains as wheat, oats, and rye were cut with a scythe, tied into bundles, and brought into the barn to be beaten loose from the stalks with a jointed wooden club known as a flail. Times without number I have watched the juncos harvest weed seeds in a similar fashion by using their wings as a flail. The birds hover against a dried weed top, vigorously beating it with their wings, then drop to the ground to pick up whatever seeds have been knocked loose from the plant. The performance is repeated with another weed until the birds have eaten their fill.

Whenever there has been soft snow on the ground, I have often found the chaff or hulls of weeds knocked loose in this manner and discarded by the birds. Beneath every such weed stalk the tracks of a junco can be seen crossing and crisscrossing the chaff. Once in a while the prints of the bird's primary wing feathers also appear in the snow.

These friendly birds are quick to utilize a feeding station during the winter months. They do not like a small raised platform, much preferring to feed upon the ground. Only if the surface area is large enough to make them feel secure will they utilize a raised feeder. This is not because they are afraid of falling off, but simply because they are ground-feeding birds. Chickadees and titmice customarily kick a lot of feed out of the feeder, so while these species are feeding on top of the feeder, the juncos pick up what is knocked to the ground below.

Feeding on corn, a squirrel does not eat the entire kernel but extracts the germ portion at the tip, then discards the rest. Ordinarily a corn kernel would be too large and too heavy for the juncos' small beak to crack. Since the squirrel makes the first cut, the juncos are able to cut pieces gradually from the kernel, making it sufficiently manageable for them to eat.

In the summertime, while the plants are growing their new crop of seeds, juncos feed on insects. Being creatures of the woodlands, they consume more caterpillars, ants, spiders, and beetles than they do grasshoppers. As the wild blueberries, raspberries, and elderberries ripen, juncos add these to their diet.

Some people dislike seeing the snowbirds arrive in the late fall because they bring the snow with them. The way I look at it, one of the few nice things about snow is that it brings the snowbirds, the slate-colored juncos.

White-throated Sparrow
(Zonotrichia albicollis)

FIELD MARKS:	*Mottled light and dark brown, two white bars on wings. Only sparrow with white throat and yellow spot in front of eye.*
SIZE:	*5½–6 inches with a wingspan of 10 inches.*
HABITS:	*Male defines his territory by singing from a series of different perches on its borders. Female rarely sings and does not help defend the territory.*
HABITAT:	*Brushlands, areas that have been burned and are being naturally reforested, open parklands with aspens or birches.*
NEST:	*Dead grasses, twigs, rootlets, moss, pine needles, and often deer hair.*
EGGS:	*Bluish green flecked with reddish brown spots, 4–6 in a clutch. Incubation 11–13 days.*
FOOD:	*Vegetable matters, particularly weed seeds.*
VOICE:	*Sounds like* Old Sam, Peabody, Peabody, Peabody.

To hear a white-throated sparrow sing as it should be heard, one should visit the wilderness of which the bird is such an integral part. Often, while paddling my canoe on the many little rivers and nameless lakes of Quebec, I have heard the cathedral-like silence broken by the plaintive call *Old Sam, Peabody, Peabody, Peabody.*

I have no idea who first described in these words the song of the white-throat. In some parts of the country, where this sparrow is known as the "Peabody bird," the description fits its song perfectly; in other parts, it does not.

In 1965 Donald J. Rorer and William W. Gunn studied 711 songs of white-throats, recorded from Massachusetts to British Columbia during the breeding season. They concluded that the old *Peabody* call is not being used as frequently as it formerly was in many sections of the continent. Many birds of the same species tend to have "dialects" in different parts of the country, as we humans do, so it stands to reason that variations in syllables, tone, and pitch can be developed and become dominant in different regions. Young birds hearing these aberrant calls respond in like fashion because they have no other teachers.

This sparrow is named after its distinctive white throat patch. The male's white crown usually has conspicuous black stripes; the female's frequently has tan stripes. The white-crowned sparrow has a similar head but lacks the lobes, or spots in front of the eye, displayed by the white-throat. The white-throated sparrow's back and tail are typically brown; the cheeks and breast are gray; the belly is white; and the wings have two white bars. It is about five and one-half to six inches in length and has a wingspan of about ten inches.

The white-throat is widespread, inhabiting all states east of the Rocky Mountains. In summer it nests in Canada and the New England states north to the barren ground. Its winters are spent from New Jersey and Kentucky south to the Gulf of Mexico. Some white-throats also cross the Rockies during the winter and can be found along the California coast.

Long after the juncos and chickadees have headed north in the spring, the white-throated sparrows remain in my area of New Jersey. A few are still around in mid-April, but most are on their breeding grounds by the first of May.

This bird prefers brushland to dense, continuous forests as a nesting site. Areas that have been cut or burned over and are slowly and naturally being reforested make favorite spots. The section of Quebec where I heard the white-throat's song so many times has been burned over again and again. Now there are many young stands of jack pine mixed in with the stands of

The white-throated sparrow has a clear, distinct call that sounds like "Old Sam, Peabody, Peabody, Peabody." The male uses this call to define his territory.

spruce that escaped the fire. This bird is also found in open parklands where aspens or birches are the dominant trees.

Territories are definitely established and fights between competing males frequently occur. The male defines the limits of his territory by singing from a series of different perches on its borders. Recent studies have revealed that the white-throated sparrow's home territory covers between two and three acres per family. The female seldom sings and does not help defend the territory, but she selects the nest site and performs all the work of gathering the nest material and of the actual construction. Usually built directly on the ground, at the edge of a clearing and under a clump of dense vegetation, the nest is composed of dead grasses, twigs, rootlets, moss, pine needles, and often deer hair. If the surrounding vegetation does not form a canopy over the nest, the female may build one.

The four to six heavily flecked, reddish brown spotted bluish or greenish eggs measure about one-half inch long and slightly less in diameter. The female broods them for eleven to thirteen days. Not enough is known about the nesting habits of this sparrow to say whether the male brings food to the brooding female. The parents share the task of feeding the young with insects and their larvae almost exclusively for the ten to twelve days they remain in the nest.

The white-throat's enemies are the hawk, the fox, and the red squirrel.

If the nest, eggs, or young are destroyed, the birds usually renest. If the brood is raised successfully, they consider their work done for that year.

The bulk of the white-throat's diet consists of vegetable matter, particularly weed seeds. It eats some grass seed, a little grain, and whatever wild berries are common to the area. In the early spring, when seeds become scarce, the sparrow eats the new buds of apple, maple, and beech trees. During the summer months, when the insect hordes are at their peak, they play a correspondingly important part in the white-throat's menu.

In wintertime I always have a couple of white-throats at my feeding stations. They do not care to feed at the station itself but prefer to pick up what seeds have been dropped or kicked out of the feeder by other birds. While scratching for food with both feet at the same time, these industrious little birds really make the duff fly. Scratch, scratch, scratch, then a hop backward to see if anything edible has been uncovered. Then it's back to work again.

Appendix
Where to See the Birds

A. National Wildlife Refuges in the United States[1]

Nearly 320 National Wildlife Refuges throughout the United States provide protection and habitat for waterfowl, nongame colonial waterbirds, endangered and indigenous species of big game, and other wildlife. The following listing is divided into the five geographic regions established by the Bureau of Sport Fisheries and Wildlife. For the purpose of this list, wildlife refuges managed primarily for big game, as well as references to hunting and fishing, have been omitted. Visitors should check with the refuge managers for sport and recreational information.

Descriptive leaflets and bird lists are available for most of the individual refuges and can be obtained by writing the Refuge Manager or Regional Director. Addresses for the administrative headquarters are given at the beginning of each regional listing.

Abbreviations

MA = Management Area	NWR = National Wildlife Refuge
MBR = Migratory Bird Refuge	R = Refuge
NMR = National Moose Refuge	WLFR = Wildlife and Fish Refuge

REGION I: THE FAR WEST

Administrative Headquarters: 730 N.E. Pacific Street, Box 3737, Portland, Oregon 97208.

Alaska

KENAI NMR. On Kenai Peninsula southwest of Anchorage. Waterfowl, eagles, hawks, and songbirds may be seen here, along with, the trumpeter swan, which has been brought back from the brink of extinction.

---

[1] Source: U.S. Department of the Interior, Fish and Wildlife Service, Bureau of Sport Fisheries and Wildlife.

California

Colusa NWR. 2 miles southwest of Colusa. Fall and winter concentrations of ducks and geese.

Kern NWR. 19 miles west of Delano in the southern San Joaquin Valley. This area is intensively developed for wintering waterfowl.

Also under the administration of Kern refuge is the nearby Pixley NWR. 8 miles north of Delano and 3 miles west of highway 99. It is being developed for waterfowl.

Merced NWR. 14 miles south and west of Merced in the San Joaquin Valley. Large numbers of ducks, geese (including much of the world population of Ross' geese), and cranes feed here during the late fall and winter.

Modoc NWR. In extreme northeastern California along both sides of highway 397 immediately south of Alturas. It is being developed for ducks and geese as a nesting and migration stopover point.

Sacramento NWR. 7 miles south of Willows on U.S. Highway 99W in Sacramento Valley, which comprises the most important wintering area for waterfowl of the Pacific Flyway. Often holds hundreds of thousands of ducks and geese from September to the end of the hunting season. Excellent location to see ducks, geese, and marsh birds from August through April.

Delevan NWR. Administered from Sacramento refuge and lies just southeast of it.

Farallon NWR. 91 acres of islands off San Francisco Bay. Also administered from Sacramento refuge. Used primarily by colonial nesting sea birds such as common murres, tufted puffins, Cassin's auklets, petrels, and pigeon guillemots. Not readily accessible.

Salton Sea NWR. One of the lowest spots in the United States, at the south end of the Salton Sea. Wintering area for waterfowl and other water birds.

San Luis NWR. Located in the San Joaquin Valley 8 miles north of Los Banos. Established primarily to provide a migration, wintering, and nesting area for waterfowl, it comprises a unique natural grassland and marsh. Opportunities for bird-watching and nature study are excellent.

Sutter NWR. On Sutter Bypass, 2 miles south of Sutter. Resting and feeding area for fall and winter concentrations of ducks and geese.

Tule Lake NWR. 6 miles west of Tulelake. This and the Lower Klamath refuge are extremely important feeding and resting areas for the largest concentrations of ducks and geese on the continent. Population peak in October. Excellent waterfowl production area. Good for viewing ducks, geese, swans, pelicans, grebes, shore birds, and other water birds from March through November, with seasonal variations in species, composition, and numbers.

Several other areas are under the administration of Tule Lake refuge. Clear Lake NWR. About 15 miles southeast of Tulelake. Nesting area for white pelicans, herons, and terns. Fall stopover point for migrating ducks and geese.

Klamath Forest NWR. In adjacent Oregon, 25 miles north of Chiloquin and several miles east of U.S. Highway 97. A nesting and migrating area for waterfowl.

Lower Klamath NWR. Located just south of the Oregon-California State Highway, 5 miles west of Tule Lake refuge. Excellent nesting area for waterfowl and other water birds. Resting and feeding area for large concentrations of ducks and geese.

Upper Klamath NWR. In Oregon, about 35 miles northwest of Klamath Falls. Nesting and resting area for waterfowl, water birds, and shore birds.

Hawaii

Hawaiian Islands NWR. Comprises a number of the small Leeward Islands in the Hawaiian chain, including Laysan, French Frigate Shoals, Pearl and Hermes Reef, and Lisianski. Protects albatrosses, frigate birds, shearwaters, petrels, boobies, terns, shore birds, and the rare Laysan duck, Laysan finch, and Nihoa millerbird. This refuge contains some of the greatest sea bird colonies in the world. Administered from a headquarters in Honolulu. Permission to visit is required.

Idaho

Camas NWR. Located just west of U.S. Highway 91, approximately 38 miles north of Idaho Falls in Jefferson County. Nesting, resting, and feeding area for ducks, geese, and other water birds.

Deer Flat NWR. 5 miles southwest of Nampa on Lake Lowell, this refuge also includes many islands in the Snake River from the vicinity of Marsing to below Weiser. Concentration area for migrating and wintering waterfowl, especially mallards and Canada geese. The Snake River islands are used by nesting geese and ducks.

Grays Lake NWR. Approximately 27 miles north of Soda Springs. Nesting and migrating waterfowl, primarily the western race of the Canada goose, greater sandhill crane, and ducks.

Kootenai NWR. Located on the flood plain of the Kootenai River 2 miles northwest of Bonners Ferry. The refuge is in the process of developing marsh and cropland for nesting and migrating waterfowl. Bird-watching and nature study opportunities available.

Minidoka NWR. Located on Lake Walcott, a Bureau of Reclamation reservoir on the Snake River about 13 miles north and east of Rupert. Excellent nesting and migration area for waterfowl and various water birds, marsh birds, and shore birds.

Montana

Benton Lake NWR. About 8 miles north of Great Falls. A nesting, resting, and feeding area for geese, ducks, shore birds, and upland game.

Also administered from Benton Lake refuge are two smaller refuges. Pishkun NWR. On Pishkun Reservoir 15 miles southwest of Choteau. Ducks, sharp-tailed grouse, gray partridges, and shore birds. Willow Creek NWR. On a Bureau of Reclamation reservoir approximately 5 miles north of Augusta. Geese, ducks, sharp-tailed grouse, and shore birds.

Bowdoin NWR. 8 miles east of Malta on U.S. Highway 2. Valuable nesting, resting, and feeding area for geese, ducks, and other water birds.

Small waterfowl refuges administered from Bowdoin include Black Coulee NWR, Blaine County; Creedman Coulee NWR and Lake Thibadeau NWR, Hill County; and Hewitt Lake NWR, Phillips County.

Charles M. Russell NWR. On Fort Peck Reservoir and adjoining public lands, occupies a 22-mile stretch of the Missouri River. A rugged area with grassy plateaus surrounded by highly eroded precipitous slopes of bare clay and weathered shale. Provides habitat for sharp-tailed grouse and sage grouse. Portions of the reservoir provide nesting, resting, and feeding areas for waterfowl.

The following lesser waterfowl areas are administered from the Charles M. Russell Range: HAILSTONE NWR and HALFBREED LAKE NWR, Stillwater County; LAKE MASON NWR, Musselshell County; and WAR HORSE NWR, Petroleum County.

MEDICINE LAKE NWR. 2 miles south of Medicine Lake. Nesting, resting, and feeding area for waterfowl and native upland game birds.

THE LAMESTEER NWR. Small waterfowl area in Wibaux County, administered from the Medicine Lake refuge.

NINEPIPE NWR. On Indian Irrigation Service Ninepipe Reservoir 9 miles north of St. Ignatius. Primarily for waterfowl. PABLO NWR. A waterfowl refuge lying on Pablo Reservoir north of the Ninepipe refuge. These two refuges are administered from the National Bison Range, 6 miles north of Dixon.

RAVALLI NWR. A new area near Stevensville. Being developed as a migratory waterfowl refuge.

RED ROCK LAKES NWR. 30 miles east of Monida at the base of the Centennial Mountains. Established mainly for the protection and propagation of the Rocky Mountain population of the rare trumpeter swan, which remains here the entire year.

Nevada

DESERT NWR. An extensive area north of U.S. Highway 95, northwest of Las Vegas. Set aside primarily for desert bighorns but also provides habitat for other desert mammals, Gambel's quail, and varied desert birds.

Also administered from the Desert NWR is the PAHRANAGAT NWR. New waterfowl area in the Pahranagat Valley about 70 miles northeast of Las Vegas.

RUBY LAKE NWR. Approximately 60 miles south and east of Elko alongside the Ruby Mountains. Marsh, lake, and sagebrush habitat for trumpeter swans, Canada geese, ducks, sandhill cranes, shore birds, and sage grouse.

STILLWATER NWR and MA. North and east of Fallon. Although in a dry, alkaline desert, return flow from the Newlands Irrigation Project provides water for about 35,000 acres of marsh and ponds, which contain excellent resting and feeding habitat for waterfowl, marsh birds, and shore birds. A very good birding area for these groups.

Also administered by the Stillwater refuge are the adjoining FALLON NWR and the ANAHO ISLAND NWR. Anaho Island consists of a rocky island in Pyramid Lake 7 miles northwest of Nixon. It contains possibly the largest white pelican nesting colony in North America as well as cormorant and gull colonies.

Oregon

ANKENY NWR. (See William L. Finley—Oregon.)

BASKETT SLOUGH NWR. (See William L. Finley—Oregon.)

CAPE MEARES NWR. (See Willapa—Washington.)

COLD SPRINGS NWR. (See McNary—Washington.)

KLAMATH FOREST NWR. (See Tule Lake—California.)

MALHEUR NWR. 32 miles south of Burns. Managed primarily for nesting and migrating waterfowl, but also provides excellent habitat for marsh birds (including sandhill cranes), shore birds, and other water birds, as well as upland game birds. Outstanding for bird-watching and wildlife photography. Museum with mounted bird specimens and display pond with photographic blind at headquarters.

McKAY CREEK NWR. (See McNary—Washington.)

OREGON ISLANDS NWR. (See Willapa—Washington.)

THREE ARCH ROCKS NWR. (See Willapa—Washington.)

UPPER KLAMATH NWR. (See Tule Lake—California.)

UMATILLA NWR. Located on both sides of the Columbia River in the vicinity of Boardman, Oregon, and Paterson, Washington. Developed primarily to replace waterfowl production habitat flooded by the project reservoir and to provide food and protection to migrating, wintering, and resident waterfowl.

WILLIAM L. FINLEY NWR. Two other refuges in the Willamette Valley are administered from the William L. Finley refuge 12 miles south of Corvallis: the ANKENY R, located south of Salem, and BASKETT SLOUGH R, 10 miles west of Salem. Mainly for waterfowl, these refuges are also managed for resident game and small birds.

Washington

COLUMBIA NWR. In the Columbia River Basin about 50 miles north of Pasco and approximately 10 miles north and west of Othello. Provides habitat for nesting and migrating waterfowl.

McNARY NWR. Located on McNary Reservoir south of Pasco. Nesting area for ducks and geese.

Two smaller refuges administered from McNary are in Oregon; COLD SPRINGS NWR. 7 miles east of Hermiston, Oregon. Resting and feeding area for a large concentration of Canada geese and ducks during the late fall. McKAY CREEK NWR. 5 miles south of Pendleton, Oregon. Resting and feeding area for tens of thousands of Canada geese and ducks during the fall.

RIDGEFIELD NWR. A new refuge in the process of acquisition and development. Primarily for migrating and wintering ducks and geese, it is on the Columbia River flood plain. Improved pastures and shallow marshes are managed for western, lesser, and dusky Canada geese and widgeon.

TOPPENISH NWR. In the acquisition stage, this marsh and meadow area near Yakima is slated primarily for waterfowl. The CONBOY NWR. 5 miles south of Glenwood. Managed out of Toppenish.

TURNBULL NWR. 6 miles south of Cheney. Managed primarily for waterfowl. Shore birds, upland game birds, and deer are also present.

WILLAPA NWR. On Leadbetter Point of Long Beach Peninsula, and on Long Island and the adjacent mainland at the south end of Willapa Bay. Managed for black brant, Canada geese, and ducks, but also provides habitat for shore birds and grouse.

A number of smaller refuges are administered from the Willapa refuge. The COPALIS NWR. A series of small offshore islands extending along 23 miles of coastline north of Grays Harbor. FLATTERY ROCKS NWR and QUILLAYUTE

Needles NWR. Extending south for 49 miles from Cape Flattery on the northwest coast. These three refuges are for comorants, petrels, murres, auklets, oystercatchers, guillemots, puffins, shore birds, and gulls.

Dungeness NWR. On Dungeness Spit and adjoining tidelands, about 7 miles northwest of Sequim. Provides habitat for black brant, ducks, and shore birds.

Located in Puget Sound are the Jones Island, Matia Island, San Juan, and Smith Island NWRs. Habitat for white-winged scoters, shearwaters, glaucous-winged gulls, band-tailed pigeons, guillemots, cormorants, puffins, and harlequin ducks.

Cape Meares NWR. A small coastal area 5 miles west of Tillamook. Cliffs and rocks bordering the ocean provide habitat for tufted puffins, black oystercatchers, black turnstones, and surfbirds. A timbered area supports band-tailed pigeons.

Oregon Islands NWR. Numerous islands and rocky prominences off the Oregon coast set aside primarily for tufted puffins, common murres, and other sea birds.

Three Arch Rocks NWR. A group of rocky islands, just off the coast at Oceanside, Oregon. Primarily for western gulls, tufted puffins, petrels, cormorants, common murres, and northern sea lions.

Region II: The Southwest

Administrative Headquarters: P.O. Box 1306, Albuquerque, New Mexico 87103.

Arizona

Cibola NWR. Along the lower Colorado River between Blythe, California, and Yuma, Arizona. Farm crops and pasturage are being provided for geese that winter in the Colorado River valley as well as for several species of ducks and for sandhill cranes.

Havasau NWR. Along the lower Colorado River in Mohave County, Arizona, and San Bernardino County, California, and a small section in Yuma County, Arizona. Primarily for waterfowl. Supports doves and quail.

Imperial NWR. On the lower Colorado River in Yuma County, Arizona, and Imperial County, California. Primarily for waterfowl; also supports quail and other wildlife. Important wintering area for Canada geese and other waterfowl.

Colorado

Alamosa NWR. Along the Rio Grande in Alamosa and Costilla Counties. Supports pheasants and waterfowl nesting.

Arapahoe NWR. Waterfowl nesting area located along the Illinois River, about 6 miles south of Walden. Administered by Hutton Lake refuge manager, Laramie, Wyoming.

Browns Park NWR. Along the Green River in Moffat County. Waterfowl nesting area.

Monte Vista NWR. Alamosa and Rio Grande Counties. Waterfowl nesting and wintering area; supports pheasants.

Kansas

FLINT HILLS NWR. Waterfowl refuge 11 miles northwest of Burlington. Provides food and protection for migrating ducks and geese.

KIRWIN NWR. 2 miles west of Kirwin on Kirwin Reservoir. Waterfowl, bobwhite, and pheasants the predominant game species.

QUIVIRA NWR. 18 miles north of Stafford. Waterfowl refuge with some quail and pheasants.

New Mexico

BITTER LAKE NWR. 15 miles northeast of Roswell along the Pecos River. Winters large numbers of sandhill cranes; supports quail and pheasants.

BOSQUE DEL APACHE NWR. 5 miles south of San Antonio along the Rio Grande. Important waterfowl wintering area; winters America's largest flock of greater sandhill cranes; is a natural nesting area for the endangered Mexican duck; supports quail and pheasants.

LAS VEGAS NWR. 3 miles southeast of Las Vegas. Food and a resting area for migrating and wintering waterfowl.

MAXWELL NWR. 5 miles northwest of Maxwell. Established in 1966 to provide migrating and wintering waterfowl with food and resting area. Will serve as a nesting area also.

Oklahoma

SALT PLAINS NWR. 10 miles north of Jet. Includes Great Salt Plains Reservoir and adjacent lands. Waterfowl wintering area; supports bobwhite and pheasants.

TISHOMINGO NWR. 6 miles southeast of Tishomingo on Washita arm of Lake Texoma. Important waterfowl wintering area; supports quail and small mammals. Popular for waterfowl observation; no hunting on refuge portion of lake.

WASHITA NWR. 12 miles from Clinton, on the upper Washita River. The refuge attracts ducks and geese during fall migration and carries many of them into the winter.

Texas

ANAHUAC NWR. In Chambers County on the upper Gulf Coast. Wintering ground for four species of geese, many waterfowl, and the yellow rail, and a year-round home for mottled ducks. Consists of valuable fresh and salt water marshlands.

ARANSAS NWR. 8 miles south of Austwell. Famed as the wintering ground of the endangered whooping crane. Supports the endangered Attwater's prairie chicken and serves as a wintering ground for migratory waterfowl.

BRAZORIA NWR. 15 miles southeast of Angleton along the Texas Gulf Coast. Waterfowl wintering area. Supports limited numbers of mourning doves and bobwhite.

BUFFALO LAKE NWR. On outskirts of Unbarger in the Texas Panhandle. Important resting area for waterfowl during migrations. Winter populations occasionally reach 1,000,000 ducks. Canada geese abundant, numbering up to 40,000.

HAGERMAN NWR. 15 miles southwest of Denison on the Big Mineral arm of Lake Texoma. Waterfowl migration and wintering area; bobwhite present.

LAGUNA ATASCOSA NWR. 25 miles northeast of San Benito, in the lower Rio Grande Valley. This waterfowl area winters 1,000,000 ducks, often including the continent's largest concentration of redheads. Popular with bird watchers in winter. More than 300 bird species have been recorded.

MULESHOE NWR. 20 miles south of Muleshoe, in the Texas Panhandle. Important to waterfowl in fall and winter; often winters 750,000 ducks and large concentrations of sandhill cranes.

SANTA ANA NWR. On the bank of the Ric Grande near Alamo, the refuge is well known for its many birds that are found elsewhere, mainly in Mexico.

Utah

BEAR RIVER MBR. At the mouth of Bear River. An outstanding waterfowl nesting area; attracts 1,000,000 or more ducks and large flocks of whistling swans and geese in migrations. National attraction for bird watchers and photographers.

FISH SPRINGS NWR. On the Great Salt Lake Desert. An isolated natural marsh supplied by permanent springs, used by nesting and migrating ducks and geese. Some birds winter on the warm springs.

OURAY NWR. In east-central Utah on the Green River, 25 miles south of Vernal. This isolated area provides nesting habitat and fall food and protection for migrating ducks and geese.

Wyoming

BAMFORTH NWR. 11 miles northwest of Laramie. Waterfowl nesting area.

HUTTON LAKE NWR. 12 miles southwest of Laramie. Waterfowl nesting and feeding area.

PATHFINDER NWR. On Pathfinder Reservoir. Waterfowl habitat.

SEEDSKADEE NWR. Along the Green River. Being established to provide nesting habitat for ducks and geese.

REGION III: THE NORTH CENTRAL STATES

Administrative Headquarters: Federal Building, Fort Snelling, Twin Cities, Minnesota 55111.

Illinois

CHAUTAUQUA NWR. Rural Route 2, 9 miles north of Havana, on the Illinois River. Large concentrations of waterfowl, principally mallards, can be seen here in fall and winter.

CRAB ORCHARD NWR. Located ½ mile south of the junction of state routes 13 and 148, approximately 5 miles west of Marion. Recreational areas include facilities for hunting. Large concentrations of Canada geese and ducks use the refuge from October through February.

MARK TWAIN NWR. This refuge includes lands in Illinois, Iowa, and Missouri, and extends along the Mississippi River from Rock Island 250 miles south to Grafton, Illinois. Public waterfowl hunting is available under state sponsorship on areas of the river outside the closed refuge units.

UPPER MISSISSIPPI RIVER WLFR. (See Minnesota.)

Indiana

MUSCATATUCK NWR. Located near Seymour, this refuge will ultimately contain

8,000 acres. The area has a history of extensive wood duck use. Focus is on the wood duck and on providing suitable habitat for other waterfowl including Canada geese.

Iowa

DE SOTO NWR. The refuge, at Missouri Valley, is on a former bend of the Missouri River, 13 miles upstream from Omaha. This flood plain has traditionally attracted migratory waterfowl. The refuge is a major source of recreational opportunity to some 500,000 people within a 30-mile radius, in addition to serving as a major resting and feeding area for waterfowl during migrations.

MARK TWAIN NWR. (See Illinois.)

UNION SLOUGH NWR. 6 miles west of Titonka, this refuge comprises about 2,100 acres on a natural slough between two watersheds in north-central Iowa. Five dikes control water levels in small impoundments. An average of 100,-000 ducks and several thousand geese stop here each year.

UPPER MISSISSIPPI RIVER WLFR. (See Minnesota.)

Michigan

SENEY NWR. North of Germfask on state highway 77. The refuge, in the Great Manistique Swamp, is a vast open marsh with shallow pools interspersed with sand ridges supporting stands of red and jack pine. Canada geese nest here as well as black ducks, mallards, and ring-necked ducks.

THE HURON NWR. Also administered from Seney. Comprises 5 islands along the south shore of Lake Superior near the village of Big Bay, Michigan. Cormorants, gulls, and terns are the main species found here.

SHIAWASSEE NWR. 7 miles southwest of Saginaw, just off state highway 13, this refuge was established as a northern link in the Mississippi Flyway chain of waterfowl refuges. Here 6 rivers converge to form Saginaw River, which flows north into Saginaw Bay of Lake Huron. A system of dikes and pumps helps to maintain agricultural lands and waterfowl habitat.

Two other refuges are administered from Shiawassee. WYANDOTTE NWR. Island-and-water area in the Detroit River between Ecorse and Grosse Ile, is used extensively during migrations by diving ducks. MICHIGAN ISLANDS NWR. In Alpena and Charlevoix Counties. Consists of 3 islands in Lake Huron and Lake Michigan for herons, gulls, and terns.

Minnesota

AGASSIZ NWR. At Middle River, 11 miles east of Holt. More than 500,000 waterfowl stop annually. The refuge is valuable nesting habitat for many species of ducks as well as Canada geese. This is a popular area for sightseers and ornithologists in spring, summer, and fall.

RICE LAKE NWR. 5 miles south of McGregor, 2 miles west of state highway 65, in a low bog country surrounding Rice Lake proper. This was a historic Indian hunting and camping ground. Great blue heron and double-crested cormorant colonies are present. The refuge has a sizable breeding population of ducks and is becoming important as a Canada goose nesting area. Ruffed grouse are common.

Also administered by Rice Lake is the MILLE LACS NWR. It comprises two small rocky islands off the south shore of Lake Mille Lacs. This area is one of the few places in North America where purple martins breed in large numbers in rocks. Terns and gulls also nest here.

SHERBURNE NWR. In developmental stage, the refuge is located on county road N. 9, 9 miles southwest of Princeton. Sherburne refuge will restore wildlife habitat that has been lost to agricultural drainage, urban expansion, and highway construction.

UPPER MISSISSIPPI RIVER WLFR. Extends from Wabasha, Minnesota, along both sides of the Mississippi River approximately 280 miles to Rock Island, Illinois, where it adjoins Mark Twain NWR. Approximately 75 percent of the refuge is open to public hunting. The remaining lands are designated as "closed areas" where waterfowl are protected during hunting seasons. Large concentrations of waterfowl are present during migration periods.

Missouri

MARK TWAIN NWR. (See Illinois.)

MINGO NWR. 1½ miles northeast of Puxico on state highway 51. The refuge occupies the former Mingo Swamp, an ancient channel of the Missouri River at the edge of the Ozarks. It consists of lowland bordered by limestone bluffs and rolling hills. The refuge serves primarily as a wintering area for waterfowl.

SQUAW CREEK NWR. At Mound City, in northwest Missouri, halfway between Kansas City and Omaha. The refuge is a traditional stopping place for migrant ducks and geese, especially snow and blue geese, Canada geese, and mallards. Goose populations frequently reach 300,000 during the spring migration. The area is popular with midwestern ornithologists.

SWAN LAKE NWR. 1 mile south of Sumner at the junction of Yellow and Grand Rivers in the north-central part of the state. The refuge serves as a major resting and feeding area for one of the largest single concentrations of Canada geese in North America, at times exceeding 100,000 birds.

Nebraska

CRESCENT LAKE NWR. Located at Ellsworth, this refuge is near the southwest edge of one of the larger tall-grass prairie regions remaining in the United States —Sandhills of Nebraska. A large variety of waterfowl uses the area as well as sharp-tailed grouse and long-billed curlews.

Also administered from Crescent Lake is the NORTH PLATTE NWR, about 8 miles northeast of Scottsbluff. This refuge provides some nesting, although it is primarily used as a resting area during migration.

DE SOTO NWR. (See Iowa.)

VALENTINE NWR. 17 miles south of Valentine on U.S. Highway 83, then 13 miles west and south on state highway 483. This refuge is another "sandhills" area made up of lakes, meadows, marshes, and rolling hills. It is an excellent nesting location for a variety of waterfowl and upland game. A great blue heron rookery and nesting long-billed curlews are of special interest.

North Dakota

ARROWWOOD NWR. West side of Arrowwood Lake, 6 miles east of Edmunds, and

24 miles north of Jamestown. Many species of waterfowl rest and nest here. Sharp-tailed grouse are common.

CHASE LAKE NWR. Administered from Arrowwood, comprises 4,385 acres in Stutsman County, and is primarily for waterfowl. It is also used by large numbers of nesting white pelicans. Smaller refuges also administered from Arrowwood are the HALF-WAY LAKE, HOBART LAKE, STONEY SLOUGH, and TOMAHAWK NWRs.

AUDUBON NWR. (Formerly Snake Creek Refuge.) About 2½ miles east of Coleharbor, on a county road just south of the Snake Creek embankment. Consists of rolling hills with grasslands, meadows, cropland, and one major impoundment maintained primarily by water from the Garrison Reservoir.

CAMP LAKE, COTTONWOOD LAKE, LAKE NETTIE, LAMBS LAKE, LOST LAKE, and WINTERING RIVER NWRs. Administered from Audubon NWR.

DES LACS NWR. 1 mile west of Kenmare. This is a long narrow refuge consisting of wooded coulees, river bottom marshes, and grassy uplands, following Des Lacs River Valley for 30 miles to the Canadian border. Waterfowl are found in abundance during spring, summer, and fall.

Three smaller refuges are administered from Des Lacs primarily for waterfowl. They are PRETTY ROCK, STEWART LAKE, and WHITE LAKE NWR.

LAKE ILO NWR. 1½ miles west of Dunn Center. A small but important refuge heavily used by waterfowl.

LONG LAKE NWR. 3 miles southeast of Moffit on U.S. Highway 83, administered from Slade Lake NWR (see below), the area was established to aid in controlling botulism. This disease, affecting waterfowl and shore birds, has on occasion caused heavy losses of birds. Mallards, gadwalls, pintails, and blue-winged teal are common nesting species. Canada and white-fronted geese frequent the area during migrations. Sandhill crane populations are increasing.

LOSTWOOD NWR. About 18 miles west of Kenmare, this refuge is in a prairie pothole region containing native grasslands pitted with thousands of small lakes and potholes. It is one of the best waterfowl production refuges, but also has many nesting shore birds and other marsh birds and water birds of interest to photographers and ornithologists.

Also administered from Lostwood are the HIDDENWOOD, McLEAN, and SHELL LAKE NWRs. They provide food and sanctuary for waterfowl, shore birds, and upland game birds.

J. CLARK SALYER NWR. 3 miles north of Upham on state highway 14, this area is predominantly river bottom marsh with managed pools and upland surrounding the Souris River for about 50 miles to the Canadian border. It is also a haven for large concentrations of migrating ducks and geese. Sharp-tailed grouse, Canada geese, and most duck species nest here.

J. Clark Salyer personnel administer 4 small waterfowl refuges. They are the LORDS LAKE, RABB LAKE, SCHOOL SECTION LAKE, and WILLOW LAKE NWR.

SLADE NWR. 2 miles south of Dawson, the refuge consists of about 3,000 acres of rolling prairie dotted with lakes and potholes. It is used by waterfowl 7 months of the year for resting, feeding, and nesting.

7 small refuges are administered from Slade refuge. They are the APPERT LAKE,

CANFIELD LAKE, FLICKERTAIL, FLORENCE LAKE, LAKE GEORGE, SPRINGWATER and SUNBURST NWRs.

TEWAUKON NWR. 4 miles southwest of Cayuga. Nesting, feeding, and resting area for migratory waterfowl. Heavy use by many species of ducks, Canada geese, blue and snow geese.

Tewaukon administers 5 small waterfowl areas—the BONE HILL, LAKE ELSIE, MAPLE RIVER, STORM LAKE, and WILD RICE LAKE NWRs.

UPPER SOURIS NWR. Located at Foxholm, this refuge extends for almost 30 miles along the Souris River. An important waterfowl production area.

Ohio

OTTAWA NWR. The project, lying 15 miles east of Toledo, comprises some of the best waterfowl habitat remaining in the Lake Erie marshes. The refuge is adjacent to the Magee Marsh Wildlife Area administered by the Ohio Division of Wildlife. Principal waterfowl species associated with the area are mallards, black ducks, widgeon, blue-winged teal, redheads, scaups, Canada geese, and whistling swans.

Two other refuges are administered from Ottawa. CEDAR POINT NWR. Established 1964 in a historic duck club marsh near Toledo through the generosity of its owners. WEST SISTER ISLAND NWR. Located in Lake Erie, supports an important black-crowned night heron rookery.

South Dakota

LACREEK NWR. Southeast of Martin in the historic Pine Ridge Sioux Indian Reservation region near the Nebraska border. Lakes and marshes make up the main area. Spring and fall waterfowl migrants and the late summer concentrations of shore birds and swallows attract many visitors.

BEAR BUTTE NWR. In Meade County. Established primarily for the benefit of waterfowl. Administered from Lacreek.

LAKE ANDES NWR. At Lake Andes. Important resting and feeding area for waterfowl. Large numbers of mallards and Canada geese spend the fall and winter at Lake Andes and nearby portions of the Fort Randall Reservoir on the Missouri River.

SAND LAKE NWR. Approximately 30 miles from Aberdeen and north of Columbia. This area, long known as an important waterfowl gathering place, has spectacular concentrations of geese and ducks during spring and fall migration periods. It also supports a substantial breeding population of ducks and a small nesting flock of Canada geese. Shore birds frequent the area in great numbers. A large breeding colony of Franklin's gulls is present, and western grebes nest.

DAKOTA LAKE NWR. In adjacent North Dakota. Waterfowl area administered from Sand Lake refuge.

WAUBAY NWR. 1 mile east and 8 miles north of Waubay, which in Sioux language means "nesting place for birds." This aptly describes the high-rolling prairie hills dotted with thousands of potholes surrounding Waubay refuge, which supports a number of species of nesting ducks and a local breeding flock of Canada geese.

Wisconsin

HORICON NWR. Located at Mayville, this joint federal-state project lies in the heart of the Wisconsin dairyland. The area receives tremendous use by migrating Canada geese, mallards, blue-winged teal, and many other species of ducks. Production of ducks, coots, and gallinules is high.

Two small refuges are administered from Horicon. GRAVEL ISLAND NWR and GREEN BAY NWR. in Door County. These refuges are for herons, gulls, Caspian terns, and waterfowl.

NECEDAH NWR. 7 miles west of Necedah, the area is characterized by numerous ponds and marshes, separated by sandy ridges and islands. Spring and fall migrations of waterfowl.

UPPER MISSISSIPPI RIVER WLFR. (See Minnesota.)

Also administered from the Upper Mississippi River WLFR is the TREMPEALEAU NWR. In Trempealeau County. Located in west-central Wisconsin, this area is primarily for the benefit of waterfowl and common egrets.

REGION IV: THE SOUTHEAST

Administrative Headquarters: Peachtree-Seventh Building, Atlanta, Georgia 30323.

Alabama

CHOCTAW NWR. On the west bank of the Tombigbee River, 2 miles upstream from the Jackson Lock and Dam, Coffeeville. Under active management for waterfowl since 1962.

EUFAULA NWR. Headquarters in Eufala. Superimposed on the Walter F. George Reservoir on the Chattahoochee River. Farming and water management programs are directed toward the establishment of wintering flocks of Canada geese and several species of ducks.

WHEELER NWR. 3 miles southeast of Decatur on state highway 67. The first large federal refuge to be located on a TVA reservoir, this area is an excellent example of multiple land use. Thousands of waterfowl have been attracted to the refuge through intensive management.

Arkansas

BIG LAKE NWR. 2½ miles northeast of Manila on state highway 18. Many species of waterfowl and other birds.

HOLLA BEND NWR. Russellville. Thousands of ducks and a small Canada goose flock.

WAPANOCCA NWR. Headquarters located ¼ mile south of Turrell, less than 4 miles from the Mississippi River. Wintering area for thousands of mallards and other waterfowl. The main topographic feature is the beautiful cypress-edged Wapanocca Lake.

WHITE RIVER NWR. At DeWitt, along the White River in eastern Arkansas. The natural lakes and streams that traverse the refuge, along with numerous "green tree" reservoirs, provide habitat and resting areas for approximately 200,000 ducks, and 2,000 Canada geese.

Florida

CHASSAHOWITZKA NWR. 4½ miles south of Homosassa on U.S. Highway 19. Principally for waterfowl. Managed waterfowl hunts in season. CEDAR KEYS R. Administered by the Chassahowitzka refuge off the Gulf Coast, provides sanctuary and nesting habitat for many colonial birds.

LAKE WOODRUFF NWR. At DeLeon Springs, 5 miles northwest of Deland along the east side of the St. Johns River. Extensive marsh and hardwood swamp areas and some pinelands. Managed for wintering waterfowl and wood ducks.

MERRITT ISLAND NWR. Located on Merritt Island, the refuge provides sanctuary for large numbers of migratory waterfowl, shore birds, and other wildlife. Home of the rare dusky seaside sparrow.

PELICAN ISLAND R. The first refuge established, in 1903, is in the Indian River east of Sebastian. Under the administration of Merritt Island NWR. Although famous for its historic nesting colony of pelicans, the island is used by thousands of other water birds, too, for nesting and loafing.

ST. MARKS NWR. 4 miles south of Wakulla, on U.S. Highway 98. The refuge includes the major Florida wintering area for Canada geese, and sanctuary is provided for many other waterfowl and wildlife species.

ST. VINCENT NWR. Headquarters in Apalachicola. This island refuge, accessible only by boat, is located on the Gulf Coast between Apalachicola and Port St. Joe. Important habitat for many species of waterfowl and other migratory birds, resident wildlife, and such rare and endangered species as the bald eagle.

SOUTH FLORIDA NWR. Headquarters on Loxahatchee R, 1 mile west of highway 441, 3.2 miles north of intersection of 441 and state road 806 (Delray Beach road). The following Florida refuges are under the administration of South Florida NWR:

Lower East Coast Areas LOXAHATCHEE R. A major wintering and production area of the Everglades for colonial and other waterbirds. Wintering waterfowl plus the resident mottled and wood ducks make it a primary waterfowl area. Other resident wildlife of particular interest includes Florida sandhill crane, limkin, gallinules, anhinga, and smooth-billed ani. The extremely rare Everglade kite uses the area and has recently nested.

Lower Keys KEY DEER, GREAT WHITE HERON, and KEY WEST NWRs. Administered from the Key Deer refuge headquarters, Big Pine Key. These refuges provide protection for the great white heron, white-crowned pigeon, roseate spoonbill, Wurdemann's heron, and other wading and shore birds.

West Coast Refuges J. N. "DING" DARLING NWR. Situated on Sanibel Island in the Gulf of Mexico, 5 miles off the coast. Also under the refuge manager's supervision are ANCLOTE, PINELLAS, ISLAND BAY, and PASSAGE KEY NWR. North of Sanibel. All areas provide important nesting grounds for colonial birds and winter sanctuary for waterfowl.

Georgia

OKEFENOKEE NWR. Headquarters in Waycross. This refuge, containing more than 80 percent of one of the oldest and most primitive swamps in America, was established to preserve this wilderness as a sanctuary for white ibises, sandhill cranes, wood ducks, and other wildlife inhabiting the area. The flora of Okefenokee is also well known and is beautiful at all seasons.

PIEDMONT NWR. 3 miles from Round Oak off state highway 11. Managed for the benefit of waterfowl and upland wildlife, including turkeys and bobwhites.

BLACKBEARD ISLAND NWR. Contact Savannah NWR, Hardeeville, South Carolina 29927, before visiting. This 5,600-acre island lies off the Georgia mainland between Sapelo Sound and the Atlantic Ocean. It provides good habitat for waterfowl and many marsh and wading birds.

Harris Neck NWR. Administered by Savannah NWR, Hardeeville, South Carolina. This Georgia coastal refuge, 50 miles south of Savannah, off U.S. Highway 17 on route 131, is directed toward the establishment of a wintering Canada goose flock. Other than waterfowl, many species of land and water birds are found.

Louisiana

Catahoula NWR. At Jonesville on the east end of Catahoula Lake. Established primarily as a sanctuary for wintering waterfowl but also for other species of wildlife.

Delta NWR. On the east bank of Mississippi River, 7 miles below Venice. Many thousands of blue and snow geese and other species of waterfowl arrive each fall from the northern breeding grounds to winter on the Delta marshes.

East Timbalier NWR. Under the administration of Delta NWR. Provides nesting and resting habitat for shore birds, gulls, and terns.

Lacassine NWR. 11 miles southwest of Lake Arthur off state highway 14. Waterfowl wintering area. Largest concentration of white-fronted geese in the Mississippi Flyway, and one of the larger populations of fulvous tree ducks in the United States.

Shell Keys NWR. Small colonial nesting bird island offshore in the Gulf of Mexico, under the administration of Lacassine NWR.

Sabine NWR. 6 miles southwest of Hackberry on state highway 27. The refuge includes 3 large artificial freshwater impoundments, and is bounded on the west and east by 2 large brackish lakes—Sabine and Calcasieu. Winter home for thousands of geese and ducks. Flocks of blue and snow geese may be seen in the marshes adjacent to the highway.

Maryland

Blackwater NWR. 10 miles south of Cambridge, on the eastern shore of Chesapeake Bay, the area serves as an important waterfowl resting and feeding grounds. Canada geese, black ducks, blue-winged teal, mallards, wood ducks, and shore birds nest here. Also under supervision of Blackwater refuge are the smaller Susquehanna and Martin NWRs in Chesapeake Bay.

Eastern Neck NWR. 8 miles south of Rock Hall. An important wintering area for waterfowl and a nesting area for black ducks.

Mississippi

Gulf Island NWR. Headquarters at Point Cadet Area, Biloxi. Gulf Island includes 3 refuges in the Gulf of Mexico off the Louisiana-Mississippi Coast—Horn Island, Petit Bois, and Breton NWRs. Many waterfowl and shore birds frequent the islands, and sea turtles nest on their shores.

Noxubee NWR. At Brooksville, approximately 18 miles south of Starkville. "Green timber" reservoirs have been constructed that, with agricultural lands, provide sanctuary for thousands of ducks in winter. Upland areas are managed for wild turkeys and bobwhites.

Yazoo NWR. 12 miles southwest of Hollandale. Waterfowl and upland game birds.

North Carolina

CEDAR ISLAND NWR. Headquarters are in the Beaufort Post Office Building, 25 miles south of the refuge. Wintering area for waterfowl, principally puddle ducks, and nesting area for black ducks.

MATTAMUSKEET NWR. ½ mile north of New Holland on U.S. Highway 264. With its dominant feature the 40,000-acre Mattamuskeet Lake, this well-known refuge is a mecca for thousands of ducks, geese, and swans during the winter.

SWANQUARTER NWR. Lying on the mainland and including island and water areas off the coast, this refuge serves as an important sanctuary for diving ducks.

PEA ISLAND NWR. Headquarters are in Manteo. A narrow strip of barrier beach, extending from Oregon Inlet to near Rodanthe, Pea Island was established primarily as a winter home for greater snow geese. Many other species of waterfowl and shore birds frequent the area. It is within Cape Hatteras National Seashore.

PEE DEE NWR. Headquarters are in the Post Office Building, Wadesboro, approximately 6 miles south of the refuge. Currently under acquisition. Following development, Pee Dee will serve as an important Canada goose and puddle duck wintering area, and will provide nesting habitat for the indigenous wood duck.

South Carolina

CAPE ROMAIN NWR. 1 mile east of U.S. Highway 17 in McClellanville. Cape Romain contains 60,000 acres in Charleston County, including Bulls Island. The refuge accommodates waterfowl and shore birds during migrations and in winter. The variety of summer resident birds contributes to the refuge's year-round attractiveness.

CAROLINA SANDHILLS NWR. 3 miles north of McBee on U.S. Highway 1. Emphasis toward management for Canada geese and ducks. In addition to wild turkey, bobwhites, and other upland wildlife, the refuge is home or a resting place to 175 species of songbirds and migratory nongame birds.

SANTEE NWR. 7 miles south of Summerton. Managed primarily for waterfowl, this refuge winters the southernmost major Canada goose flock.

SAVANNAH NWR. Route 1, Hardeeville, off highway 17 near the Georgia line, with the refuge divided between the 2 states. The refuge has been developed to provide excellent habitat for wintering waterfowl and serves also as an important wood duck nesting area. TYBEE and WOLF ISLAND NWRs, located off the coast of Georgia, are important shore bird refuges under the administration of Savannah NWR. BLACKBEARD R and HARRIS NECK R are also administered by Savannah refuge.

Tennessee

CROSS CREEKS NWR. 3½ miles southeast of Dover off state highway 49. This refuge was established in 1962 to replace waterfowl habitat flooded at the former Kentucky Woodlands NWR by Barkley Reservoir. An intensive waterfowl management program is in progress.

HATCHIE NWR. 10 miles south of Brownsville on the Hatchie River. When acquisition is complete, Hatchie will be one of the better bottomland hardwood timbered refuges in the entire system. Important wood duck protection and waterfowl migration and wintering area.

REELFOOT NWR. Headquartered in Samburg, this refuge lies partly in Kentucky. LAKE ISOM NWR. 5 miles south. Also administered by Reelfoot refuge. Serving primarily as sanctuaries for waterfowl, these 2 areas attract thousands of ducks and geese each winter.

TENNESSEE NWR. Headquarters in Paris. Sanctuary for many forms of waterfowl and other wildlife. A large farming program to provide supplemental waterfowl foods.

Virginia

BACK BAY NWR. Headquarters in Princess Anne. The refuge is located 5½ miles south of Sandbridge Beach. Sanctuary for wintering populations of whistling swans, greater snow geese, Canada geese, and various species of ducks. A number of shore birds are year-round residents.

CHINCOTEAGUE NWR. This refuge, occupying the south third of Assateague Island National Seashore, was established for waterfowl, and is an outstanding shore bird area. A small portion extends into Maryland.

MACKAY ISLAND NWR. Headquarters for Mackay Island and Back Bay refuges are combined in an office in Princess Anne, Virginia. This refuge is located in North Carolina and Virginia. State route 615 runs through the refuge. Sanctuary for wintering populations of whistling swans, greater snow geese, Canada geese, and various species of ducks. Snow geese using the marsh provide a spectacular sight.

PRESQUILE NWR. Headquarters located in Hopewell. Located on an island in the James River. Sanctuary is provided for a variety of waterfowl and shore birds.

REGION V: THE NORTHEAST

Administrative Headquarters, U.S. Post Office and Courthouse, Boston, Massachusetts 02109.

Delaware

BOMBAY HOOK NWR. Smyrna, 10 miles northeast of Dover. Waterfowl populations reach peaks of 25,000 Canada geese and 25,000 ducks, October through December.

PRIME HOOK NWR. Located at Milford, 28 miles southeast of Dover. Under supervision of Bombay Hook. Important resting and feeding site for ducks and geese and other wildlife.

Maine

CARLTON POND NWR. Located at Troy. Waterfowl protection area under supervision of Moosehorn.

COASTAL MAINE NWR. 9 separated units of salt and brackish marsh extending from near Portland, Maine, south to York Village, adjacent to U.S. Highway 1 and Interstate 95. Under supervision of Parker River in Massachusetts. Establishment is primarily for preservation of valuable habitat threatened by commercial development. Land acquisition is incomplete.

MOOSEHORN NWR. Located 6 miles southwest of Calais on route 1. This timbered area, interspersed with lakes, marshes, and streams, provides habitat for 200 species of birds and waterfowl.

Massachusetts

GREAT MEADOWS NWR. Located at Concord, 20 miles west of Boston, this marsh
and river bottomland along the Concord and Sudbury rivers constitutes one
of the most important freshwater marsh areas in the state. The refuge provides resting and feeding areas for migrating waterfowl, and wading and
other birds.

MONOMOY NWR. Located on Monomoy and Morris islands at the "elbow" of
Cape Cod. Under supervision of Great Meadows. The Massachusetts Audubon Society conducts guided tours from the mainland. The refuge is a resting
and wintering area for migrating waterfowl. Small fresh and brackish
marshes dot the island along with dune grass, brush, stunted pine, and oak.
The area is famous for shore bird migrations in the spring.

PARKER RIVER NWR. Located at Newburyport, 32 miles northeast of Boston.
Many species of waterfowl, shore birds, and other birds can be viewed in
their natural habitat. More than 300 bird species have been recorded.

New Jersey

BARNEGAT NWR. A coastal area of primarily salt marsh at Manahawkin. Under
supervision of Brigantine. Nesting habitat for waterfowl and marsh birds,
and food and shelter for waterfowl in migration are provided.

BRIGANTINE NWR. At Oceanville, 8 miles west and north of Atlantic City. Nesting
habitat for waterfowl and marsh and shore birds. Hosts thousands of ducks,
geese, and brant during migrations. More than 250 bird species have been
recorded. Visitors may follow a 7-mile tour route. The Holgate Unit on Long
Beach Island provides nesting habitat for colonies of skimmers, terns, and
oystercatchers, and is noted for shore bird flights.

GREAT SWAMP NWR. Located at Gillette, 15 miles west of Newark. More than 175
species of birds have been recorded. Great Swamp will be managed as a
protection and resting area for migratory waterfowl and as a major center
for conservative education. Two trails and a center for observing and photographing wildlife are now open. Land acquisition still underway.

New York

IROQUOIS NWR. Located at Basom, 15 miles northwest of Batavia. Flanked on the
east and west by the state's Oak Orchard and Tonawanda Game MAs, Iroquois refuge lies at the center of a contiguous conservation complex. As many
as 30,000 Canada geese and many species of ducks can be seen in March and
April.

MONTEZUMA NWR. Located near Seneca Falls, at the north end of Cayuga Lake,
Montezuma is bordered on the north and east by the New York Barge Canal.
Diverse habitat, from cattail marshes to green timber impoundments, pro-
vides excellent environment for migrating and nesting waterfowl.

MORTON NWR. Located at Sag Harbor, 125 miles east of New York City on Long
Island, this refuge is a resting area for waterfowl and shore birds.

TARGET ROCK NWR. Huntington, Long Island. In developmental stage.

Pennsylvania

ERIE NWR. Located at Guys Mills, 40 miles south of the city of Erie. Established
as a protection and resting area for migratory waterfowl, the area includes

open fields, timbered upland, swamp, and marsh along the narrow valley at the headwaters of Woodcock and Lake Creeks.

Vermont

MISSISQUOI NWR. Located at Swanton, 40 miles north of Burlington on the Missisquoi River delta near the Canadian border. Protection and resting area for ducks, especially black and wood ducks. Migrant waterfowl include snow and Canada geese. Many species of songbirds and water and marsh birds are present in season.

B. Other Places to See the Birds

Following is a selected list of places, other than National Wildlife Refuges listed in the first part of the appendix, to see birds in the United States and Canada. Further information on these and other areas can be obtained on the local or regional level from state and provincial departments of parks and conservation and municipal chambers of commerce and park departments. On the national level, information on U.S. areas is available from the National Audubon Society, 1130 Fifth Avenue, New York, N.Y. 10028, and from the National Park Service, Department of the Interior, Washington, D.C. 20240. In Canada, important sources include the following: Canadian Audubon Society, 46 St. Clair Ave. E., Toronto 7, Ontario; Canadian National Park System, 400 Laurier Ave. W., Ottawa, Ontario; and Canadian Wildlife Service, 400 Laurier Ave. W., Ottawa, Ontario.

Although dated in some respects, Olin S. Pettingill's two-volume work, *Guide to Bird Finding East of the Mississippi* and *Guide to Bird Finding West of the Mississippi*, is still recognized as the best source available on where to find North American birds. Published in 1951 and 1953 respectively by the Oxford University Press, the books are available at libraries and through your local bookstore.

Abbreviations

BR = Bird Refuge	R = Refuge
BS = Bird Sanctuary	S = Sanctuary
FP = Forest Preserve	SP = State Park
NF = National Forest	WR = Wildlife Refuge
NM = National Monument	WS = Wildlife Sanctuary
NP = National Park	

UNITED STATES

Alabama

GULF SP. Located on a narrow, sandy peninsula between Mobile Bay and the Gulf of Mexico, southeast of Mobile on state route 59. An area of beaches, dunes, scrub oaks, and grass that attracts a variety of shore birds, waterbirds, and marsh birds.

Arizona

GRAND CANYON NP. In northwest corner of state, off state routes 64 (to south rim) and 67 (to north rim). A variety of species is found in different zones and elevations alongside and within the canyon. The Naturalist's Workshop, at Park Headquarters on south rim, displays 500 species found in area.

ORGAN PIPE CACTUS NM. Southwest of Phoenix on state route 85. Desert setting for viewing owls, flickers, doves, phoebes, and other land birds.

California

GRIFFITH PARK. The largest municipal park in Los Angeles includes chaparral slopes and oak woodlands, where woodpeckers, jays, vireos, and humming-birds can be seen.

LAKE MERRITT WS. Located on a tide-replenished, salt-water lake in the heart of Oakland, this municipal preserve attracts wintering ducks, gulls, and coots.

LOS PADRES NF. Located in the Sierra Madre Mountain chain, inland from Santa Barbara. A condor refuge has been established at its southern edge in the Sespe Wildlife Area.

MONTEREY BAY. Between Point Lobos, west of Monterey, and Santa Cruz. Murres, guillemots, loons, shearwaters, and albatrosses are among the sea birds attracted by the nutrient upwellings of the submarine canyon off the end of the bay.

SAN DIEGO ZOO. Located on Park Boulevard in Balboa Park in downtown San Diego. Huge cages, which encompass trees, contain more than 1,000 flying birds. The Natural History Museum, also in the park, houses an extensive collection of mounted birds from the Southwest and Baja California.

SANTA CATALINA ISLAND. 20 miles offshore from Long Beach, on San Pedro Bay. Hummingbirds, larks, wrens, shrikes, and other birds can be seen near the town of Avalon, where the ferry lands. Nearby Bird Park houses exotic species from all over the world in an outdoor zoo.

YOSEMITE NP. East-central part of state, on route 140 east from Merced. Woodpeckers, tanagers, wrens, warblers, and other land birds amid spectacular scenery of cliffs, cascades, and forests. The great gray owl and golden eagle are added attractions for bird-watchers.

Colorado

GRAND MESA NF. East of Grand Junction in west-central part of Colorado, on state route 65. Hawks, swallows, quail, and pheasants fly over an alternating landscape of wastelands, meadows, and pygmy forests.

MESA VERDE NP. In extreme southwest corner of state, west of Durango on U.S. Highway 160. Prehistoric Indian ruins are the focal point here, but a variety of desert birds can be seen on the north edge along the entrance road.

ROCKY MOUNTAIN NP. North-central part of state, 65 miles northwest of Denver. Ptarmigan and other alpine birds reside here.

Connecticut

EAST ROCK PARK. A municipal park surrounding the rock cliffs on the northeast edge of New Haven. Best birding areas are the tree groves and cattail marshes bordering Mill River on the west and south of the park, and the Quinnipiac River marshes to the east.

LITCHFIELD-MORRIS WS. Between Litchfield and Morris off state route 61. This privately owned sanctuary, with wildlife rights controlled by the State Board of Fisheries and Game, attracts a variety of land birds and waterfowl to its woods, marshes, ponds, and river and lake shorelines. Migrating warblers in May and September.

Florida

CORKSCREW SWAMP S. At the northern tip of the Big Cypress Swamp, 35 miles southeast of Fort Myers, Corkscrew is the most important sanctuary of the National Audubon Society. The largest colony of wood ibises in the United States finds protection here.

EVERGLADES NP. This swamp and wilderness area of the southwest peninsular tip of Florida comprises America's third largest national park. Reached by state road 27, south and west from Homestead. Semitropical paradise of wading and water birds.

FLORIDA BAY. Small islands for great white herons near Everglades National Park run by the National Audubon Society. Boat tours available.

FLORIDA KEYS. A group of islands stretching south and west from Miami and culminating in Key West, the southernmost city in the United States. Excellent waterfront for observing pelicans, man-o'-war-birds, herons, terns, and gulls. Contains three national wildlife Refuges.

ST. JOHNS RIVER MARSHES. A freshwater marsh area along the St. Johns River, 7 miles west of Melbourne on U.S. Highway 192. Includes water bird rookery on Lake Washington, north of 192.

Georgia

JEKYLL ISLAND SP. Off Atlantic Coast, connected to mainland by U.S. Highway 84 and state route 50 from Brunswick. This semitropical island, with extensive beaches and forests, is an excellent place to observe water birds, waterfowl, shore birds, and land birds during spring migration.

Illinois

BIRD HAVEN. In southeastern Illinois on state route 130 at Olney. A resident director manages this woods and meadows sanctuary for the University of Chicago.

COOK COUNTY FOREST PRESERVE. Municipal preserve bordering the Des Plaines River, adjoining Chicago on the west. The forest preserve also controls the ORLAND WR and PALOS HILLS FP southwest of the Loop on U.S. Highway 45.

HORSESHOE LAKE WR. In southwestern extremity of state, on state route 3 near Olive Branch. This stage-owned refuge, on a lake in the Illinois farm country, attracts large concentrations of migrating and wintering Canada geese.

LINCOLN PARK. A north-south strip along Lake Michigan in Chicago. In addition to a variety of resident and migrating birds, this municipal park offers ornithological exhibits at the Museum of Natural History and exotic birds and water birds at the Lincoln Park Zoo.

MORTON ARBORETUM. About 20 miles west of downtown Chicago via the East-West Tollway. A variety of land birds, including owls and hawks. A favorite birding area in winter.

STARVED ROCK SP. A narrow strip of woodland along the Illinois River west of Ottawa off interstate highway 80. Ducks, hawks, cuckoos, orioles, and other birds can be seen there regularly.

Indiana

INDIANA DUNES SP. 15 miles east of Gary on south shore of Lake Michigan. Beaches, wooded dunes, and cattail lowlands attract a variety of migrating and resident birds.

Kansas

CHEYENNE BOTTOMS. North of Great Bend in central part of state. This state-operated waterfowl marsh draws large concentrations during spring and fall migrations. Hawks, rails, and coots are among the summer residents.

Kentucky

AUDUBON MEMORIAL SP. In northwestern Kentucky along the Ohio River north of Henderson on U.S. Highway 41. Woodlands and two artificial lakes attract waterfowl, water birds, and land birds. The Audubon Museum in the park contains original paintings by Audubon and members of his family.

KENTUCKY DAM SP. At north end of Kentucky Lake in western part of state. Migrating waterfowl and wintering ducks, geese, and gulls can be seen here.

MAMMOTH CAVE NP. In south-central part of state, northeast of Bowling Green. Reached by U.S. Highway 31 and state routes 255 and 70. A medley of warbler songs from a variety of species can be heard in this wooded park. Nighttime serenades from owls and whip-poor-wills.

Louisiana

JUNGLE GARDEN AND BIRD CITY. On Avery Island in Iberia County. An abundance of birds, especially herons and egrets, can be found on this private sanctuary, amid an abundant array of exotic plants. Admission fee charged.

Maine

ACADIA NP. On Mount Desert Island, off eastern coast. Both temperate and sub-Arctic birds are found on this biological boundary line between two zones. Park naturalists conduct nature walks around the island and up Cadillac Mountain, the highest peak on the Atlantic Coast.

BAXTER SP. 20 miles northwest of Millinocket, in north-central part of state. Including Mount Katahdin, the state's highest mountain, this park is a good place to see ducks, woodcocks, woodpeckers, flycatchers, ravens, and warblers. Birding is best in June and July.

MATINICUS ISLAND. Largest island in archipelago on outermost fringe of Penobscot Bay, can be reached by passenger ferry from Rockland from June to September. Excellent place to observe gulls, terns, cormorants, eiders, ospreys, guillemots, and other oceanic birds. (Plans to visit Matinicus Rock, 5 miles south of Matinicus Island, should be cleared with the U.S. Coast Guard station in Rockland.)

Massachusetts

MARTHA'S VINEYARD. South of Cape Cod reached by ferry from Woods Hole. The ponds along the south side of the island attract large gatherings of waterfowl in winter.

PLEASANT VALLEY S. 3 miles north of Lenox. The Massachusetts Audubon Society owns this refuge in the Berkshire Hills, managed by a resident superintendent. A museum on the premises houses Audubon prints.

Michigan

W. H. KELLOGG BS. Private waterfowl area 12 miles northwest of Battle Creek. For many years this sanctuary had the only trumpeter swans in captivity in this country.

KIRTLAND WARBLER R. A cooperative management area has been established for this endangered species 3 miles south and 3 miles east of Mio.

ST. CLAIR FLATS. A group of islands at the delta where St. Clair River empties into Lake St. Clair. A year-round gathering place for waterfowl and marsh birds. Use state routes 29 and 154.

UNIVERSITY OF MICHIGAN BIOLOGICAL STATION. Located on Douglas Lake, 25 miles south of Mackinaw City. This extensive field station has two laboratories for ornithological research. Lowlands setting is excellent for bird finding.

Minnesota

CARLTON COLLEGE ARBORETUM. North of the campus at Northfield. Best birding area is the Nature Trail, which follows the Cannon River for three miles. Best season is migration time in May.

MINNESOTA MUSEUM OF NATURAL HISTORY. University and 17th Avenues, Minneapolis. Extensive bird exhibits in strikingly realistic environmental settings.

NERSTAND WOODS SP. Northeast of Faribault in southeastern part of state, off state route 60. Warblers and other woodland birds inhabit this deciduous forest.

THEODORE WIRTH PARK. On western edge of downtown Minneapolis, via Wayzata Boulevard. Bird watchers are rewarded by a diversity of birdlife amid a varied landscape.

Missouri

EAST ASHLAND CONSERVATION AREA. East of Ashland, off U.S. Highway 63. This wildlife area, administered by the University of Missouri, attracts prairie chickens and a variety of migrating and breeding warblers, tanagers, and sparrows.

FOREST PARK. This large municipal park, on the western edge of downtown St. Louis, is a year-round center for birds and bird watchers alike. The St. Louis Zoo, in the park, features a large outdoor bird cage, a tropical bird house, and waterfowl lakes.

Montana

WATERTON-GLACIER INTERNATIONAL PEACE PARK. Includes Glacier National Park. In Rocky Mountains of northwestern Montana and Waterton Lakes National Park in southwestern Alberta. The landscape collects a variety of birds of the prairies, forests, mountain streams, and alpine zones.

New Jersey

LONG BEACH ISLAND. This 18-mile-long sand barrier island off the Jersey coast is a favorite vantage point for brant, grebes, ducks, and loons. Connected to the mainland by bridge via state route 72.

Stone Harbor Heron Rookery. A municipally operated preserve on the southern edge of Stone Harbor near the Cape May peninsula attracts a great variety of nesting herons, egrets, and ibises.

Troy Meadow. A vast freshwater marsh in the metropolitan area of New Jersey. Attracts wood ducks, bitterns, rails, gallinules, snipes, and other marsh birds.

New York

Braddock's Bay. North of Rochester, at the mouth of the Genesee River. This area on the southern shore of Lake Ontario provides abundant opportunity to see migrating waterfowl while exploring cattail marshes, ponds, and sand spits.

Central Park. This large municipal park in the center of New York City attracts large numbers of migrating land birds in late April and May. The best place to see them is the Ramble between 72nd and 79th Streets in the midsection between the East and West Drives.

Jamaica Bay WR. On Jamaica Bay, adjacent to the John F. Kennedy International Airport. Abundant concentrations of shore birds and waterfowl. Visitors must obtain permit from Department of Parks, 830 Fifth Avenue, New York City, N.Y. 10021.

Prospect Park. Municipal park in downtown Brooklyn. Migrating land birds in fall and spring.

North Carolina

The Great Dismal Swamp. A large marsh, including Lake Drummond, near U.S. Highway 17 in northeastern North Carolina and southeastern Virginia. Prothonotary and other warblers, herons, owls, and woodpeckers are numerous.

Great Smoky Mountain NP. This forested mountainous terrain, about equally divided between Tennessee and North Carolina, is the home of owls, flycatchers, ravens, chickadees, kingfishers, nuthatches, warblers, and a variety of other birds which normally nest hundreds of miles to the north. The Appalachian Trail stretches for 60 miles along the high divide between the two states.

Lockhart Gaddy Wild Goose R. Private sanctuary near Ansonville on U.S. Highway 52. This area attracts large numbers of Canada geese.

Mt. Mitchell SP. Northeast of Asheville in western part of the state. Located on the highest elevation in the eastern U.S., this park is of interest because it attracts northern woodland birds.

North Dakota

Theodore Roosevelt National Memorial Park. This park is comprised of three separate units off U.S. Highway 85 in the Badlands of North Dakota. Wooded areas of the northern unit are best for bird finding.

Ohio

Buckeye Lake. South of interstate highway 70, between Columbus and Zanesville. This artificial lake is a haven for nesting land birds and migrating waterfowl. Shore birds can be seen on the mud flats in late summer and early fall.

Lake St. Marys (also called Grand Lake). Located in western part of state near

Salina, east of U.S. Highway 127. Geese and ducks stop here in early spring, followed by land birds and gulls in April and shore birds in May. Bird-watching is recommended year-round.

O'Shaughnessy Reservoir. 20 miles northwest of Columbus on state route 257. Water birds and waterfowl stop here in March and November.

Rocky River Reservation. This municipal reservation winds along the river for 20 miles at the western edge of the city of Cleveland. A forest-and-grove setting for migrating and nesting birds.

Oregon

Crater Lake NP. Southwestern part of state on state route 62. Tourists roll peanuts down the edge of the volcano to attract the gray jays and Clark's nutcrackers.

Pennsylvania

Fairmount Park. A large municipal park in downtown Philadelphia bordering the Schuylkill River and Wissahickon Creek. Best bird-watching in Wissahickon section.

Hawk Mountain S. North from Hamburg on U.S. Highway 122. Private haven for migrating hawks and eagles in Appalachian chain in eastern part of state.

Pennsylvania SP at Erie. This hook-shaped peninsula, which stretches northeast into the lake from the city of Erie, is a favorite stopping place for shore birds.

Pymatuning State Game R. A water, marsh, and land area on the Pymatuning Reservoir on the Ohio border. An abundance of waterfowl, marsh birds, and shore birds, as well as land birds that seek moist areas.

Tinicum Swamp. Located along the Delaware River between the Philadelphia Airport and Essington. This municipal sanctuary, run by the city of Philadelphia, is a wintering and migration area for waterfowl, hawks, and shore birds. In spring and fall, pintails, teal, and sandpipers gather there.

Rhode Island

Block Island. Reached by ferry from Rhode Island coast. A magnet to birds and bird watchers alike, this treeless island is on many species' spring and fall migration routes.

The Great Swamp. West and south from West Kingston off state route 2. An area of shrubs, bogs, and wetlands, bordered on the south by Worden Pond. Breeding species include ducks, warblers, nuthatches, redstarts, tanagers, and hawks.

South Dakota

Custer SP and Mount Rushmore National Memorial. Southwest of Rapid City, off U.S. Highway 16. Jays, juncos, tanagers, nuthatches, and other birds of Black Hills region.

Tennessee

Fall Creek Falls SP. Reached by state route 30 west of Pikeville in Cumberland Plateau. Hawks, owls, and wild turkeys can be seen regularly amid the spectacular canyons, creeks, and falls.

GREAT SMOKY MOUNTAIN NP. (See North Carolina.)

SHELBY STATE FOREST PARK. 12 miles north of Memphis, this thickly forested state park on bluffs above the Mississippi is frequented by land birds of many species.

Texas

BIG BEND NP. 70 miles south of Marathon on state route 385. This desert and mountain park, bordered on the south by a bend in the Rio Grande, hosts a variety of birds, including hawks, doves, roadrunners, hummingbirds, phoebes, and flycatchers. More birds (537 species) have been seen in this park than anywhere else in the U.S.

PALO DURO CANYON SP. Reached via U.S. Highway 87 and state route 217 south and east from Amarillo. Excellent bird finding in any season in this panhandle park along the colorful walls of the Palo Duro Canyon.

VINGT'UN ISLANDS S. In Galveston Bay on Gulf of Mexico. The nation's largest nesting colony of roseate spoonbills, once nearly extinct, can be seen in this National Audubon Society sanctuary.

Utah

OGDEN BAY WATERFOWL AREA. State-run preserve, on the Great Salt Lake west of Ogden, attracts large numbers of migratory ducks, geese, ibis, avocets, and pelicans.

ZION NP. Located in the southwestern corner of the state on state route 15. Quail, roadrunners, mockingbirds, and hummingbirds are among the species that can be seen along the deep canyons cut by the Virgin River and its tributaries. The best bird trails are along the valley floor.

Virginia

THE GREAT DISMAL SWAMP. (See North Carolina.)

SHENANDOAH NP. Stretching for 75 miles northeast from Waynesboro, this scenic park curves along the backbone of the Blue Ridge Mountains. Many nature trails traverse the park, but those in the Skyland and Big Meadows areas are especially recommended.

Washington

MT. RANIER NP. 40 miles southeast of Tacoma, on the state's highest elevation. Birds are especially abundant in the sub-Alpine zones between 5,000 and 6,000 feet.

OLYMPIC NP. Northwestern Washington, on Olympic Peninsula. Reached by spur roads from U.S. Highway 101, which circles park. Hummingbirds, wrens, thrushes, warblers, and tanagers are among the inhabitants of the park's meadows and coniferous forests. Auklets, guillemots, cormorants, and murres are found along the Olympic Ocean Strip.

Wyoming

YELLOWSTONE NP. Northwest corner of Wyoming, overlapping slightly into the adjoining states of Idaho and Montana. More than 200 species of birds—including ducks, hawks, eagles, and trumpeter swans—frequent America's oldest and largest national park.

Canada

Alberta

Waterton-Glacier International Peace Park. (See Montana.)

Nova Scotia

Cape Sable Island. Southernmost tip of the island. Stop-over place for migrating shore birds from July to November.

Eastern Shore BS. Small group of coastal islands run by the Nova Scotia Bird Society, reached from the village of Moser River on route 7 on the southern shore. A nesting place for ducks, eiders, guillemots, gulls, and cormorants.

Ontario

Jack Miner BS. Private conservation-education center in Kingsville, Ontario. Has attracted as many as 25,000 Canada geese.

Point Pelee NP. Located off route 2, southeast of Windsor, Ontario. This narrow point of land, jutting southward into Lake Erie, attracts large concentrations of migrating birds in the spring and fall.

Algonquin Provincial Park. A vast wilderness and lake area 170 miles north of Toronto. The rugged landscape is the home of a number of northern forest species and the nesting area for loons, hawks, sapsuckers, and other birds seen only as migrants farther south.

Quebec

Bonaventure Island. Located in the Gulf of St. Lawrence, 3 miles off the village of Percé, on the eastern coast of the Gaspé Peninsula. Gannets, murres, and other sea birds nest among the island's towering cliffs and dive into the sea for food.

Saskatchewan

Last Mountain Lake BS. At northern end of 50-mile lake northwest of Regina. Located on spring and fall migration routes for sandhill cranes, ducks, and geese.

Bibliography
and Suggested Reading

ALLEN, ARTHUR A., *The Book of Bird Life*. D. Van Nostrand Co., Inc., New York, 1930.

————, *Stalking Birds with Color Camera*. National Geographic Society, Washington, D.C., 1951.

ALLEN, GLOVER M., *Birds and Their Attributes*. Marshall Jones Co., Francestown, New Hampshire, 1925.

AMERICAN ORNITHOLOGIST'S UNION, *Check-List of North American Birds*. American Ornithologists' Union, Cornell University, Ithaca, New York, 1957.

ARMSTRONG, EDWARD A., *Bird Display: An Introduction to the Study of Bird Psychology*. The Macmillan Co., New York, 1942.

————, *The Way Birds Live*. Dover Publications, Inc., New York, 1967.

AUSTIN, OLIVER L., *Birds of the World*. Golden Press, New York, 1961.

BARTON, ROGER, *How to Watch Birds*. McGraw-Hill Book Company, New York, 1956.

BEEBE, WILLIAM, *The Bird, Its Form and Function*. Dover Publications, Inc., New York, 1965.

BENT, ARTHUR CLEVELAND, *Life Histories of North American Birds*. (Entire Series 25 Volumes) Dover Publications, Inc., New York, 1919–1958.

BUMP, GARDINER; DARROW, ROBERT; EDMINSTER, FRANK; and CRISSEY, WALTER, *The Ruffed Grouse*. New York State Conservation Dept., Albany, New York, 1947.

BURTT, HAROLD E., *The Psychology of Birds*. The Macmillan Co., New York, 1967.

CHAPMAN, FRANK M., *Handbook of Birds of Eastern North America*. Dover Publications Inc., New York, 1940.

CRAIGHEAD, JOHN J., and CRAIGHEAD, FRANK C., *Hawks, Owls and Wildlife*. Wildlife Management Institute, Washington, D.C., 1956.

CRUICKSHANK, ALLAN D., *Birds Around New York City*. The American Museum of Natural History, New York, 1942.

————, *Wings in the Wilderness*. Oxford University Press, New York, 1948.

————, *Pocket Guide to the Birds*. Dodd, Mead and Co., New York, 1953.

CRUICKSHANK, ALLAN D., and CRUICKSHANK, H. G., *1001 Questions Answered About Birds*. Dodd, Mead & Co., New York, 1958.

DAY, ALBERT M., *North American Waterfowl*. Stackpole and Heck, Inc., Harrisburg, Pa., 1949.

DAVISON, VERNE E., *Attracting Birds*. Thomas Y. Crowell Co., New York, 1967.

DORST, JEAN, *The Migration of Birds*. Houghton Mifflin Company, Boston, 1963.

EATON, ELON HOWARD, *Birds of New York*. New York State Museum, Albany, 1910.

FABLES, DAVID, *Annotated List of New Jersey Birds*. Urner Ornithological Club, Newark, New Jersey, 1955.

GODFREY, W. EARL, *The Birds of Canada*. National Museum of Canada, Ottawa, 1966.

GRISCOM, LUDLOW, *The Birds of Concord*. Harvard University Press, Cambridge, Mass., 1949.

———, *Modern Bird Study*. Harvard University Press, Cambridge, Mass., 1945.

GROSSMAN, MARY L., and HAMLET, JOHN, *Birds of Prey of the World*. Clarkson N. Potter, Inc., New York, 1964.

HALL, HENRY MARION, *A Gathering of Shore Birds*. Bramhall House, New York, 1960.

HAUSMAN, LEON AUGUSTUS, *Birds of Prey of Northeastern North America*. Rutgers University Press, New Brunswick, New Jersey, 1948.

HESS, GERTRUD, *The Bird: Its Life and Structure*. Greenberg, New York, 1952.

HICKEY, JOSEPH J., *A Guide to Bird Watching*. Oxford University Press, New York, 1943.

HOCHBAUM, H. ALBERT, *Travels and Traditions of Waterfowl*. University of Minnesota Press, Minneapolis, 1955.

HOWARD, LEN, *Birds as Individuals*. William Collins Sons & Co., Ltd., London, 1952.

JOHNSGARD, PAUL A., *Handbook of Waterfowl Behavior*. Comstock Publishing Associates, Ithaca, New York, 1965.

———, *Waterfowl: Their Biology and Natural History*. University of Nebraska Press, Lincoln, 1968.

KORTRIGHT, FRANCIS H., *The Ducks, Geese and Swans of North America*. The American Wildlife Institute, Washington, D.C., 1942.

LEMMON, ROBERT S., *Our Amazing Birds*. Doubleday & Company, Inc., Garden City, New York, 1952.

MACDONALD, J. D.; GOODWIN, DEREK; and ADLER, HELMUT E., *Curiosities of Bird Life*. Castle Books, Inc., New York, 1967.

MARTIN, ALEXANDER C.; ZIM, HERBERT S.; and NELSON, ARNOLD L., *American Wildlife and Plants*. Dover Publications, Inc., New York, 1951.

MATTHIESSEN, PETER, *The Shorebirds of North America*. The Viking Press, Inc., New York, 1967.

MCELROY, THOMAS P., *Handbook of Attracting Birds*. Alfred A. Knopf, Inc., New York, 1950.

MURIE, ADOLPH, *Birds of Mt. McKinley National Park, Alaska*. Mt. McKinley Natural History Assoc., McKinley Park, Alaska, 1963.

MURPHY, ROBERT C., and AMADON, DEAN, *Land Birds of America*. McGraw-Hill Book Company, New York, 1953.

PEARSON, T. GILBERT (Ed.), *Birds of America*. University Society, Inc., New York, 1917.

PETERSON, ROGER TORY, *A Field Guide to the Birds.* Houghton Mifflin Company, Boston, 1934.

———, *Birds Over America.* Dodd, Mead & Co., New York, 1964.

PETTINGILL, OLIN SEWALL, *A Guide to Bird Finding East of the Mississippi.* Oxford University Press, New York, 1951.

———, *A Guide to Bird Finding West of the Mississippi.* Oxford University Press, New York, 1953.

POUGH, RICHARD H., *Audubon Bird Guide: Small Land Birds of Eastern and Central North America.* Doubleday & Company, Inc., 1949.

———, *Audubon Water Bird Guide.* Doubleday & Company, Inc., Garden City, New York, 1951.

REED, CHESTER A., *North American Birds' Eggs.* Dover Publications, Inc., New York, 1965.

ROBBINS, CHANDLER; BRUNN, BERTEL; and ZIM, HERBERT S., *Birds of North America: A Guide to Field Identification.* Golden Press, New York, 1966.

SIMPSON, D. P., *Cassell's New Latin Dictionary.* Funk & Wagnalls, New York, 1960.

SPRUNT, ALEXANDER, *Florida Bird Life.* Coward-McCann, Inc., New York, 1954.

———, *North American Birds of Prey.* Harper & Bros., New York, 1955.

STEFFERUD and NELSON, *Birds in Our Lives.* United States Government Printing Office, Washington, D.C., 1966.

STONE, WITMER, *Bird Studies at Old Cape May.* Dover Publications Inc., New York, 1965.

TERRES, JOHN K., *Songbirds in Your Garden.* Thomas Y. Crowell Co., New York, 1968.

———, *The Audubon Book of True Nature Stories.* Thomas Y. Crowell Co., New York, 1958.

VAN TYNE, JOSSELYN, and BERGER, A. J., *Fundamentals of Ornithology.* John Wiley & Sons, Inc., New York, 1966.

VESEY-FITZGERALD, BRIAN S., *Bird Biology for Beginners.* Cassell & Co., Ltd., London, England, 1948.

WALLACE, GEORGE J., *An Introduction to Ornithology.* The Macmillan Co., New York, 1955.

WELTY, JOEL CARL, *The Life of Birds.* Alfred A. Knopf, Inc., New York, 1963.

WETMORE, ALEXANDER, *Water, Prey, and Game Birds of North America.* National Geographic Society, Washington, D.C., 1965.

WING, LEONARD W., *Natural History of Birds.* The Ronald Press Company, New York, 1956.

WORMINGTON, HANNAH M., *Birds of Arctic Alaska.* Denver Museum of Natural History, 1948.

Index